Dedication

To Kin-Man Chung and Herbert Yuen, whose labor of love brings
the power of Pascal to home computer users.

PASCAL

No. 1205
$15.95

PASCAL

BY DAVID L. HEISERMAN

TAB TAB BOOKS Inc.

BLUE RIDGE SUMMIT, PA. 17214

FIRST EDITION

FIRST PRINTING—JULY 1980

Copyright © 1980 by TAB BOOKS Inc.

Printed in the United States of America

Library of Congress Cataloging in Publication Data

Heiserman, David L.   1940-
    PASCAL.

    "TAB#1205."
    Includes index.
    1. PASCAL (Computer program language) 2. TRS = 80
(Computer)—Programming. I. Title.
QA76.73.P2H44   001.64′24   80-14309
ISBN 0-8306-9934-1
ISBN 0-8306-1205-X (pbk.)

Cover Photo Courtesy of Highland Industries.

Preface

Pascal has always been a computer language with great promise and potential. Much of that promise and potential has already been realized, and many experts describe it as the ideal programming language.

Indeed, it appears that Pascal takes the best of all other languages and rejects their shortcomings. Pascal is essentially simple to learn, understand and apply. It can fit into just about any sort of computer environment.

Unless a computer system is specifically designed to work in Pascal, however, its compiler takes up a great-deal of memory space. In a personal computer environment, the full-blown version requires at least 32k of RAM and two disk drives. Such systems are now available, but relatively few personal computer users can afford so much hardware.

Two computer researchers and graduate students at the University of Illinois came to the rescue in 1978, developing a scaled-down version of Pascal that is now commonly known as Tiny Pascal. Kin-Man Chung and Herbert Yuen published a complete summary of their Tiny Pascal in the September, October and November 1978 issues of *Byte* magazine.

Tiny Pascal, the subject of this book, fits into a 16k personal computing system. The articles just cited, as well as a few subsequent ones, present Tiny Pascal compilers in North Star BASIC and 8080 assembly language.

As far as more casual home computer users are concerned, the next breakthrough in Pascal came about in 1979 when Supersoft began marketing a simple cassette tape version of Tiny Pascal for both the North Star and TRS-80 systems. The material in this book is specifically aimed toward using Supersoft's TRS-80 version of Tiny Pascal. It is thus possible to work through this entire book, learning the fundamentals of Pascal and having a lot of fun with the examples, having no more equipment than a Level II, 16k TRS-80 system and Supersoft's Tiny Pascal cassette tape.

That does not mean users of other personal computing systems are left in the dark, though. With the exception of some graphics routines that are unique ot the TRS-80, all the material in this book can be carried over to any other system that will adapt Tiny Pascal compilers in the future.

On a personal note, I have studied, used and written about many other computer languages for personal computers, but I have never had such an impression of computing "power" that I get from Tiny Pascal. It is exciting to be able to share this impression with you.

David L. Heiserman

Contents

Chapter 1

Using This Book

Learning to use a new programming language is always a rather involved process. Sometimes it is fun and sometimes it is extremely frustrating. Always it is hard work.

The general subject of this book is learning to use the relatively new Pascal programming language. More specifically, the book is about Tiny Pascal. Even more specifically, it is about Supersoft Tiny Pascal for the TRS-80 personal computer system.

BASIC AND PASCAL

It takes a lot of work to learn how to use Pascal, Tiny Pascal and Supersoft Tiny Pascal. You will find the task easier if you have already mastered the BASIC programming language, however. Obviously the job will be even easier and more fun if you have access to a computer system that can handle the examples and exercises included in this book.

Assuming you already have some working acquaintance with BASIC, you are going to find Pascal is quite different and, in some respects, rather confusing at first. But your knowledge of BASIC will most likely be more of a help to you than a hindrance.

BASIC, you see, is a very down-to-earth programming language. It is possible to build BASIC programs using a kind of thinking that isn't much different from everyday analytical thinking. All you have to do is learn the almost plain English BASIC syntax forms, play with them to see exactly how they work, and then start putting things together. BASIC, in fact, was invented for beginning programmers who have no real feeling for formal programming language structures.

Pascal, on the other hand, demands a very rigorous and fairly abstract approach. While there might be a dozen suitable ways to do a given job in BASIC, Pascal's formal structure might allow only two approaches at the most.

The more experience you've had with BASIC, however, the more smoothly you can ease into Pascal. The idea here is that a lot of experience with BASIC gradually forces you to think in highly structured and analytical terms. If you have done more than simply copy BASIC programs others have written for you or if you have written programs having more than a handful of steps, you've at least brushed against the kind of thinking required for programming in Pascal.

So a previous knowledge of BASIC is a two-edged sword when it comes to learning Pascal. On one hand, you will find that the kind of thinking that goes into developing moderately sophisticated BASIC programs will serve as a firm stepping stone for getting started in Pascal. On the other hand, you will have to break some old habits, especially some questionable programming habits that BASIC can tolerate but Pascal cannot.

Sure, it is going to be a lot of hard work. It is going to get frustrating at times. But it can be a lot of fun, too. Judging from the rate that Pascal is growing in popularity, your work will pay off big dividends in the long run.

LIMITATIONS OF A PROGRAMMING BOOK

It is virtually impossible, or certainly impractical, to write a computer programming book that covers all possible ways in which the language is used. No language of any significance is perfectly portable. None can be perfectly transferred from one kind of computing machine to another. There are always minor variations.

For example, Standard Pascal, as originally developed by Niklaus Wirth and others between 1968 and 1973, is not at all suitable for small personal computers. At the time of this writing, a Standard Pascal or UCSD (University of California at San Diego) version calls for a personal computing system having 32k of RAM and two disk drives. Those specifications are far beyond the reach of most home computer users.

In an attempt to reach people who have more modest computers, Kin-Man Chung and Herbert Yuen developed a trimmed-down version of Standard Pascal. They called it Tiny Pascal, and it seems likely that name is going to stick.

Tiny Pascal works exactly like its parent, but simply has fewer features available. Tiny Pascal, for instance, works only with integer arithmetic and cannot handle string variables very well. It retains the powerful structural nature of Standard Pascal, however. So whatever procedures you learn with Tiny Pascal carry directly over to the Standard version.

Tiny Pascal, though, was originally developed on a North Star computing system. And while that might be a fine system, it has operating characteristics that do not carry over directly to other personal computers.

There is a need to refine the language even further. The Tiny Pascal featured in this book has *all* the features of Chung and Yuen Tiny Pascal. The differences involve mainly some special commands for doing graphics and getting programs loaded to and from cassette tape. Aside from these machine-dependent differences, what you learn about Tiny Pascal in this book applies to Tiny Pascal on any personal computing system.

The final specifications are these. You will need a TRS-80 with at least 16k of RAM and Level II capability. That's the most popular TRS-80 format, anyway. Plus, you will need a Tiny Pascal program package from Supersoft.

Current economic difficulties in the world make it rather pointless to specify the price of a Supersoft Tiny Pascal package for the TRS-80. Perhaps it is enough to say that it costs no more than three conventional BASIC computer game cassettes. To get a current price, write Supersoft, P.O. Box 1628, Champaign, IL 61820.

What you are about to learn is Tiny Pascal for the TRS-80. With the exception of a few machine-dependent commands, what you learn here is applicable to Tiny Pascal on any machine. And what you learn about Tiny Pascal can be applied to full-blown Standard or UCSD Pascal systems.

In other words, you won't be learning *all* there is to know about Pascal from this book. What you do learn will serve you well if you are ever confronted with a Standard Pascal system. In any event, you will be learning how to cope with the special quality of Pascal and that's the most difficult part of the job.

BOOK FORMAT

Pascal is a highly structured language. It is very systematic, and the layout of this book reflects that special character. Just as you are forced to build Pascal programs in a particular fashion, you will find that you must go through the text, examples and exercises in this book from beginning to end.

You should not try to step into the middle of the book and start from there. You are going to miss some important ideas if you try to skip around.

Bear with the scheme setup here. It works, even if it occasionally seems to get a little boring or tedious. Just pretend there is a teacher watching over your shoulder. Work out all the exercises, whether you think you have to or not.

While you will find a lot of exercises and examples written out for you in this book, you will see few suggestions concerning ideas for making up your own programs. It's simply taken for granted that you will want to make up your own programs as you go along. Do it! Try making up your own Pascal programs as you learn new things. You can learn a lot more from making your own mistakes than from the immediate success offered by the specific examples in this book.

Chapter 2
Getting Started With Pascal

The purpose of this chapter is twofold. I want to get you acquainted with the ways Supersoft Tiny Pascal is loaded and handled, and give you something of an intuitive feeling for Pascal.

The first part of the chapter is really a how-to manual for loading and using the Supersoft Tiny Pascal package. It describes how to get the program from cassette tape and into your machine, how to write in programs, how to use the editing features and how to execute programs in Pascal.

The second part of this chapter offers a series of fun-and-games Pascal programs that you can write into the computer yourself. If you wish, you can save them on cassette tape for future use.

The point of the examples is to show you what Pascal programs look like and, of course, to give you some experience working with the Tiny Pascal package. The programs are presented without any technical discussion. You'll start getting plenty of that in Chapter 3.

GETTING TINY PASCAL INTO YOUR TRS-80

Place the Supersoft Tiny Pascal cassette tape into your cassette machine and make sure it is rewound to the start. To obtain the tape, write to Supersoft at the address given in the first chapter.

Initialize your TRS-80 to get the MEMORY SIZE? message. At this time, you won't have to reserve any memory space, so simply respond by striking the ENTER key.

Then type SYSTEM and do an ENTER. You should see a *? on the screen.

Set the cassette player to PLAY, type PASCAL and strike the ENTER key. The cassette player should begin running immediately.

If all is going well, you should soon see two asterisks in the upper right-hand corner of the screen. These are the same asterisks you see whenever loading any cassette program on the TRS-80. The second asterisk will blink on and off at 4-second intervals.

Take a break at this point. The program loads in something on the order of 3 minutes.

When the program is loaded, you will see another *? on the screen and the cassette player will stop running. Type a slash symbol, /, do an ENTER, and you're in business.

Actually the instructions to this point are identical to loading any SYSTEM program into the TRS-80. The only unique feature is the file name, PASCAL.

After entering the slash symbol, the screen will clear. You will see the message, TINY PASCAL, followed by a version number in the upper left-hand corner of the screen.

The Supersoft cassette loads a sample program as well as the Pascal programming. If you want to see it run, enter Q and then enter R. The program will begin running, drawing all sorts of nifty graphics on the screen. The message, THE SHOW IS OVER, appears when the program is done.

You can run this program again by simply entering R. Yes, entering R amounts to doing a RUN command.

Of course, you haven't bought the Supersoft Tiny Pascal tape just to watch this one program. It is time to clear out that program and try entering a different one from the keyboard.

WIPING OUT AN OLD PROGRAM

To erase any program written into the Tiny Pascal system, first enter a Q. In Supersoft Tiny Pascal, Q means to quit whatever you are doing. Maybe you have been running a Pascal program and now you want to erase it. First you have to QUIT the running phase. So enter Q.

After entering the Q, you will see some information on the screen that says things about the number of lines in the current program, the number of bytes it occupies and the absolute (actual) memory locations. There is also a phrase, PTR AT LINE, followed by a number. That one tells you where the program counter is setting at the moment. If all this doesn't make much sense at this point, don't worry about it.

You still haven't wiped out the program. You have simply QUIT doing the RUN operation and returned to the system monitor. So enter an E.

Entering an E puts the system into its EDIT mode. The system prints out the same general information about number of lines, bytes and so on. You'll see, however, that the pointer is set to line 1 of the program. That's still not really relevant to what you are trying to do now, which is wipe out the program.

While you're at it, though, notice something else. After you entered the Q, the system skipped a line on the screen and printed a period symbol. *The period symbol is the prompt character whenever the system is in the monitor mode.* Whenever you see a period used as the prompt symbol, you know the system is in its monitor mode.

You responded to the period by entering an E. The system repeated the technical information about the program, and then printed a greater-than symbol. *The greater-than symbol is the prompt character whenever the system is in the edit mode.*

So you've gone to the monitor mode and then to the edit mode. Now here is where you wipe out the existing program. Enter D*. This time you don't see a lot of technical information, just the comment, EMPTY FILE . . . ENTER TEXT.

So the old program is gone and the system is waiting for a new program. The prompt character is now a question mark. *The question mark is the prompt character whenever the system is in the programming mode.* Whenever you see a question mark prompt character, you know the system is expecting you to enter some new information.

In summary, here's how to wipe out an existing program.

- ENTER Q
- ENTER E
- ENTER D*

ENTERING A NEW PROGRAM FROM THE KEYBOARD

Suppose you have wiped out all existing programs by using the procedures described in the previous section. Doing so, you are left with the message:

EMPTY FILE. . .ENTER TEXT
?—

The message tells you there are no programs in the current file. It's wide open for a new one. Try entering this program. Copy it one line at a time, ending each line by striking the ENTER key.

Example 2-1
    BEGIN
    WRITE (28, 31, 'YOU HAVE JUST ENTERED A PASCAL
    PROGRAM')
    END.

When you are through, the screen should look something like this:

    EMPTY FILE . . . ENTER TEXT
    ?BEGIN
    ?WRITE ?28, 31, 'YOU HAVE JUST ENTERED A PASCAL
    PROGRAM')
    ?END.
    ?—

The system is still in the PROGRAM mode. How do you know that? The question mark prompt symbol tells you so.

Now strike the ENTER key again, and you should get this message:

    FILE HAS 3 LINES   66 BYTES   (498E-49CF)   PTR
    AT LINE 3

Sure enough, the program has three lines. Count them. It also occupies 66 bytes of memory in hexadecimal address locations 498E to 49CF. The program pointer happens to be at the last line.

You cannot add any more lines of information at this time because the system is no longer in the PROGRAM mode. It happens to be in the EDIT mode as signaled by the greater-than prompt character.

If you have made any mistakes in writing the program, wipe out the whole works by entering D* and starting over.

In summary, to enter a new program from the keyboard:

● Delete the existing program.
● Enter the new lines of text.
● Strike the ENTER key to get to the EDIT mode.

For the time being, correcting any errors in the program is a matter of deleting the whole thing from the EDIT mode and starting over from scratch. You will find out how to modify a program and correct minor errors later on.

COMPILING A PROGRAM

A Tiny Pascal program cannot be run immediately after it is written. It must be compiled first. It must be translated from the Pascal character text or *source* program into machine language or *object* program. Standard and UCSD Pascal takes care of the compiling job automatically, but Tiny Pascal does not. *You must tell the system to compile a new program before it can be run.*

To compile your new program, return to the MONITOR mode by entering a Q. How can you be sure the system has returned to the MONITOR mode? It uses a period for the prompt symbol.

Now enter C. In Supersoft Tiny Pascal, entering a C from the MONITOR mode tells the system to compile the existing source program.

Using the program suggested in the previous section, the system prints out this information when you compile it:

```
.C
BEGIN
WRITE (28, 31, 'YOU HAVE JUST ENTERED A PASCAL
PROGRAM')
END.
56 CODES. 49D0-4A07
.-
```

If you have made any syntax errors in the Pascal source program, the system will pick them up during the COMPILE phase. In fact, Tiny Pascal won't complete the compiling operation until the program is error free.

The little message at the end of the program listing tells you that the machine language version of your program occupies memory locations hex 49D0 through 4A07. That really isn't important information at this point, but it might be mildly interesting if you have ever done any machine language programming before.

To compile a program:

- Get into the MONITOR mode by entering Q.
- Enter C.
- Hope the whole thing gets compiled without any error messages.

RUNNING A PROGRAM

A Tiny Pascal program can be run only from the MONITOR mode. In other words, you cannot expect to run a program unless the current prompt symbol is a period. After compiling a program, the system is automatically in the MONITOR mode. That means a program is ready to run the moment the compiling operation is done.

To run a program, simply enter R for "run."

If you run the program that is used as an example through these discussions, it clears the screen and then prints:

YOU HAVE JUST ENTERED A PASCAL PROGRAM

Incidentally, Pascal programs do not automatically clear the screen when they are run. It so happens that the program you entered contained some instructions that told the system to clear the screen. (No more CLS, dear BASIC buffs).

When the computer has executed the entire program, it prints the period prompt character, followed by the cursor. That signifies that the system is still in the MONITOR mode, and that you can run the program again by simply entering an R.

Now you can wipe out that program by going to the EDIT mode, entering an E. Then enter D*. The system is ready to receive the next program from the keyboard.

SHORT PASCAL PROGRAMS

Here are a few simple Pascal programs that are intended to give you some exercise in entering, compiling, running and erasing programs. If you make any mistakes, just get into the EDIT mode and enter D*. That will erase the entire program and set up the system for entering it again, without the error this time.

Some of these programs are set up to end automatically after doing just one or two short operations. Whenever a program ends, you will see the MONITOR mode prompt symbol, a period, on the screen.

A few of the programs do not end at all on their own accord, or they run for a very long time. To halt an ongoing program, simply strike the BREAK key one time. If you want the program to resume from that point, just strike any other key.

Whenever you want to stop an ongoing program and return to the MONITOR mode, strike the BREAK key twice in succession. You'll know it worked when you see the period prompt symbol.

Example 2-2

```
(* COUNTER *)
VAR L, N: INTEGER;
BEGIN
WRITE (28, 31, 'COUNTER');
FOR L:=1 TO 8 DO
```

```
                WRITE (13);
        N:=0;
        WHILE N<1000 DO
                BEGIN
                WRITE (220, N#);
                FOR L:=1 TO 500 DO
                        L:=L+1;
                WRITE (29, 30);
                N:=N+1;
                END
        END.
```

Example 2-3

```
        (* SUMS *)
        VAR FIRST, SECOND: INTEGER;
        BEGIN
        WRITE (28, 31, 'SUMS', 13, 13);
        WRITE ('ENTER AN INTEGER BETWEEN −15000 AND
        +15000', 13);
        READ (FIRST#);
        WRITE ('ENTER ANOTHER INTEGER IN THE SAME
        RANGE', 13);
        READ (SECOND#);
        WRITE (28, 31, 13, 13, 13, FIRST#, '+', SECOND#, '=',
        FIRST+SECOND#);
        FOR FIRST:=1 TO 8 DO
                WRITE (13);
        WRITE ('ENTER TO DO AGAIN')
        END.
```

Example 2-4

```
        (* STAIRS *)
        VAR H, H0, V, V0:INTEGER;
        BEGIN
        WRITE (28, 31, 210, 'STRIKE SPACE BAR TO EXIT THIS
        PROGRAM');
        H0:=0; V0:=0;
        REPEAT
                FOR V:=V0 TO 47 DO
                        BEGIN
                        FOR H:=H0 TO H0+4 DO
                                PLOT (H, V, 1)
                        END;
                H0:=H0+4; V0:=V0+2;
```

```
UNTIL VØ:=47;
REPEAT;
UNTIL INKEY=32
END.
```

Example 2-5

```
(* POWERS OF N *)
VAR LINE, N: INTEGER;
BEGIN
WRITE (28, 31, 215, '** POWERS OF N **', 13);
WRITE ('N', 2Ø7, 'N 2ND', 2Ø7, 'N 3RD', 13);
FOR LINE:=Ø TO 63 DO
        WRITE ('3');
FOR N:=Ø TO 1Ø DO
        WRITE (N#, 2Ø7, N*N#, 211, N*N*N#, 13);
WRITE (27)
END.
```

SUMMARY OF BASIC OPERATING PROCEDURES

The information presented thus far in this chapter can be summarized as follows:

- —Load the Supersoft TRS-80 Tiny Pascal tape as a SYSTEM program having the file name PASCAL.
- —There are three basic operating modes, each having its own prompt character: MONITOR, period prompt symbol; EDIT, greater-than prompt symbol; PROGRAM, question mark prompt symbol.
- —The MONITOR mode is "home base." Programs are compiled and run from MONITOR.
- —To get into MONITOR from EDIT or PROGRAM, enter Q.
- —To get into EDIT from MONITOR, enter E. To get into EDIT from PROGRAM, strike the ENTER key twice in succession.
- —One way to get into PROGRAM is to enter D* while in the EDIT mode.
- —A complete program is delected by entering D* while in the EDIT mode.
- —All programs must be compiled before they can be run. Programs are compiled by entering C while in the MONITOR mode.
- —Compiled programs are run by entering R while in the MONITOR mode.

MODIFYING PROGRAMS WHILE IN EDIT

Programmers, no matter how much experience they have, make programming errors. So far in this chapter, it has been suggested that you deal with program errors by deleting the entire program and rewriting it from scratch. Obviously that isn't the most efficient way to deal with errors, especially when the program is fairly long.

Tiny Pascal includes a rather nice editing feature that lets you correct programming errors by either inserting a new line of information or deleting an old one. Quite often you will deal with an error by applying both procedures in succession, deleting a line containing an error and then inserting a corrected version in its place.

You have probably guessed by now that the system must be in the EDIT mode in order to make deletions and insertions. You're right. In the EDIT mode, entering a D deletes a line of text. Entering and I allows you to insert any number of lines of text.

To get a feeling for how Tiny Pascal editing works, enter this little program.

Example 2-6A

```
(* ERROR PROGRAM *)
VAR X, Y: INTEGER
READ (X#, Y#);
WRITE ((X+Y)#)
END.
```

Example 2-6A has an error in it. Don't worry about what the error is at this time. Pretend you don't know it exists, and try compiling the program.

The compiler will pick up the error, and you will see something like this on the screen:

```
.C
(* ERROR PROGRAM *)
VAR X, Y: INTEGER
READ<ERROR 14
 ·-
```

ERROR 14-Missing Semicolon

ERROR 14 . . . ? What is that? Look back at the listing of Tiny Pascal syntax errors in the Appendix, and you will find that ERROR 14 means that a semicolon is missing.

It so happens that the line reading VAR X, Y: INTEGER should end with a semicolon. It should read VAR X, Y: INTEGER;.

Unfortunately the system does not know for sure that you have omitted the semicolon until the compiler has moved on to the next program statement. For that reason, the less-than pointer and error message appear on the next line.

It would be nice if the error message pointed directly to the problem, but it rarely does. It usually shows up in the next program statement. You'll simply have to get used to that little feature.

At any rate, the compiler prevents you from fully compiling a program that contains a syntax error. It spells out the nature of the error for you. Now you have to correct the error before the program can be compiled properly and run.

When the compiler picked up the error for you, it returned a period prompt symbol. That means the system is still in the MONITOR mode. Remember that compiling is a MONITOR operation. So you have to get into the EDIT mode in order to make the necessary correction.

Enter E to get into EDIT, and you will see something like this on the screen:

```
.C
(* ERROR PROGRAM *)
VAR X, Y:INTEGER
READ<ERROR 14
.E

FILE HAS 5 LINES 67 BYTES (498E-49D∅) PTR AT LINE 1
>_
```

Now the system is in the EDIT mode as signaled by the greater-than prompt character.

There are several different ways to handle this particular editing job—inserting the semicolon at the end of the VAR line. In any event, the general idea is to get to the line containing the error, delete that line, and replace it with a corrected version.

Editing in BASIC is made rather simple because all lines of text carry line numbers. In BASIC, you can get to a particular line by simply specifying its line number. Pascal, however, does not use line numbers, so you have to home in on a particular line by more subtle means.

In this case, notice that the EDIT data message, that automatically printed line that contains information about the number of lines and bytes, says the pointer (PTR) is at line 1. The system, in other words, is "looking" at line 1 at the moment.

The error, however, is in the second line of the program. To get to that line, enter N. *Entering an N while in the EDIT mode moves the pointer down one line.* Here is what you will see on the screen:

```
>N
VAR X, Y: INTEGER
>—
```

Sure enough. There's the next line printed out for you. That happens to be the line that contains the error, so delete it by entering D. *Entering D in the EDIT mode deletes the current program line.* The information on the screen now looks like this:

```
>N
VAR X, Y: INTEGER
>D
>—
```

The faulty line is now gone, and the next step is to insert a corrected version in its place. Begin by entering I, for "insert." *Entering an I in the EDIT mode sets up the system for inserting a new line of text.*

```
>N
VAR X, Y: INTEGER
>D
>I
?__
```

Now the system is prepared to accept a new line of text. In this instance, you should enter VAR X, Y: INTEGER;.

```
N
VAR X, Y: INTEGER
D
I
? VAR X, Y: INTEGER;
?__
```

Compiling

The revised line is now inserted into the program. The presence of the question mark prompt character indicates the system is ready to accept yet another line of text. But since this particular program calls for just a one-line correction, it is time to try compiling again.

First, you have to get out of the insert mode (actually the PROGRAM mode—see the question mark?). Strike the ENTER key one more time, and you will see the greater-than prompt character:

```
N
VAR X, Y: INTEGER
D
I
? VAR X, Y: INTEGER;
? _
```

That means the system is back in the EDIT mode. You have to compile from MONITOR, so enter Q. Sure enough, there's the period signaling the MONITOR mode. Now compile by entering C.

```
.C
(* ERROR PROGRAM *)
VAR X, Y: INTEGER;
READ<ERROR 18
._
```

ERROR 18 and Its Correction

Rats! There is another error in the program. According to the error listing in the Appendix, ERROR 18 means there is an error in the declaration part of the program. You probably don't know what that means at this point in the game, but it seems that a BEGIN statement ought to appear between VAR X, Y: INTEGER; and READ (X#, Y#);. So go back to the EDIT mode.

The information text indicates that the program pointer is at line 1. The new line of text, however, should be inserted between the second and third lines. You want to work it out so that VAR X, Y: INTEGER; is the current line, and then insert BEGIN.

You can get down to that second line by entering N. Then enter I to get into the INSERT mode, and respond to the question mark by entering BEGIN.

Get out of the INSERT/PROGRAM mode by striking the ENTER key, return to the MONITOR by entering Q, and then compile by entering C. The compiler ought to make it all the way through this time. There are no more syntax errors.

The corrected version of the program in Example 2-6A should look like this:

Example 2-6B

```
(* ERROR PROGRAM *)
VAR X, Y: INTEGER;
```

```
BEGIN
READ (X#, Y#);
WRITE ((X+Y)#)
END.
```

Getting To the Right Line

All you can really do in the EDIT mode is delete and insert lines of text. The trick to editing in Tiny Pascal is getting to the desired line of text.

In the examples just cited, getting to the desired place in the program was a matter of moving down one line, by entering an N for "next." But what if you want to move down maybe 20 lines in a long program? Does that mean you have to enter N 20 times in succession? No, not really. You can move down any number of program lines by entering Nn, where n is the number of lines you want to move. Entering N12, for example, moves the pointer down 12 lines below the current one. N1 is the same thing as just plain N.

You can also move upward any number of lines by entering Un. Entering U6 moves the pointer 6 lines above the current one. Entering just plain U moves the pointer to the next line above the current one.

So by entering Us and Ns, it is possible to move up and down any desired number of lines in the program—only while in the EDIT mode, of course. Once you get to the desired place in the program in this fashion, you can do the necessary delete and insert operations.

More Editing Tricks

There is yet another handy operation that is possible in the EDIT mode. Enter P*, and the system prints the entire program listing. That operation is the same as doing a LIST in BASIC.

There are a couple of more editing tricks available in the Supersoft Tiny Pascal package. You have enough at your disposal for the time being, however. If you want to see how some of the other procedures work, consult the Supersoft manual.

Here is a brief summary of the editing procedures described in this section:

- To delete a line of text, enter D. To delete the entire program listing, enter D*.
- To insert one or more new lines of text, first enter I and then enter the new lines.
- To move the program pointer downward n number of lines, enter Nn.

- To move the program pointer upward *n* number of lines, enter U*n*.
- To view the entire program listing, enter P*. To view *n* lines of text in succession, enter P*n*.

LEARNING BY DOING

There is a lot of material presented in this chapter. And there is little doubt that many readers are confused by the whole thing.

The best way to clear up the confusion and get some good Pascal programming under way is by doing it. Dig in and make mistakes. You'll learn from your mistakes, and the material in this chapter should help bail you out of some of the problems. In fact, some people learn better by setting aside the book and doing everything on their own, referring back to the book only when all theories have been exhausted.

So what if you don't know exactly how to do things in the most efficient manner? As long as you can get the job done, that's adequate for the time being. You will most likely find yourself perfecting the necessary skills as you go along and get more first-hand experience.

SAVING PASCAL PROGRAMS ON CASSETTE TAPE

Suppose you have entered and compiled a Tiny Pascal program that you would like to save on cassette tape. The job isn't difficult.

First, make sure the system is in the MONITOR mode. Then set up the cassette machine for recording.

Enter WS, followed by a file name of your choosing. The file name cannot have more than six characters; other than that, you are free to invent file names of any sort.

Suppose, for example, you want to record the Pascal program called FUNNY1. Set the system to the MONITOR mode, set up the cassette machine for recording, and enter WS FUNNY1.

The cassette machine starts running and continues running until the program is recorded. At that time, the cassette machine stops and you see the MONITOR prompt symbol on the screen. The job is done.

To load a Pascal program from cassette tape, make sure the program file is empty. Get the computer into the MONITOR mode and set the cassette machine for playback. Then enter LS, followed by the program's file name.

The cassette machine stops when the program is fully loaded. All you do after that is compile the program and run it.

Remember: every program must be compiled before it can be run.
A new program entered from the keyboard must be compiled. A program that has been edited must be compiled. And a program entered from cassette tape must be compiled.

The procedures for getting Pascal programs onto tape and from tape into the machine are nearly identical to the ways you handle BASIC recording. Simply remember the job has to be done in the MONITOR mode. You enter WS and a file name to record, and LS and a file name to load the program from tape.

TESTING YOUR SKILLS WITH MORE PROGRAMS

Here are a few more Tiny Pascal programs. Give them all a try. If you make any mistakes, correct them by using the editing procedures rather than wiping out the whole thing. Also, try saving some of the more interesting ones on cassette tape.

Example 2-7

```
(* NESTED RECTANGLES *)
VAR HØ, H1, VØ, V1:INTEGER;
PROC DRAW;
      VAR H, V:INTEGER;
      BEGIN
      FOR H:=HØ TO H1 DO
             BEGIN
             PLOT (H, VØ, 1); PLOT (H, V1, 1)
             END;
      FOR V:=VØ TO V1 DO
             BEGIN
             PLOT (HØ, V, 1); PLOT (H1, V, 1)
             END;
      END;
BEGIN
HØ:=Ø; H1:=127; VØ:=Ø; V1:=47;
WRITE (28, 31);
REPEAT
      WHILE (HØ<H1) AND (VØ<V1) DO
             BEGIN
             DRAW;
             HØ:=HØ+4; H1:=H1-4; VØ:=VØ+2; V1:
             =V1-2;
             END;
      UNTIL INKEY=32;
   END.
```

Example 2-8

```
(* DICE ROLL *)
VAR LINE: INTEGER;
PROC RANDOM;
    VAR M, N, P: INTEGER;
    BEGIN
    REPEAT
        M:=N*25;
        IF M Ø THEN
            M:=ABS(M);
        N:=M;P:=M
        P:=P MOD 7;
    UNTIL P Ø;
    WRITE (P#)
END;
BEGIN
WRITE(28, 31, 22Ø, 'DICE ROLL');
FOR LINE:=1 TO 8 DO
    WRITE (13, 22Ø);
RANDOM;
WRITE (32, 32);
RANDOM;
WRITE (13, 13, 13, 13, 'ENTER R TO ROLL AGAIN')
END.
```

Example 2-9

```
(* ASCII DEMO *)
VAR N: INTEGER;
BEGIN
WRITE (28, 31, 'HERE IS THE COMPLETE TRS-80 ASCII
CHARACTER SET:');
WRITE(13, 13);
FOR N:=32 TO 191 DO
    WRITE (N);
END.
```

OUT-OF-MEMORY ERROR SIGNAL

When you get to the point where you are developing rather long and involved Tiny Pascal programs, you are bound to come across an ERROR 1ØØ1 when attempting to compile them. This is the system's "out-of-memory" error signal.

Under normal circumstances, both your source program and its P-code version will reside in the memory. When compiling very long source programs, however, it is entirely possible to run out of memory space before the P-code version is completely compiled.

What can you do about it? Basically, the idea is to tell the system to give up the source program, writing over it with the P-code version. This version is absolutely necessary for running the program. The disadvantage is that your written-out source program is lost in the process.

There are a couple of ways to handle the situation, but here is the one I have found to be most helpful in the long run. First, compile your finished source program by entering C/-P instead of C. That will compile the program, checking for syntax errors, without actually generating the P-code. The idea is to iron out all the syntax errors.

Then save the entire source program on cassette tape by doing a WS *file name*. The source program is thus saved for future use and, debugging.

With the source program still residing in memory, compile the P-code version by entering P/-S. This operation generates the P-code right over your source program. It will destroy the source program. Remember, though, that you have saved it for future use on cassette tape.

Now the program can be run and tested for programming errors. Hopefully, you won't find any programming errors. Certainly there won't be any syntax errors. Running the C/-P routine should have taken care of that little matter.

If you decide you want to change something in the program, you must reload the source version from the cassette tape. The P-code version, itself, cannot be altered from the keyboard. Once you make the necessary corrections in the source program start the sequence all over again. Do a C/-P to check for syntax errors. Save the source program on cassette tape. Compile the program with P/-S. Run the P-code version.

Eventually, you will end up with a recorded version of the source program that satisfies you. It can be loaded into the system, compiled with C/-S and run at any later time. None of this applies, of course, if you do not see an ERROR 1001 when attempting to compile with an ordinary C command.

Chapter 3
Begin With BEGIN

One of the hallmarks of Pascal, including Tiny Pascal, is the orderly and logical fashion in which programs must be written. There is a whole family of syntax rules that you must follow in precise detail, and you are probably going to stumble over some of them at first. Once you begin grasping the idea of Pascal syntax, you will find the rules are, themselves, very logical and rather easy to remember.

The task of learning and recalling Pascal syntax rules can be made much easier when you learn to read *syntax diagrams*. In fact, the whole essence of Pascal can be summarized in about three pages of syntax diagrams.

So even though it is possible to write a book of this sort without making any references to syntax diagrams, it would be foolish to try it. Knowing how to read these diagrams makes it possible to learn Pascal much more effectively. This chapter introduces a few of the most fundamental Pascal programming steps and, at the same time, shows how to read syntax diagrams.

READING SYNTAX DIAGRAMS

Figure 3-1 is the syntax diagram for absolutely any program written in Pascal. The term BLOCK enclosed in the rectangle represents everything that goes into the structure of the program.

Reading the syntax diagram in Fig. 3-1 in the direction the arrows are pointing, —from left to right, —every Pascal program first consists of a *block*.

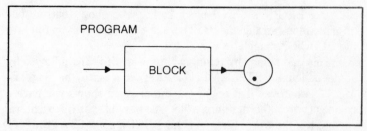

PROGRAM

BLOCK

Fig. 3-1. Syntax diagram for any Pascal program.

After the BLOCK comes a circle with a period inside it. That symbol indicates that *every* Pascal program must end with a period. Look back through the examples in Chapter 2, and you should find every one of them ending with a period.

Thus any Pascal program begins with a block of operations and concludes with a period. That's what the syntax diagram in Fig. 3-1 says.

Symbols

But what is that BLOCK? On a syntax diagram, any expression enclosed within a rectangular figure represents something that has to be defined somewhere else. The BLOCK in Fig. 3-1, in other words, has to be defined. Putting it even more simply, someone, somewhere along the line, has to specify the operation to be included in the BLOCK.

On the other hand, terms enclosed in circles or rectangles with rounded corners indicate things that do not require definition. The period in the circle in Fig. 3-1 says a period character must end a Pascal program. The "period" doesn't need further defining. A period is a period, no matter how you look at it.

There is a third kind of symbol appearing on a syntax diagram: arrows. Arrows indicate the direction of flow of events.

And that's all, just three symbols. There is a rectangle that indicates operations that are defined elsewhere, a circle or rounded rectangle enclosing self-defined steps, and arrows indicating the direction of activity.

Seem too simple? Maybe it is, because nothing can be done until block is defined better.

Defining BLOCK

The simplest way to define BLOCK and have a program that does anything useful is to apply the syntax diagram in Fig. 3-2.

31

The BEGIN ... END block in Fig. 3-2 shows one of four possible block arrangements. These are the elements that fit into the BLOCK rectangle in Fig. 3-1.

This one begins by telling you to print BLOCK, followed by some undefined STATEMENT. After you write the STATEMENT, whatever that might be, the diagram shows you have a choice of two different things to do. One possible path is to a literal rendition of the word, END. Writing BEGIN, some STATEMENT and END terminates this block operation.

But if you wish, the diagram shows you can loop back to another statement, provided you write a semicolon along the way. Here are some valid BEGIN ... END block sequences:

        BEGIN
        statement
        END

        BEGIN
        statement;statement
        END

        BEGIN
        statement; statement; statement; statement
        END

The syntax diagram in Fig. 3-2 shows that you can include any number of statements, just as long as you insert a semicolon between them. Apparently the work isn't done yet, however. The STATEMENT block in Fig. 3-2 is not defined.

WRITE Statement Formats

Figure 3-3 is the syntax diagram for one of 12 Tiny Pascal statements. This is a WRITE statement, one of the simplest that does anything useful at all.

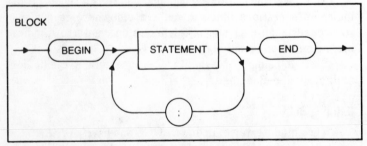

Fig. 3-2. Syntax diagram for the BEGIN ... END block.

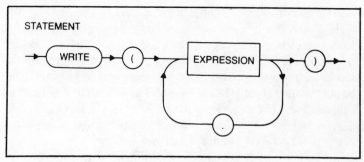

Fig. 3-3. Syntax diagram for the Pascal WRITE statement.

The syntax diagram in Fig. 3-3 says a statement can be made up of the word WRITE and EXPRESSION enclosed in parentheses. Some valid WRITE statements would have these formats:

WRITE (expression)

WRITE (expression, expression)

WRITE (expression, expression, expression)

A WRITE statement can include any number of expressions, as long as the expressions are separated by commas and *all* the expressions are enclosed in a single set of parentheses.

String Constant

But EXPRESSION is left undefined in Fig. 3-3. Will this ever end? To keep this discussion to manageable proportions, the analysis of several more syntax diagrams shows that it is possible to build an expression from a STRING CONSTANT. Figure 3-4 is the syntax diagram for a string constant.

Finally, you see a syntax diagram that is completely self-defined. There are no rectangles with sharp corners.

Writing a string constant is a matter of enclosing one or more keyboard characters within a set of apostrophes. The characters can be alphanumerics, spaces and any other symbols on the keyboard. Note from the syntax diagram that the characters are not separated by commas.

Here are some valid string constants:

'PASCAL IS FUN—WHEN YOU GET TO KNOW HIM!'

E EQUALS MC SQUARED'

'SOME COMPUTER PEOPLE GO CRAZY IN AN IN-TERESTING WAY'

Go back to Fig. 3-1 and work your way through to Fig. 3-4 again. Figure 3-1 says that a complete Pascal program consists of a block that ends with a period. Figure 3-2 indicates that a block can be composed of BEGIN, followed by any number of statements, and concluded with END. Figure 3-3 says the STATEMENT can be put together from WRITE, followed by any number of expressions enclosed in a single set of parentheses. And Fig. 3-4 indicates that an expression can be composed of any number of keyboard characters enclosed within a set of apostrophes.

The whole thing fits together like a Tinker Toy set. Whatever is left undefined at one stage is at least partly defined by the next one. The entire process continues until every step is fully defined. Figure 3-5 shows everything assembled into one syntax diagram.

SIMPLE PROGRAM EXAMPLES

Here are some simple Pascal programs that are written according to the overall diagram in Fig. 3-5. Try them; they work.

Example 3-1
    BEGIN
    WRITE('HELLO THERE')
    END.

Example 3-2
    BEGIN
    WRITE('HOW ABOUT THIS?', 'IT WORKS')
    END.

Example 3-3
    BEGIN
    WRITE('THIS WORKS');
    WRITE('TOO')
    END.

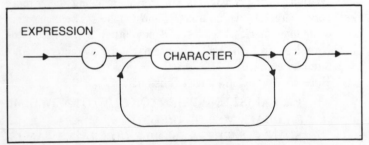

Fig. 3-4. Syntax diagram for the STRING CONSTANT expression.

34

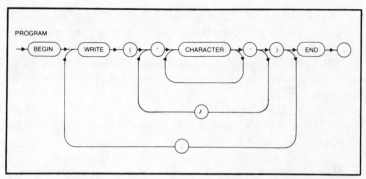

Fig. 3-5. A complete syntax diagram for Pascal programs using a BEGIN ...END block, WRITE statements and STRING CONSTANT expressions.

Example 3-1 represents a BEGIN ... END block operation. It includes a single WRITE statement which, in turn, is composed of a single string constant.

Example 3-2 is also a BEGIN ... END block operation with a single WRITE statement; but the statement is made up of two expressions. The expressions in that case are both string constants.

Example 3-3 uses two WRITE statements. Each contains a single string constant.

The three examples just cited hardly cover all possible programs that can come out of the syntax diagram in Fig. 3-5. Work through each of the examples yourself, carefully noting how they follow the syntax diagram. And then try making up some programs of your own. If you goof up, the compiler will let you know about it.

STEP-BY-STEP ANALYSIS OF WRITE STATEMENTS

For the sake of readers who are still hazy about how to interpret syntax diagrams, this is a good place to analyze them one step at a time. Refer to the diagram in Fig. 3-5 again, and see how it is a very specific guide to writing Pascal programs.

Beginning at the left-hand side of the drawing (where the reading of syntax diagrams usually begins), the first step is to enter BEGIN. And then the diagram says the next step is to write WRITE.

For the sake of clarity, rather than necessity, these words are usually printed on separate lines. For instance:

BEGIN
WRITE

Next, the diagram says that every WRITE must be followed by a left parenthesis. Since the purpose of the diagram is to write some string characters, the next item on the list is an apostrophe.

Thus far, the diagram says you must do this:

BEGIN
WRITE('

There has been no choice in the selection of words and symbols to this point.

CHARACTER Phase

A CHARACTER of some sort comes after the first apostrophe. It can be any keyboard character you want to use. After writing the first character, you reach the first choice point in the diagram. You have the choice of going to the right, entering an apostrophe and ending the CHARACTER phase of the job, or looping back to the beginning of the CHARACTER phase. In actual practice, you can loop around through the CHARACTER phase about 250 times before leaving it.

To keep things simple, suppose you loop through the CHARACTER phase often enough to write the characters for HELLO. So when you're through with the CHARACTER phase, the program looks like this:

BEGIN
WRITE('HELLO

The diagram says you must conclude a character writing phase with an apostrophe. There's no choice in the matter.

BEGIN
WRITE('HELLO'

Choice Points

Now comes another choice point, the one between the second apostrophe and right parthenseis character. This choice point gives you the option of either writing a right parenthesis and concluding the WRITE statement, or looping back through a comma symbol to the beginning of an entirely new CHARACTER phase.

Assuming you want to write another set of characters, you must write a comma, an apostrophe, another set of characters and another apostrophe. For example:

```
BEGIN
WRITE ('HELLO', 'THERE'
```

Now you are at the choice point between the apostrophe and right-parenthesis symbol again. Opting to write another set of characters, you must enter a comma, an apostrophe, and another set of characters concluded with an apostrophe. See this:

```
BEGIN
WRITE('HELLO', 'THERE'. 'HOW ARE YOU?'
```

Suppose this time you want to conclude the WRITE statement, rather than looping back through the comma to generate yet another string of characters. The diagram says you must enter a right-parenthesis character. Thus:

```
BEGIN
WRITE('HELLO', 'THERE', '.HOW ARE YOU?' )
```

You are now at another choice point. You can either conclude the program by entering END and a period, or loop back through a semicolon to begin an entirely new WRITE statement.

If you choose to loop back to do another WRITE statement, enter the semicolon, enter WRITE, followed by a left parenthesis, an apostrophe and a whole new set of string characters. Using just one string expression this time, the overall program looks like this:

```
BEGIN
WRITE('HELLO', 'THERE','. HOW ARE YOU?');
WRITE( 'I AM FINE, THANK YOU.')
```

At this time, you are back to the choice point between ending the program or entering a semicolon to begin yet another WRITE statement. Opting to end the program, you must write the word END, followed by a period.

```
BEGIN
WRITE('HELLO', 'THERE','. HOW ARE YOU?');
WRITE( 'I AM FINE, THANK YOU.')
END.
```

You have worked your way through the syntax diagram in Fig. 3-5 from beginning to end. And that makes up a complete Pascal program. Compile and run it to see something like this on the screen:

```
HELLO THERE. HOW ARE YOU? I AM FINE, THANK
YOU.
```

VARYING FORMATS

The syntax of the program is critical. The syntax diagram must be followed to the tiniest detail. Aside from the actual syntax, however, you can write out the program in just about any sort of format you choose. For instance, there is no critical reason why BEGIN, WRITE, WRITE and END should start on separate lines of the program. Also, the expressions within the parentheses could be written on lines separate from their respective WRITE statements. In fact, the whole program could be written as a one-liner:

```
BEGIN WRITE('HELLO', 'THERE','. HOW ARE YOU?');
WRITE('I AM FINE, THANK YOU.') END.
```

The program still follows the syntax rules, and it will run the same way as the 4-line version. But the 1-liner is terribly confusing to anyone trying to understand what the program is supposed to do. Even if you aren't interested in what others think of your programs, you will find that long-line programs are very difficult to edit.

So an orderly program format pays off in the long run. Generally, that means beginning each new statement on a new line.

Chapter 4
Screen Control and
Graphics With WRITE

The WRITE statement described in Chapter 3 is good for more than simply writing out simple string constants. It is also one of the primary screen control statements, and that is what this chapter is about.

CONTROLLING THE CURSOR WITH WRITE

You have probably noticed by now that the CLEAR key on your TRS-80 has no effect on Tiny Pascal screen operations. All of your programs, compile listings and general doodling on the screen cannot be cleared away in the usual fashion. It remains on the screen until it is scrolled off the top by subsequent keyboard operations.

It turns out that the screen cannot be cleared while the system is accepting commands from the keyboard, but it is altogether possible to insert a screen clearing operation into a Tiny Pascal program. The operation works just like the CLS statement in BASIC.

To see the Tiny Pascal version of CLS at work, enter, compile and run the following program:

Example 4-1

    BEGIN
    WRITE (28, 31)
    END.

Upon executing this program, the system clears the screen and places the MONITOR prompt symbol, a period, at the cursor's home position at the upper left-hand corner of the screen. That's it. WRITE (28, 31) is the Tiny Pascal version of BASIC's CLS.

The program in Example 4-1 follows the syntax rules that are painstakingly drawn out for you in Chapter 3. The only difference of special note is that this new program uses integer constants as expressions. The examples in Chapter 3 all used string constants as expressions. Figure 4-1 shows the syntax diagram for EXPRESSION, extended to include both string and integer constants.

The big question now is this one. What is so special about the constants 28 and 31 that makes the system clear the screen and drive the cursor to its home position?

If you take a look at the Appendix in this book or the listing of *Control Codes: 1-31* in your TRS-80 user's manual, you will find that code 28 homes the cursor and code 31 clears the screen to the end of the screen frame. Performing those two control operations in succession amounts to doing a CLS in BASIC.

You will want to use this screen clearing WRITE statement rather often in your Pascal program writing experience. Just about every program ought to begin that way, clearing unnecessary text from the screen before writing out information that is more relevant to the programming task at hand.

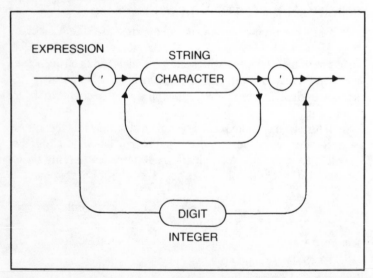

Fig. 4-1. Syntax diagram for an EXPRESSION offering STRING and INTEGER options.

Figure 4-2 shows the complete evolution of Pascal syntax diagrams that eventually leads to writing string constants, integer constants or both. The diagrams are identical to those in Chapter 3, up to Fig. 4-2D. At that point, the programmer has the option of writing either a STRING or INTEGER expression.

STRING Expression

Writing a STRING expression (Fig. 4-2E) is a matter of entering an apostrophe, followed by any delivered combination of keyboard characters and concluded with another apostrophe. The diagram in this case is no different from that in Fig. 3-4.

Figure 4-2F is the syntax diagram for writing an integer constant. In this instance, there are no apostrophes enclosing the expression; it is simply any combination of keyboard digits, 0 through 9, written in succession.

The little screen clearing program in Example 4-1 follows the syntax evolution in Fig. 4-2. The BLOCK is a BEGIN . . . END operation. The STATEMENT is a WRITE; and in this particular case, the EXPRESSION is a series of two INTEGER entries, 28 and 31.

The STRING expression option is not used in Example 4-1. Take a look at these examples, however. Try them on your machine to convince yourself that they work.

Example 4-2A

```
BEGIN
WRITE (28, 31);
WRITE ('NOW THE SCREEN IS CLEARED')
END.
```

Example 4-2B

```
BEGIN
WRITE (28, 31, 'NOW THE SCREEN IS CLEARED')
END.
```

Examples 4-2A and 4-2B do the same job. They clear the screen, home the cursor and write the message NOW THE SCREEN IS CLEARED in the upper left-hand corner of the screen. The only programming difference is that Example 4-2A carries the screen clearing and message printing operations at two separate WRITE statements, while Example 4-2B combines those two operations into a single WRITE statement. Whether you choose to apply the 2-line or 1-line WRITE statement is purely a matter of personal preference.

Of course the entire program could be written on a single line without violating any of the syntax rules:

Example 4-2C

BEGIN WRITE (28, 31, 'NOW THE SCREEN IS CLEAR')
END.

But again, the problem with the single-line programming approach is that the entire line must be altered if you happen to make any mistakes.

You ought to make a note of the fact that string expressions must be enclosed in apostrophes, while integer expressions are not. That's the only way the computer can tell the difference between the two.

WRITE/INTEGER Statements

Interpreting these programming examples in the light of the syntax diagrams in Fig. 4-2 is important. But the main issue is now that you can gain complete control over cursor operations by means of WRITE/INTEGER statements.

Suppose you not only want to clear the screen, but write a string message near the center of the top line. Try this:

Example 4-3A

BEGIN
WRITE (28, 31, 25, 25, 25, 25, 25, 25, 25, 25, 25, 25, 25);
WRITE ('THIS MESSAGE IS CENTERED ON THE TOP LINE')
END.

First convince yourself that the Pascal program in Example 4-3A follows the syntax evolution in Fig. 4-2. There are two WRITE statements that are properly separated by a semicolon. The first WRITE statement contains a series of 2-digit INTEGER operations, each separated by commas. That comes about by combining Figs. 4-2C and 4-2F. The second WRITE statement is composed of a single STRING expression.

25 Codes

The first WRITE statement includes three different control codes: 28, 31 and 25. By beginning the integer sequence with the 28, 31 combination, the system first homes the cursor and clears the entire screen. After that you find twelve 25 codes. What do 25

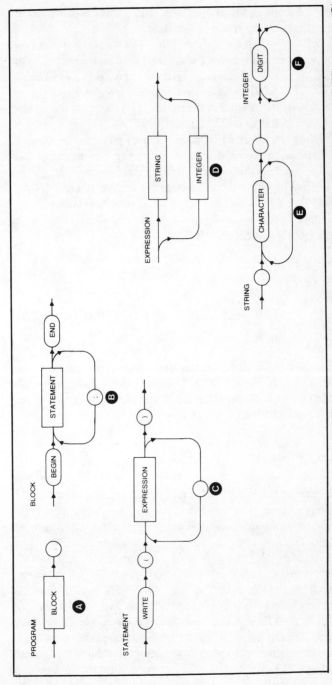

Fig. 4-2. (A) Syntax diagram for any Pascal program. (B) Syntax diagram for the BEGIN...END block. (C) Syntax diagram for WRITE statement. (D) Syntax diagram showing the option of writing either a STRING or INTEGER expression. (E) Syntax diagram for writing a STRING expression. (F). Syntax diagram for writing an integer constant.

43

codes do? According to the Appendix, a 25 control code moves the cursor one character space to the right.

The first WRITE line in Example 4-3A thus homes the cursor, clears the screen and moves the cursor 12 character spaces to the right. As a result, the message THIS MESSAGE IS CENTERED ON THE TOP LINE does indeed describe itself. Of course, you can vary the starting point of the message by changing the number of 25 codes in the first WRITE line.

Writing out so many 25 codes, just to position the message some distance to the right, can be something of a nuisance. Certainly the idea does the job, and is often a handy notion; but there is a more efficient way to move messages to the right. The improved method takes advantage of a set of TAB code numbers.

Try the program in Example 4-3A, and then compare the results with this version:

Example 4-3B

```
BEGIN
WRITE (28, 31, 204);
WRITE ('THIS MESSAGE IS CENTERED ON THE TOP
LINE')
END.
```

Example 4-3B does exactly the same thing as 4-3A, and without having to enter twelve 25 codes in succession. That 204 control code in Example 4-3B does the same job as the twelve successive 25s in Example 4-3A.

TAB Control Feature

To see the meaning of code 204, refer to the Appendix. You will see that control codes 192 through 255 are reserved for TAB operations. The cursor is automatically tabbed some number of spaces to the right, depending on which number you enter between 192 and 255.

If you use 192, you will find that the cursor isn't moved at all. But if you use the high extreme (255), you will find the cursor tabbed all the way to the end of the line. The control number 204 used in Example 4-3B falls within this range. Since 204 is the sum of 192 plus 12, it follows that code 204 tabs the cursor 12 spaces to the right. Getting the TAB feature to space 20 spaces to the right, by way of another example, is a matter of using control code 192+20, or 212.

To get a feeling for this TAB control feature, edit Example 4-3B several different times, using control numbers other than 204 in each case. Naturally, if you use control numbers that are too large, you will find the system breaking the message at the end of the first line and printing the rest of it at the beginning of the second line.

Line Feed Operations

So to this point, you know how to use WRITE/INTEGER statements to home the cursor (code 28), clear the screen (code 31 following 28), and position the cursor anywhere on the top line of the screen (codes 192 through 255). The next control code trick of special importance is the one that sends the cursor downward any desired number of lines. This is a downward line feed operation caused by control code 26. Try this example:

Example 4-4

```
BEGIN
WRITE (28, 31, 26, 26, 26, 26, 26, 26, 26, 26);
WRITE ('THIS MESSAGE IS ON THE MIDDLE LINE')
END.
```

The first WRITE statement homes the cursor, clears the screen, and then does eight downward line feeds in succession. Those eight successive line feed operations carry the cursor downward eight lines from its home position, very near the middle of the screen.

Unfortunately, there is no simple control code trick for eliminating the need for writing a bunch of 26s in sequence. If you want to move down 10 lines, you must write ten 26 codes in succession.

This is, however, an entirely different approach to simplifying the notion of doing a number of line feeds in succession, but it involves a Pascal repetitive statement that isn't described until later in this book. In the meantime, you'll have to live with the process of writing a 26 control code for each downward line feed you want to do.

Play around with the program in Example 4-4, altering the number of line feed codes. Remember that your TRS-80 screen can handle only 16 lines at a time. After that, see if you can figure out what Example 4-5 is supposed to do and how it does it.

Example 4-5

```
BEGIN
WRITE (28, 31, 26, 26, 26, 26, 26, 26, 26, 26, 202);
```

WRITE ('THIS MESSAGE IS IN THE CENTER OF THE
SCREEN')
END.

Code 13

Another control code of special importance to Tiny Pascal
programming is code 13: line feed with carriage return. The following examples demonstrate the value of this particular control code.

Example 4-6A

```
BEGIN
WRITE (28, 31, 'FIRST MESSAGE', 'SECOND MESSAGE')
END.
```

Enter, compile and run the program in Example 4-6A, and you
will see something like this on the screen:

FIRST MESSAGESECOND MESSAGE

Now that's a mess. The second message is butted up against
the end of the first one. Of course, you could separate them by
inserting a space control code between the two string messages:

Example 4-6B

```
BEGIN
WRITE (28, 31, 'FIRST MESSAGE', 25, 'SECOND MES-
SAGE')
END.
```

Or:

Example 4-6C

```
BEGIN
WRITE (28, 31, 'FIRST MESSAGE', 32, 'SECOND MES-
SAGE')
END.
```

Examples 4-6B and 4-6C both insert a space between the two
messages, resulting in a display that looks like this:

FIRST MESSAGE SECOND MESSAGE

The only difference between those two programs is that they
use different control codes for inserting the space. Example 4-6B
uses a 25 code to advance the cursor one space to the right, while
Example 4-6C does the same thing with a control code version of
striking the SPACE BAR (code 32). It makes no difference which
code you use.

But here is the real point of this discussion. How can you get the two messages printed at the beginning of separate lines? How do you get a display that looks like this?

FIRST MESSAGE
SECOND MESSAGE

Writing Messages As Separate WRITE Statements

It might seem logical to do the job by writing the two messages as separate WRITE statements:

Example 4-6D

```
BEGIN
WRITE (28, 31, 'FIRST MESSAGE');
WRITE ('SECOND MESSAGE')
END.
```

Enter, compile and run Example 4-6D, and you see this on the screen:

FIRST MESSAGESECOND MESSAGE

No, writing messages on separate WRITE lines doesn't help matters at all. Standard Pascal handles this sort of problem by offering two different WRITE statements: WRITE and WRITELN. Tiny Pascal cannot offer such an option, however, and *it is necessary to specify a line feed/carriage return control code* whenever lines of text are to be printed on successive lines. Try either of the following programs, and you'll see things working out better:

Example 4-6E

```
BEGIN
WRITE (28, 31, 'FIRST MESSAGE', 13, 'SECOND MES-
SAGE')
END.
```

Example 4-6F

```
BEGIN
WRITE (28, 31, 'FIRST MESSAGE', 13);
WRITE ('SECOND MESSAGE')
END.
```

Examples 4-6E and 4-6F do exactly the same thing:

FIRST MESSAGE
SECOND MESSAGE

47

Tiny Pascal does not perform a line feed/carriage return operation without being told to do so by means of a control code 13.

Study the complete list of control codes in the Appendix and try some of them in WRITE statements for yourself. Most of them are self explanatory. With a bit of playing around, you can get a good understanding of their nice features and shortcomings.

Virtually all of these control codes are used a number of times throughout this book. For the most part, they will be presented with little or no further comment.

PRINTING ASCII CHARACTERS WITH WRITE

Every character key on your TRS-80 keyboard is assigned an unique ASCII character code number. These codes can be represented by decimal numbers 32 through 128, and you will find them completely summarized in the Appendix and in your TRS-80 user's manual.

Just as it is possible to do cursor control operations by including some control code numbers in WRITE statements, it is possible to print any keyboard character by including their respective code numbers in WRITE statements. Here is a little demonstration of that fact:

Example 4-7

```
BEGIN
WRITE (28, 31, '*', 13, 13, 42)
END.
```

Example 4-7 is a legitimate and complete Pascal program. It follows the syntax rules, using a WRITE statement composed of five integer expressions and one string expression.

Reading that WRITE statement from left to right, it says:

Home the cursor (control code 28)
Clear the fram (control code 31)
Print an asterisk (* string constant)
Do two successive linefeed/carriage returns (control code 13)
Do control 42.

Control/42

What is "control 42?" According to the ASCII character listings, doing a 42 is the same thing as printing an asterisk. So this program clears the screen and homes the cursor, prints an asterisk by means of a string constant, skips down two lines and prints another asterisk by means of an ASCII command.

The program in Example 4-7 clearly shows that you have the option of printing a keyboard character as either a string constant or ASCII integer. Incidentally, the example shows how powerful WRITE statements can be when it comes to controlling screen activity. You can cram a lot of different kinds of operations into a single WRITE statement.

At any rate, whether you choose to print a keyboard character as a string or ASCII integer constant is a matter of personal preference and common sense. For example, there is little point in using ASCII code integers for writing messages having a lot of characters in them. The system can write BILL two different ways:

WRITE ('BILL') or WRITE (66, 73, 76, 76)

Obviously, using the string version, 'BILL', is both easier to write and understand after it is inserted into the program. Using the ASCII version is both cumbersome and difficult to interpret.

Advantages of ASCII Codes

So why bother with ASCII codes at all? There are a couple of reasons.

For one, it is slightly easier to write a single character message in ASCII form than as a string. You don't have to enclose the ASCII code in apostrophes. Doing ASCII 42 is somewhat simpler and faster than programming the string version, '*'.

A second advantage of using ASCII integer codes is that it becomes possible to print all four arrow characters. Using the string feature, it is possible to print only the up arrow (▲). Trying to fit the other three arrow figures into apostrophes causes some unwanted cursor motions.

To see what this is all about, try these two little programs.

Example 4-8A

```
BEGIN
WRITE (28, 31, 91, 92, 93, 94)
END.
```

Example 4-8B

```
BEGIN
WRITE (28, 31, '↑', '↓', '←', '→')
END.
```

Upon entering, compiling and running the Pascal program in Example 4-8A, you should see all four arrow characters on the screen:

↑↓ ← →

But you cannot even get Example 4-8B entered into the machine. You can only get as far as specifying the up-arrow character. As soon as you try to enter the down-arrow character as a string constant in Example 4-8B, you will find that the cursor simply drops down one line without printing the arrow at all. The same sort of thing happens when trying to specify the left- and right-arrow characters as string constants.

Now the fact that you can, indeed, print all four kinds of arrows using ASCII codes as integer constants in Pascal might seem to be a trivial advantage. Don't you imagine, however, that little arrows pointing in different directions will make handy characters for Pascal computer games and things of that sort? Sure they will.

DOING TRS-80 GRAPHICS WITH WRITE

Applying WRITE commands to cursor control and ASCII characters is a matter that is identical to all kinds of computer systems using any version of Pascal. The TRS-80, however, has an unique graphics format that is accessed in an identical fashion, by means of WRITE/INTEGER statements.

TRS-80 graphics symbols are built into integer locations 128 through 191. These 64 different graphics are summarized in the Appendix.

Each of these little characters occupies a single character space on the screen, and they can be called by a WRITE statement. Doing a WRITE (153), for example, causes a little vertical, zig-zag figure to appear on the screen, while doing a WRITE (170) makes a narrow vertical line appear. So it is possible to play with the graphics to generate some interesting patterns on the screen.

Example 4-9

BEGIN
WRITE (28, 31, 153, 13, 153, 13, 153, 13, 153)
END.

Example 4-9 generates the simple, but potentially useful, figure illustrated in Fig. 4-3. The WRITE statement first homes the cursor, clears the field, prints character 153, does a line feed/carriage return, then prints another 153 character and so on.

This is a cumbersome way to go about generating a complex set of figures on the screen. Most of the tedium will be eliminated when you've had a chance to work with some Pascal statements that do repetitive operations for you.

Fig. 4-3. Results of running the graphics program in Example 4-9. Note that blacks and whites are reversed for clarity.

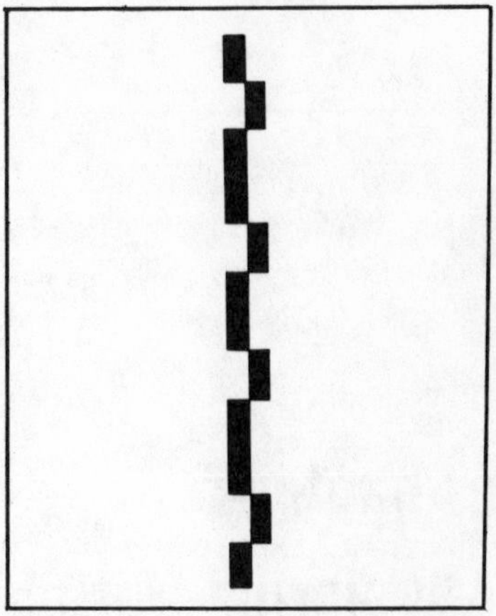

In the meantime, you will find it fun and instructive to write short Pascal programs that include WRITE statements calling the figures from the Appendix. If you want to see the entire graphics character set printed out on the screen, go back to Example 2-9. That little program in Example 2-9 prints out the entire ASCII and graphics format between code 32 and 191.

SOME THOUGHTS ABOUT THE WRITE STATEMENT

You have just spent two chapters of this book working with the Pascal WRITE statement. Figure 4-2 is especially important in this respect because it shows how the WRITE statement fits into a BEGIN . . . END BLOCK, and further shows how WRITE statements can be specified as STRING constants or INTEGER constants.

The importance of the WRITE statement in Pascal warrants two chapters in this book and even more, as you will see later on. A WRITE statement in Pascal carries far more weight than a PRINT statement in BASIC. A single compound WRITE statement—one made up of a number of different string and integer expressions—can carry the burden of a lot of programming operations.

In practice, the only thing that limits the length and complexity of a WRITE statement is the fact that Tiny Pascal can accept only 255 characters (*only* 255?) in a "single line." In a practical sense, however, a WRITE line should be kept relatively short so that you, as the programmer, can make editing changes without having to wipe out dozens of expressions. Lengthy WRITE sequences, in other words, should be broken up into a series of successive, relatively short WRITE statements.

51

Chapter 5
Declaring Variables
And Inputting With READ

Writing computer programs without using variables is like having cars without wheels. They look nice and make a lot of noise, but they can't really go anywhere. Then, too, some of the most interesting and useful programs are those giving the operator a chance to interact from the keyboard.

None of the examples cited in Chapters 3 and 4 includes variables or on-line keyboard operations. You aren't going very far in the business of writing and understanding Pascal programs until you know how to handle both of these situations.

Unfortunately, it is impossible to do anything meaningful with keyboard inputs until you understand Pascal variables. Most information entered from the keyboard is entered as values for variables. So you must study variables before doing anything with keyboard inputs.

Now that, in itself, isn't bad. The problem is that you are not yet in a position to work with Pascal variables without knowing how to work with keyboard inputs.

It looks like one of those crazy catch-22 situations. But there is a way around it. We will simply describe the nature of Pascal variables first, reserving specific, working examples until later in the chapter.

What this means is that you won't be able to test your understanding of Pascal variables until you get to the second part of the chapter. You will probably end up going through this chapter at least two times—once to get the general idea, and then again to test the ideas on a first-hand basis. Here goes.

DECLARING VARIABLES

Every variable used in a Pascal program must be declared, or specified, before it is used. In BASIC, you can pop a new variable into a program as the mood and need arise. Not so in Pascal. The machine must know in advance the name of every variable it will encounter in the operating portion of the program.

IDENTIFIER FORMAT

Pascal variables are declared in a BLOCK operation, and the syntax diagram in Fig. 5-1 shows how it works. According to that diagram, you first write VAR (for VARiable, of course), followed by something called an IDENTIFIER.

The IDENTIFIER rectangle in Fig. 5-1A is the only portion of that diagram that isn't completely defined. It is a fairly simple affair, however; and it is defined for you in Fig. 5-1B.

An IDENTIFIER consists of a letter—any one of the 26 letters of the alphabet—followed by nothing at all, or any combination of letters and digits. According to Fig. 5-1B, some valid identifiers would be:

ALPHA 1
SNOOPY
FUNNY9
NUMBER
SIM1DO

The syntax diagram for IDENTIFIER does not allow spaces or any other special keyboard characters, just alphanumerics between A and Z and Ø and 9. However, A2345 would be valid even though it appears to contain a number larger than 9. Actually, it is a letter followed by a sequence of four digits. That's okay.

An IDENTIFIER can be of any length, but in Tiny Pascal only the first four characters are significant. Any beyond the fourth are ignored. The significance of this fact is that you must be careful to distinguish two similar identifiers within the first four characters. The machine, for instance, cannot tell the difference between identifiers NUMBER1 and NUMBER2. FIRSTNO and SEC-ONDNO, on the other hand, are perfectly distinguishable.

One of the nice things about the Pascal IDENTIFIER format is that the identifiers, or variable names, can be literally descriptive, something rarely possible in BASIC. You can, for example, specify a variable for synchronizing operations with SYNCHNO or spell out a line drawing variable with LINEDRW.

Variable Declaration Block

It is the great flexibility in the selection of variable names that gives Pascal programs a peculiar and sometimes confusing appearance. All those nifty variable names, or identifiers, appear to be names of statements. "What does SYNCHNO do?" It looks like some sort of command or program statement, especially to people schooled in BASIC. But they search the Pascal literature for a description of SYNCHNO and cannot find it. It is simply a variable name the programmer dreamed up. At any rate, begin a variable declaration block by writing VAR, followed by an IDENTIFIER.

According to the syntax diagram in Fig. 5-1A, if you are specifying only one variable, the next step is to write a colon, followed by writing INTEGER and a semicolon. Here is an example of a declaration block for a single variable identifier, SNOOK.

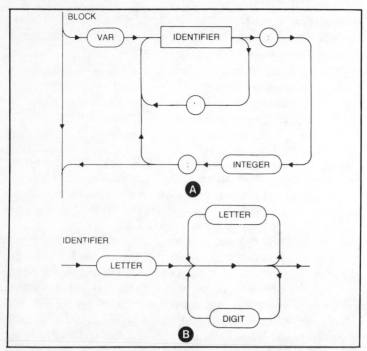

Fig. 5-1. Syntax diagram for declaring Pascal variables. (A) Main syntax diagram. (B) Syntax diagram for IDENTIFIER.

VAR SNOOK:INTEGER;

More often than not, however, you will have to specify more than one variable. That begin the case, the syntax diagram in Fig. 5-1A tells you to separate them with a comma. Here is a declaration block that specifies five different variables:

VAR X,XØ,Y,Z,Z2:INTEGER;

The syntax diagram also shows that you can write more than one variable line:

VAR DE,DF,DG,E:INTEGER;
    SNOOK,HOOK,SOME1:INTEGER;

Being able to split up the variable declaration lines as shown in that last example comes in handy on several occasions. For one, it is handy when specifying a very long list of variables, a list so long that it would otherwise spill off the right-hand side of the screen and onto the beginning of the next line.

There will be times when you will forget to declare some of the variables at the beginning of the program. Rather than having to edit the existing variable declaration line, simply insert another one below it.

Finally, being able to split up this block lets you specify different kinds of variable on different lines. Variables for one sort of application can be grouped on one line, while variables for an entirely different set of operations can be put onto another line.

In practice, there is no limit to the number of variables you can specify. As long as you follow the syntax rules for IDENTIFIER, the nature of the variable names is a matter of applying your own common sense and imagnation.

If you haven't noticed already, you can see that the syntax diagram for declaring variable names ends on the same line where it starts. All of the syntax diagrams shown to this point are open ended. This one is not, implying it must be used in conjunction with another BLOCK sequence. For our immediate purposes, the variable declaration block must be used with the BEGIN...END block already described in Chapters 3 and 4.

BLOCK Syntax Diagram

A variable declaration block is not adequate for defining a complete Pascal program. Figure 5-2 shows a complete BLOCK syntax diagram that incorporates both the BEGIN ... END operation and a variable declaration step.

The syntax diagram in Fig. 5-2 indicates something else of importance. The variable declaration operation must be inserted ahead of the BEGIN...END operation. See the downward direction of the arrows along the left-hand side of the drawing. This is consistent with the earlier statement that all variables must be declared before the program, itself, can be run.

A program generated from the diagram in Fig. 5-2 takes this sort of form:

```
VAR X,Y,Z:INTEGER;
BEGIN
       .
       .
       .
  (statement using variables
     X,Y and Z)
       .
       .
       .
END.
```

ENTERING INTEGERS WITH READ

One of the most common ways to assign values to Pascal variables is from the keyboard, via the READ statement. Just as Pascal's WRITE statement includes the elements of a PRINT statement in BASIC, Pascal's READ statement works much like an INPUT statement in BASIC.

Figure 5-3 is the syntax diagram for the READ statement. It begins by telling you to enter READ, followed by a right parenthesis. After that, you specify an IDENTIFIER already declared in the VAR ... INTEGER part of the program. So whatever you enter as part of the READ statement will be assigned to that particular variable, or identifier.

The READ statement always concludes with a left parenthesis. And if you are using more than one identifier in the statement, they are to be separated by commas.

At this point, you are probably wondering about the pound sign (#) and percent sign(%) characters in the READ statement. Following the flow of the syntax diagram, you can see that each IDENTIFIER can be followed by a pound sign, a percent sign, or nothing at all. For example, if the identifier happens to be variable

X1, the READ statement for evaluating that variable could be written as:

READ(X1#)
    or
READ(X1%)
    or
READ(X1)

Inserting a pound sign after the IDENTIFIER in a READ statement tells the system to expect an integer entered in a decimal format. The decimal integers can be anywhere between −32767 and +32767.

Inserting a per cent sign after the IDENTIFIER in a READ statement tells the system to expect 4-place hexadecimal number. Hex values can be anywhere between 0000 and FFFF, excluding 8000. So you have the option of entering integer values in either an ordinary decimal format or a computer-oriented hexadecimal format.

Using neither a pound sign or percent sign after the IDENTIFIER in a READ statement tells the system to assign the decimal ASCII code to whatever character is entered from the keyboard. So if you respond to READ(X1) by entering a numeral 9, X1 will take on the value of 57, the decimal ASCII code for the 9 character. By the same token, responding to READ(X1) by striking the A key gives the IDENTIFIER a value of 65, which is the decimal ASCII number for upper case A.

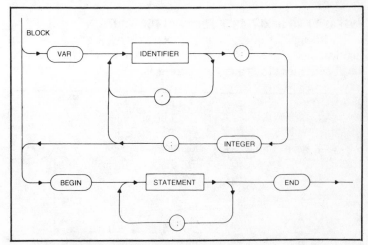

Fig. 5-2. Composite syntax diagram for variable declaration and BEGIN ... END portions of BLOCK.

This business of specifying decimal, hexadecimal or ASCII interpretation of a READ statement IDENTIFIER is unique to Tiny Pascal. Standard Pascal wouldn't know what to do with a pound sign or percent sign suffix.

Identifiers specified in the VAR ... INTEGER part of a Pascal program can thus be evaluated from the keyboard by means of a READ statement. Putting together everything described so far in this chapter, a Pascal program can take the following form:

```
VAR FOO, EXIT,SØ:INTEGER;
BEGIN
READ (FOO#,EXIT#,SØ#);
    .
    .
    .
(other Pascal statements)
    .
    .
    .
END.
```

The variables declared at the beginning of this particular program are FOO, EXIT and SØ. They are later evaluated by a READ statement, and entered as decimal numbers.

Now you are almost to a point where you can do something useful with this information. There are just a couple of points to consider yet.

INTEGER AND HEXINTEGER FORMATS FOR WRITE

Although Chapters 3 and 4 dealt almost exclusively with applications of the WRITE statement, you were promised that there was more to come. And here it is.

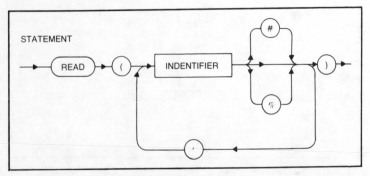

Fig. 5-3. Syntax diagram for the READ statement.

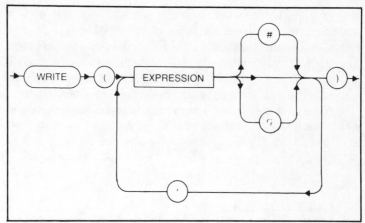

Fig. 5-4. Syntax diagram for the WRITE statement, modified to include decimal and hexadecimal renditions of integer values.

Throughout those two earlier chapters, the WRITE statement was used for printing string constants (any combination of keyboard characters enclosed within apostrophes), doing cursor control operations, printing characters from ASCII code numbers, and generating TRS-80 graphics figures from code numbers. In view of the fact that you have just learned how to evaluate Pascal variables by means of a READ statement, it is time to show how to WRITE the values of such variables. And that calls for modifying the syntax diagram for the WRITE statement.

Figure 5-4 shows the syntax diagram for the complete WRITE statement. This is it. There will be no need for further modifications later on.

The complete syntax diagram for the WRITE statement very closely resembles that of the READ statement in Fig. 5-3. You first print WRITE, followed by a left parenthesis. Then you specify an EXPRESSION. The EXPRESSION is then followed by a pound sign, a percent sign, or nothing at all. The WRITE statement always concludes with a right parenthesis; if you need more than one EXPRESSION within the statement, they are to be separated by a comma.

In Chapters 3 and 4, you were never instructed to write a pound sign or percent sign after the EXPRESSION in a WRITE statement. Using neither of these suffix characters, the WRITE statement behaves as described in those two earlier chapters.

Now here is the new stuff. The EXPRESSION part of a WRITE statement can be a variable name, or IDENTIFIER. If that kind of EXPRESSION is followed by a pound sign, the WRITE statement will print out the value of the variable in a decimal format. Following that variable EXPRESSION with a percent sign, on the other hand, tells the system to write the value of the variable in a hexadeciamal format. That is what you must know in order to do anything useful with all the material presented in this chapter.

Here are a couple of programming examples to help you see how this all works. Study them to see if you can figure out what they should do. Then enter, compile and run them. The next section of this chapter will analyze the scheme in more detail.

Example 5-1

```
VAR X:INTEGER;
BEGIN
WRITE(28,31);
READ(X#);
WRITE(13,X#)
END.
```

Example 5-2

```
VAR ASCII:INTEGER;
BEGIN
WRITE(28,31);
READ(ASCII);
WRITE(13,ASCII)
END.
```

PUTTING TOGETHER COMPLETE
READ AND WRITE PASCAL PROGRAMS

Figure 5-5 summarizes all the syntax rules embodied in the material presented thus far in this book. The diagrams are shown in a evolutionary sequence, with the undefined rectangles in operation being defined in the following diagram, or nearly so.

The elemental starting point is the PROGRAM operation in Fig. 5-5A. As you have seen before, a complete Pascal program can be represented by a BLOCK and terminated with a period. Look back at all of the complete programming examples, and you will find them ending with that period.

Figure 5-5B defines the BLOCK. Thus far, you have been considering two kinds of BLOCK operations: the variable declaration and BEGIN ... END operations.

To declare the variables for the program, first write VAR, followed by an IDENTIFIER. Now the IDENTIFIER is left undefined in Fig. 5-5B, but it is subsequently defined in a complete fashion in Fig. 5-5C.

The IDENTIFIER begins with any letter of the alphabet, and then is followed by any combination of letters and numerals. Note, however, that it is entirely possible to specify an IDENTIFIER having just that first letter. Also bear in mind that, in Tiny Pascal, only the first four alphanumeric characters in the IDENTIFIER are significant. Anything beyond four characters is simply ignored by the machine.

With the IDENTIFIER thus defined in Fig. 5-5C, you can complete the syntax rules for the variable declaration portion of BLOCK in Fig. 5-5B. Any number of identifiers can follow VAR, as long as they are separated by a comma. After specifying all of the variable identifiers, the diagram in Fig. 5-5B says you should write a colon, the word INTEGER—and a semicolon.

That particular sequence of programming characters can conclude the variable declaration part of BLOCK. But the diagram shows that you also have the option of entering another set of IDENTIFIER steps.

The main body of a Pascal program is always enclosed between the BEGIN ... END part of the BLOCK. After specifying the variables, then, you write BEGIN, followed by one or more EXPRESSION steps, and conclude with END.

Fitting together Figs. 5-5A, 5-5B and 5-5C, Pascal programs take on the general form:

```
VAR identifier, identifier:INTEGER;
BEGIN
    statement;
    statement;
    statement
END.
```

Of course this is just one example of an infinite variety.

Defining STATEMENT

The analysis is far from complete, because STATEMENT in Fig. 5-5B is not self-defined. So look at the definition of STATEMENT in Fig. 5-5D.

The Pascal statements described so far in this book fall into two categories: WRITE statements and READ statements. According to Fig. 5-5D, you build a WRITE statement by printing

WRITE, a left parenthesis, and some sort of EXPRESSION. The EXPRESSION, whatever it might be, is to be followed by a pound sign, a percent sign or nothing at all. If the WRITE statement is to include more than one EXPRESSION, the individual expressions are to be separated by commas. In any event, the WRITE statement always ends with a right parenthesis character.

The EXPRESSION part of the WRITE statement in Fig. 5-5D is not self defining. So look at Fig. 5-5E to see the syntax format for EXPRESSION.

Defining CONSTANT

According to Fig. 5-5E, EXPRESSION consists of a CONSTANT or a VARIABLE. Neither are self defining, so they have to be defined by their own syntax diagrams.

CONSTANT is defined in Fig. 5-5F as either an INTEGER, a STRING or a HEXINTEGER. Those three elements are defined in Figs. 5-5G, 5-5H and 5-5I respectively.

INTEGER is built up of a series of digits that can be prefixed by a plus sign, a minus sign or nothing at all. Using a plus sign prefix indicates a positive integer, as does no prefix character at all. A minus sign prefix, as you might have guessed by now, indicates a negative integer value. While you're at it, keep in mind that Supersoft Tiny Pascal handles INTEGER values between −32767 and +32767.

Figure 5-5H defines the STRING portion of CONSTANT. A STRING, as you have seen before, consists of an apostrophe, followed by any number of keyboard characters and concluded with another apostrophe.

Figure 5-5I defines the HEXINTEGER part of the CONSTANT diagram in Fig. 5-5F. HEXINTEGER consists of four hex digits, no more and no less. The range of hex constants in Tiny Pascal is between 0000 and FFFF. Of course, you have to know something about hexadecimal numbers before this means anything at all to you.

By this time, you've probably lost track of where this is all going. What you have been doing through the last part of the discussion is defining the CONSTANT portion of EXPRESSION in Fig. 5-5E. The process of defining CONSTANT occupied discussions of Figs. 5-5F, 5-5G, 5-5H and 5-5I.

Defining VARIABLE

What remains to be done is to define the VARIABLE part of EXPRESSION in Fig. 5-5E. That's easy at this point. VARIABLE is simply defined as an IDENTIFIER in Fig. 5-5J; and IDENTIFIER has already been defined for you in Fig. 5-5C.

So if you put all these syntax diagrams together, there are no rectangles that are left undefined. Everything, in one way or another, winds up in circle or rounded rectangular figures. And that is necessary for defining a complete Pascal program.

In theory, at least, it is possible to assemble all the syntax diagrams in Fig. 5-5 into one, giant syntax diagram that describes everything you have studied so far in this book. That would be quite a task for anyone, and Pascal users very rarely go to such trouble. Most are content looking at the evolutionary sequence.

SAMPLE PROGRAMS USING READ AND WRITE STATEMENTS
Example 5-3

```
VAR FIRST, SECOND:INTEGER;
BEGIN
WRITE(28,31, 'ENTER FIRST INTEGER',13);
READ(FIRST#);
WRITE('ENTER SECOND INTEGER',13);
WRITE(28,31, 'HERE ARE YOUR TWO INTE-
GERS:',13,13);
WRITE('YOUR FIRST INTEGER WAS', 32, FIRST#,13);
WRITE('YOUR SECOND INTEGER WAS',32,SECOND#)
END.
```

The first line in Example 5-3 declares the integer variables to be used in the program. In this case, the variables are assigned to identifiers FIRST and SECOND. That first line completely satisfies the syntax rules for the variable declaration part of a program BLOCK. See Fig. 5-5B.

The second line in the program marks the beginning of the BEGIN ... END portion of the BLOCK operation. Of course that syntax is satisfied by the END appearing on the final line of the program. The actual operating part of the program as usual, is represented by all the STATEMENT lines between BEGIN and END.

The first STATEMENT operation is a write statement appearing on the third line of the program. That particular WRITE statement includes four EXPRESSION operations. The first two expressions and the last one are unsigned constants that aren't suffixed by either a pound sign or percent sign. The system will thus interpret those numbers as ASCII-type operations, specifically control operations.

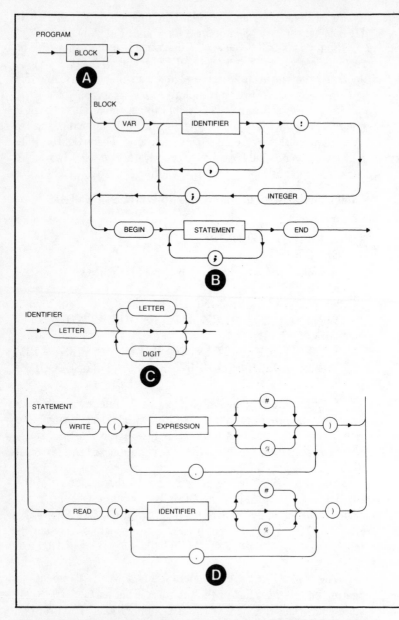

Fig. 5-5. Complete syntax evolution of Tiny Pascal. (A) PROGRAM operation. (B) Definition of BLOCK. (C) Definition of IDENTIFIER. (D) Definition of STATE-MENT. (E) Syntax format for EXPRESSION. (F) Definition of CONSTANT. (G) Definition of INTEGER. (H) Definition of STRING. (I) Definition of HEXIN-TEGER.(J)VARIABLE is defined as an IDENTIFIER.

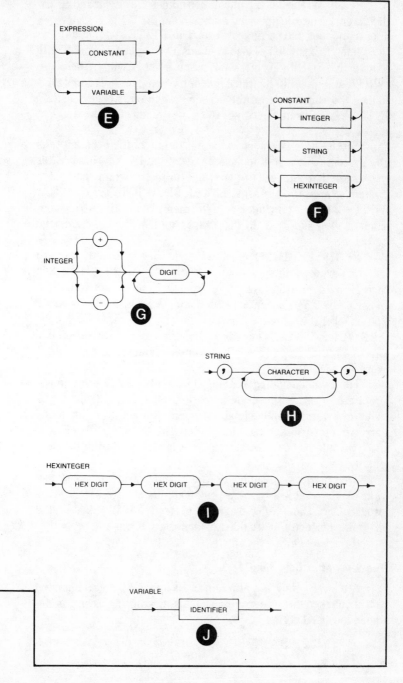

Recall that the 28,31 combination homes the cursor and clears the screen. The 13 appearing at the end of the WRITE statement does a line feed and carriage return. The WRITE statement in the third line of Example 5-3 also contains a string constant, ENTER FIRST INTEGER. From an operation point of view, then, the WRITE statement in the third line of the program in Example 5-3 homes the cursor, clears the screen, prints out ENTER FIRST INTEGER, and sets the cursor to the beginning of the next line of the screen.

The READ statement in the fourth line of the program tells the system to accept a decimal integer from the keyboard. After you enter that integer, the next line in the program causes the system to print the message, ENTER SECOND INTEGER. That WRITE statement includes both the message printing string constant as well as a code 13 that causes another line feed/carriage return.

READ(SECOND#) tells the system to wait around for you to enter a keyboard, integer value for variable SECOND. The pound sign prefix means the system is expecting the integer to be in a decimal form. The seventh line in Example 5-3 is another WRITE statement that homes the cursor, clears the screen, prints HERE ARE YOUR TWO INTEGERS, and then does two line feed/carriage return operations in succession (double spacing, in other words).

The two concluding WRITE statements simply print an appropriate message, generate a space (ASCII code 32), print the value of a variable in decimal form, and then either a line feed/carriage return or nothing. Finally, note that the program in Example 5-3 contains seven statements, each separated from the next one by a semicolon.

That particular example does not demonstrate all the syntax rules designated in Fig. 5-5. You should be able to see how the program fits the syntax diagrams perfectly. If it didn't fit the diagrams perfectly, it wouldn't compile, much less run properly.

The View After Compiling

After compiling the program in Example 5-3 and running it, you should see the screen clear and this message appearing in the upper left-hand corner:

ENTER FIRST INTEGER
? __

Whenever the system encounters a READ statement, it automatically generates a question mark prompt character. The INPUT statement in BASIC does the same sort of thing for you.

Incidentally, the only reason the question mark appears at the beginning of the next line is because of the 13 ASCII code at the end of the WRITE statement in line 3 of the program. If you didn't end that particular WRITE statement that way, the question mark would appear at the end of the word, INTEGER.

Suppose you respond to the question mark by entering decimal number 123. The screen then looks like this:

ENTER FIRST INTEGER
?123
ENTER SECOND INTEGER
?__

So far, the program is down to the second READ statement. Maybe you respond to the new question mark by entering decimal 90. After doing that, the screen clears and this sort of test appears in the upper left-hand corner of the screen:

HERE ARE YOUR TWO INTEGERS:

YOUR FIRST INTEGER WAS 123
YOUR SECOND INTEGER WAS 90

· __

And that's it. As a program, it isn't very spectacular. If you study it in conjunction with all the other material presented in this chapter (expecially Fig. 5-5), you will see how much you have all ready learned about programming in Pascal.

More Examples

The remaining examples in this chapter will not be analyzed in such great detail. You will find just a few comments about some of the special features. It is up to you to confirm their validity by comparing them with the syntax diagrams in Fig. 5-5.

Example 5-4

```
VAR ASCII:INTEGER;
BEGIN
WRITE(28,31,'ENTER AN INTEGER BETWEEN 128 AND
191',13);
READ(ASCII#);
WRITE(28,31,'HERE  IS  THE  TRS-80  GRAPHIC
FOR',32,ASCII#);
```

```
WRITE(13,13,ASCII)
END.
```

Example 5-4 allows you to select one of the graphics generating numbers for the TRS-80 system, and then it is shown to you. The variable is declared as ASCII, and it is read as a decimal value in the READ statement line. In the WRITE line that follows, the value of the decimal number is written out for you be means of the ASCII# expression.

Note, however, that the ASCII variable in the final WRITE statement does not carry a percent sign suffix. Without that suffix, the system is instructed to carry out the ASCII-type operation designated by the number you entered. In other words, the ASCII expression in the final WRITE statement causes the TRS-80 graphics symbol, itself, to appear on the screen. Contrast that effect with ASCII# expression appearing in other places in the program.

Example 5-5

```
VAR XØ,X1,X2,X3:INTEGER;
BEGIN
WRITE(28,31,'RESPOND TO THE QUESTION MARKS BY
ENTERING AN INTEGER',13);
READ(XØ#,X1#,X2#,X3#);
WRITE(XØ#,32,X1#,32,X2#,32,X3#,13,13,'DONE')
END.
```

Example 5-5 shows the application of a multiple IDENTIFIER READ statement. The four variables are to be entered from the keyboard as decimal values and in the order specified in the READ statement. The final WRITE statement simply reprints those values, inserting a space between them and concluding the program by writing DONE.

Example 5-6

```
VAR DEC:INTEGER;
BEGIN                 .
WRITE(28,31,215,'DECIMAL-TO-HEX  CONVERSION,
13,13);
WRITE('ENTER  ANY  DECIMAL  INTEGER  BETWEEN
-32767 and +32767',13);
READ(DEC#);
WRITE(13,13,13,13,'THE  HEX  VERSION  OF',DEC#,'is
',DEC%)
END.
```

The fact that Tiny Pascal works so easily in both decimal and hexadecimal numbering formats brings up the possibility of writing small programs that convert between the two numbering systems. In Example 5-6, the READ statement accepts a number in decimal terms. The WRITE statement that concludes the program prints out the number, both in a decimal and then in a hex format. Contrast the DEC#and DEC% expressions in that WRITE statement.

Here is a similar sort of program that converts from hex to decimal:

Example 5-7

```
VAR HEX:INTEGER;
BEGIN
WRITE(28,31,215,'HEX-TO-DECIMAL CONVER-
SION',13,13);
WRITE('ENTER ANY HEX INTEGER BETWEEN 0000
AND FFFF',13);
READ(HEX%);
WRITE(13,13,13,13,'THE DECIMAL VERSION OF
',HEX%,' IS ',DEC%)
END.
```

Chapter 6
Pascal Arithmetic
and Logic Operations

Arithmetic and logic operations play powerful roles in any sort of computer programming, and of course Pascal programming is no exception. Even if the purpose of a program is something far removed from performing arithmetic calculations for the operator, the routines quite often reside in the program as controlling operations. An example is counting the number of times a certain step is carried out.

In order to keep this discussion as simple and to the point as possible, it is assumed that you, the reader, already have a working understanding of the fundamental arithmetic and logical operators. Many operators carry over to Pascal from BASIC, so inequality expressions such as $<$, $>$, $<>$, $<=$ and $=$ should not be strangers to you. You should also know the technical meanings of AND, OR and NOT.

You will find brief explanations of operators that are quite different from any found in BASIC. Beyond that, you are on your own as far as the definitions are concerned.

THE ASSIGNMENT STATEMENT

Pascal uses an assignment statement that often acts a stumbling block for people accustomed to working in BASIC. The assignment statement is a 2-character statement, represented by a colon immediately followed by an equal sign. It looks like this:

$$:=$$

It is a bona fide Pascal statement that ranks right up there in importance with WRITE and READ statements. The purpose of the assignment statement is to assign a value to a variable.

The statement, A:=2, means that the value of 2 is assigned to variable A. A slightly more complex assignment statement might take the form, A:=X+Y. In that case, the sum of variables X and Y (assuming they have been assigned constant values in an earlier operation) is assigned to variable A.

Here is a short Pascal program that uses the assignment statement:

```
VAR FOO:INTEGER;
BEGIN
READ(FOO#);
FOO:=FOO+10;
WRITE (FOO#0
END.
```

What does the program above do? Well, FOO is declared as the only variable for the program. Then after beginning the program, the system accepts a decimal value for FOO from the keyboard that comes about by the READ statement.

The assignment statement appears in the fourth line, where variable FOO is assigned its old value plus 10. The program then writes the decimal value of FOO, just so you know it really did the intended job.

It is at this point that some people get a little bit confused. They ask, "Why use that complicated, 2-character assignment statement when a simple equal sign should do the job?"

It turns out that an equal sign, used alone, expresses a logical equality between two factors. An equal sign cannot be used for setting the value of a variable. A=10 means that A *is* equal to 10, and it *does not mean*, "set A equal to 10."

Whenever you want to set the value of a variable, you must use an assignment operator. That holds true in BASIC as well as Pascal.

"Hold on there!" you say. "Doesn't the statement A=10 in BASIC set the value of variable A to 10?" No, it doesn't; but LET A=10 does.

As BASIC evolved through the years, it began tolerating an ever increasing amount of sloppiness on the part of its programmers. In BASIC, LET A=10 is an assignment statement; and the LET part of the statement signals that fact. As time passed, it became possible to do the same thing without having to begin with the LET part of the statement. Hence, the confusion between using an equal sign as part of an assignment statement and using it (quite rightly) as a simple expression of equality between two factors.

Whether you are really confused by this matter or not, the fact remains that you must assign values to variables by means of the assignment statement, using the := characters to do the job.

Figure 6-1 is the syntax diagram for the assignment statement. It begins by stating some variable name, or identifier, then shows the assignment characters and, finally, some well-defined numerical expression.

You will be seeing more examples of assignment statements as you work your way through this chapter and, indeed, the rest of this book. They are inescapable little critters in Pascal programming.

ADDING, SUBTRACTING, MULTIPLYING AND DIVIDING

You will not find much unusual about Pascal arithmetic. Here is a listing of the four basic operators:

+   summing operator
−   subtraction operator
*   multiplication operator
DIV division operator

Only the division operator, DIV, is different from BASIC. There's a good reason for that particular difference. Tiny Pascal, you see, works with purely integer arithmetic. That means it works only with "whole" numbers. Tiny Pascal cannot deal with fractional decimals.

So whenever you specify the math expression, X:=10 DIV 2, a value of 5 is going to be assigned to variable X. That's fine. But whenever you specify a division problem such as X:=13 DIV 4, you are going to get 3 for an answer.

Whenever a division problem in Tiny Pascal has a fractional part to its answer, that fractional part is truncated. To put it in everyday terms, the fractional part is dropped.

Sorry about that. It's one of the prices that must be paid for getting Pascal into a computer having 16k of memory. Of course, Standard Pascal can handle decimals and even exponential expressions. Tiny Pascal cannot.

While Tiny Pascal has some shortcomings when it comes to division problems, it does allow you to insert math expressions

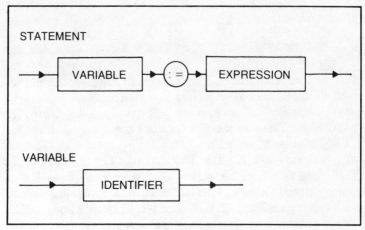

Fig. 6-1. Syntax diagram for the assignment statement.

within parentheses. Besides, parenthetical math expressions can be nested to perform some rather complex mathematical operations. You will see some examples of this later in this section.

Order of Precedence

Pascal, like all other programming languages, assigns priorities or an order of precedence to its math operators. Expressions enclosed within parentheses, for example, are always executed first. The multiplication and division have equal precedence, one order lower than parenthetical expressions.

Summing and subtraction operations take the lowest precedence. There's nothing at all unusual about this order of precedence.

Figure 6-2 shows the syntax diagrams for the four elementary Pascal math operations. This particular set of diagrams fit into the EXPRESSION rectangle for the assignment statement in Fig. 6-1.

Math Expression

According to Fig. 6-2A, a math expression begins with a plus sign (for a positive TERM), a minus sign (for a negative TERM), or no sign at all (for an implied positive TERM). After that comes one or more TERMs. If you choose to use just one TERM, the diagram in Fig. 6-2A is concluded. But if you use more than one TERM, they must be separated by summing or subtraction operators, + or –.

Here are some possible formats for Fig. 6-2A:

```
term
term+term
+term−term
−term+term−term
```

You can loop around through the second TERM rectangle in Fig. 6-2A as many times as necessary to do the math job at hand.

That's nice, but unfortunately TERM isn't self-defining in Fig. 6-2A. So you have to take into account the syntax diagram for TERM as it is shown in Fig. 6-2B.

According to Fig. 6-2B, TERM always begins with a FACTOR. You then have the option of concluding the operation or looping around through a second FACTOR and separating the two with a multiplication or division operator. Here are some possible TERM formats from the diagram in Fig. 6-2B:

```
factor*factor
factor DIV factor
factor*factor DIV factor
factor*factor*factor DIV factor
```

As in the case of the math EXPRESSION diagram in Fig. 6-2A, it is possible to build up some very complex combinations of multiplication and division operations. Loop through the second FACTOR rectangle as often as necessary to get the math job done.

More Definitions

But FACTOR is left undefined in Fig. 6-2A, so it's necessary to look at its definition in Fig. 6-2C. According to that diagram, a FACTOR can consist of a CONSTANT, a VARIABLE or a whole new EXPRESSION enclosed in parentheses.

CONSTANT and VARIABLE are not defined here because you have seen their definitions in earlier discussions. Putting it simply, a CONSTANT is some number and a VARIABLE is some previously declared IDENTIFIER that has a numerical value assigned to it.

The EXPRESSION enclosed within quotes in Fig. 6-2C brings up an intriguing point. How is EXPRESSION defined? Well, it is defined by the diagram in Fig. 6-2. In order to define EXPRESSION in Fig. 6-2C, you have to go back to Fig. 6-2A and start all over again. And if you want, you can put another EXPRESSION within EXPRESSION. That's the nested EXPRESSION idea.

The following list shows some complete Pascal assignment statements:

```
A:=10
A:=A+1
A:=-B+C*10
A:=B-C DIV E+12
A:=-(A*B+2) DIV B*B
B:=-((X-Y*Y)+2*A DIV (4*Z+10))
```

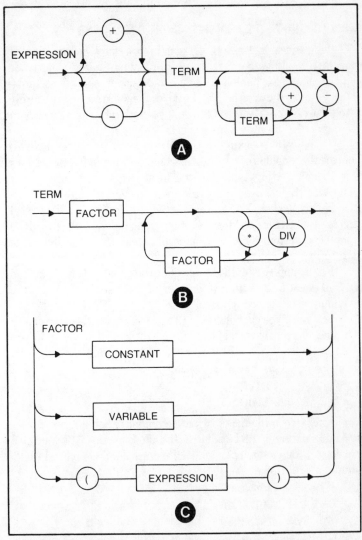

Fig. 6-2. (A) A math expression begins with a plus sign, a minus sign or no sign at all. (B) Syntax diagram for TERM. (C) Definition of FACTOR.

While the actual mathematical operations might be of questionable value in some instances, these examples at least demonstrate the workings of the syntax diagrams in Figs. 6-1 and 6-2.

All things considered, the only difference between the four fundamental arithmetic operations in Tiny Pascal and standard BASIC is Pascal's DIV operator. That difference is made necessary by the fact that Tiny Pascal works only with integer arithmetic.

MODULO, SHIFT-LEFT AND SHIFT-RIGHT OPERATIONS

Tiny Pascal includes three arithmetic-related operations that might seem altogether new to people having limited experience with computer technology. They can be handy operations, however, because they can help make up for the shortcomings of purely integer arithmetic. And you can be sure that's why Chung and Yuen have included them in Tiny Pascal.

Technically speaking, the MOD operator (short for *modulo*) returns the modulus of two expressions. So what in the world does that mean? Setting aside the technical jargon, it means that it generates the remainder created by a division operation.

Now you should recall that the DIV operation in Tiny Pascal divides two factors and leaves off any remainder. Well, the MOD operator determines the remainder that results from the division of two terms.

For example, 5 MOD 2 turns out to be equal to 1. Five divided by 2 is equal to 2, with a remainder of 1. That remainder is the modulus of the expression.

So even if you cannot divide 13 by 4 in Tiny Pascal and come up with the correct answer, at least the MOD operation will show you the remainder. Look at this sequence of operation that might be included in a Tiny Pascal program:

```
A:=23 DIV 5;
R:=23 MOD 5;
```

After executing these two statements, variable A will be set to 4 and variable R will be set to 3. In plain English, 23 divided by 5 equals 4 with a remainder of 3. DIV does the division and MOD yields the remainder.

What about this sequence?

```
A:= 100 DIV 10
R:= 100 DIV 10
```

In this case, A is set to a value of 10 and R is set to 0. One hundred divided by 10 equals 10 with a remainder of 0.

You will also find later in this book that the MOD operator is quite useful for generating psuedo-random numbers. No, Tiny Pascal does not include a RND function.

If the MOD operator seems a bit abstract, consider the shift-left (SHL) and shift-right (SHR) operators. Like the MOD operator, SHL and SHR can be quite useful for making up division programs that handle fractional parts. But understanding these two operator calls for getting down to the machine's binary working level.

Whenever your computer is working with a decimal number 27, for example, that number is represented in some memory register as an 8-bit binary number, 00011011. If, for some reason, the system shifts that binary number two places to the left, you no longer have 00011011 but 01101100. The pattern, you notice, moves two bit positions to the left. Zeros fill in the spaces thus created.

That particular operation is carried out whenever the Pascal system sees the term 27 SHL 2. The binary version of that first number is shifted to the left by a number of places specified by the second number.

Look at the situation this way:

$$27 = 00011011$$
$$27 \text{ SHL } 2 = 01101100$$

Obviously that shifted number is no longer equal to 27. In fact, the decimal rendition is 108. Thus 27 SHL 2 = 108.

The same general idea holds for shift-right (SHR) operations:

$$27 = 00011011$$
$$27 \text{ SHR } 2 = 00000110$$

SHR shifts the binary number to the right by two places in that example, and the result is decimal 6: 27 SHR 2=6.

Most Tiny Pascal users will find the SHL and SHR operators of limited usefulness, but anyone acquainted with machine language arithmetic will find them of great interest.

MOD, SHL and SHR fit into the arithmetic syntax as shown in Fig. 6-3. That diagram is actually an expanded version of the TERM diagram in Fig. 6-2B.

THE IF . . . THEN . . . ELSE CONDITIONAL STATEMENT

Returning to grounds that are perhaps more familiar to most readers, it is time to consider the Pascal IF . . . THEN . . . ELSE conditional statement. In the process, you are going to have a

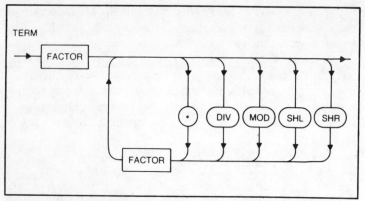

Fig. 6-3. TERM syntax diagram expanded to include MOD, SHL and SHR.

chance to see the relational operators ($=, >, >=$, etc.) at work. Figure 6-4 shows the syntax diagrams for the IF . . . THEN . . . ELSE statement and the relational expressions that are normally included in the conditional statement.

According to Fig. 6-4A, the Pascal conditional statement begins with IF, followed by some sort of EXPRESSION. After that comes a THEN and a STATEMENT.

The choice point after the first STATEMENT rectangle in Fig. 6-4A allows the option of doing an ELSE/STATEMENT combination or ending the statement. Generally, the conditional statements take forms such as these:

IF expression THEN statement;

IF expression THEN statement ELSE statement;

      or even

IF expression THEN statement
          ELSE IF expression THEN statement
          ELSE IF expression THEN statement;

In other words, it is possible to do a simple IF . . . THEN statement, a somewhat more complex IF . . . THEN . . . ELSE statement, or even a rather involved set of "nested" conditional statements.

It is diffiuclt to overrate the importance of this conditional syntax in Pascal, especially Tiny Pascal. Tiny Pascal does not have any capability of doing GOTO-like operations. One cannot jump around freely in a Tiny Pascal program. It is only through the intelligent and imaginative application of the conditionals that makes many control operations possible at all. You can certainly expect to see some examples that illustrate this particular point later on.

Syntax Definitions for EXPRESSION and STATEMENT Rectangles

In the meantime, you should round out the syntax diagram in Fig. 6-4A by coming up with syntax definitions for the EXPRESSION and STATEMENT rectangles. EXPRESSION, in this case, is at least partly defined for you in Fig. 6-4B. It consists of something called a SIMPLE EXPRESSION that is followed by nothing, or one of the six relational operators and another SIMPLE EXPRESSION.

Now, a SIMPLE EXPRESSION can be defined in terms of the diagrams you have already studied in Fig. 6-2. In other words, a SIMPLE EXPRESSION can be a constant, a variable or, indeed, any sort of math expression.

A STATEMENT, of course, is any of the four Pascal statements defined so far in this book: READ, WRITE, the assignment statement, and now the IF . . . THEN conditional statement, itself.

Here are a few examples of complete Pascal conditional statements. See if you can trace their syntax before trying some of the programming examples.

```
IF A=10 THEN
     WRITE ('DONE');

IF A DIV B > C THEN
     READ (NEWNO#)
     ELSE WRITE ('DONE');

IF A=B THEN
     WRITE (A#, 'EQUALS ', B#)
     ELSE IF A >B THEN
     WRITE (A#, ' IS GREATER THAN ', B#)
     ELSE IF A<B THEN
     WRITE (A#, ' IS LESS THAN ', B#);
```

The indentations are not at all necessary in any of these examples. Such a trick, however, tends to simplify the task of interpreting the written program.

Programs

Here is the sort of question a teacher might ask on an exam. Why aren't all the statements included in the IF . . . THEN statement ended with a semicolon? Think about that one for a little bit. It is important, and the only way to justify the right answer is by going through the appropriate syntax diagrams. Incidentally, you will find the answer to that particular question tucked away in a later discussion. Now here are some complete programs that illustrate much of what you have learned so far in this chapter.

Example 6-1

```
VAR FIRST, SECOND:INTEGER;
BEGIN
WRITE (28, 31, 'FIRST NUMBER');
READ (FIRST#);
WRITE (28, 31, 'SECOND NUMBER');
READ (SECOND#);
IF FIRST=SECOND THEN
      WRITE (28, 31, FIRST#, 32, 'AND', 32 SECOND#,
      32, 'ARE EQUAL')
END.
```

Example 6-2

```
VAR FIRST, SECOND: INTEGER;
BEGIN
WRITE (28, 31, 'FIRST NUMBER');
READ (FIRST#);
WRITE (28, 31, SECOND NUMBER');
READ (SECOND#);
WRITE (28, 31, FIRST#, 32, 'AND', 32, SECOND#, 32,
'ARE', 32);
IF FIRST=SECOND THEN
      WRITE ('EQUAL')
      ELSE WRITE ('NOT EQUAL')
END.
```

Note that the program in Example 6-1 simply ends if the two variables, FIRST and SECOND, are not equal. Example 6-2, however, expands on the idea to write something else in the even the two variables are not equal. Being able to use the ELSE portion of the conditional statement makes a lot of difference sometimes. Example 6-3 expands further on this same idea.

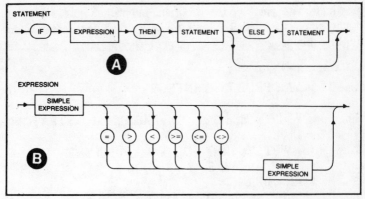

Fig. 6-4. (A) Syntax diagram for building IF...THEN...ELSE statements. (B) an EXPRESSION consists of a SIMPLE EXPRESSION that is either followed by nothing or one of the six relational operators and another SIMPLE EXPRESSION.

Example 6-3

```
VAR FIRST, SECOND:INTEGER;
BEGIN
WRITE (28, 31, 'FIRST NUMBER');
READ (FIRST#) ;
WRITE (28, 31, 'SECOND NUMBER');
READ (SECOND#);
WRITE (28, 31, FIRST#, 32, 'IS', 32);
IF FIRST=SECOND THEN
    WRITE ('EQUAL TO', 32, SECOND#)
    ELSE IF FIRST>SECOND THEN
    WRITE ('GREATER THAN', 32, SECOND#);
    ELSE WRITE('LESS THAN', 32, SECOND #);
END.
```

AN IMPORTANT ARITHMETIC/LOGIC DEMO PROGRAM

The Pascal program listed in Example 6-4 is so important at this stage of the game that it is worth devoting a special section to it. The special importance of this program lies in the fact that it embodies a number of programming procedures that have not been discussed in detail, compares some alternate procedures that have been described in several different places, and demonstrates the workings of the IF . . . THEN statement and operators DIV and MOD.

It might be a good idea to enter, compile and run this program several times before studying the rather extensive commentary. Bear in mind while entering this program that the line numbers are not legitimate parts of the program, but rather guides for the technical discussion that follows. So ignore the line numbers when putting this program into your computer.

Example 6-4

line 1   VAR PROG, X, Y:INTEGER;
line 2   BEGIN
line 3   WRITE (28, 31, 215, 'DIVISION DEMONSTRATOR', 13, 13);
line 4   WRITE ('DO YOU WANT TO SEE THE REMAINDERS—Y OR N', 13);
line 5   READ(PROG);
line 6   IF PROG=89 THEN
line 7   BEGIN
line 8   WRITE (28, 31, 215, 'DIVISION WITH REMAIN-DER', 13, 13);
line 9   WRITE ('ENTER DIVIDEND');
line 10   READ (X#);
line 11   WRITE ('ENTER DIVISOR');
line 12   READ(Y#);
line 13   WRITE (13, 13, 200, X#, '/', Y#, '=', (X DIV Y)#)
line 14   END
line 15   ELSE IF PROG=78 THEN
line 16   BEGIN
line 17   WRITE (28, 31, 215, 'DIVISION WITHOUT REMAINDER', 13, 13);
line 18   WRITE ('ENTER DIVIDEND');
line 19   READ(X#);
line 20   WRITE ('ENTER DIVISOR');
line 21   READ(Y#);
line 22   WRITE (13, 13, 200, X#, 47, Y#, 61, (X DIV Y)#);
line 23   IF X MOD Y<>0 THEN
line 24   WRITE (32, 43)
line 25   END;
line 26   WRITE (13, 13, 13, 13, 'ENTER R TO DO AGAIN')
line 27   END.

Program Function

Before getting into an analysis of how this program works, take a look at what it is supposed to do. Upon running the program, you should see the screen clear, and then the following messages:

DIVISION DEMONSTRATOR
DO YOU WANT TO SEE THE REMAINDERS —Y OR N—

The program wants to know whether you want to do division showing the remainder or division without showing the remainder. In this case, the system responds immediately when you strike a key. You will find you do not have to do an ENTER. What's more, if you strike a character other than Y or N, the program defaults to its end, telling you to ENTER R TO DO AGAIN.

Suppose you respond to the initial message by striking the Y key. The program immediately clears the screen and prints a message format that looks something like this:

DIVISION WITH REMAINDER
ENTER DIVIDEND?_

You are to respond by entering any integer between −32767 and +32767. This time you do indeed have to strike the ENTER key to keep the program rolling along. For the sake of this discussion, assume you respond by entering integer 123. After that, the screen looks like this:

DIVISION WITH REMAINDER
ENTER DIVIDEND?123
ENTER DIVISOR?_

Enter the divisor, say, 19. Here's what happens:

DIVISION WITH REMAINDER

ENTER DIVIDEND?123
ENTER DIVISOR?19

123/19=6 WITH A REMAINDER OF 9

ENTER R TO DO AGAIN

· —

So there it is: 123 divided by 19 equals 6 with a remainder of 9. The final message on the screen simply informs you that the program can be run again by entering R.

If you elect to run the program without showing the remainder (striking the N key), the final screen display would be slightly different:

DIVISION WITHOUT REMAINDER
ENTER DIVIDEND?123
ENTER DIVISOR?19

$123/19=6 +$

ENTER R TO DO AGAIN
· —

In this case, the program does the division operation, but merely prints a plus sign to indicate that a remainder exists. The plus sign does not appear if your numbers divide evenly and there is no remainder.

Certainly the program is rather trivial from an operator's viewpoint. It doesn't do anything very exciting, but the way it works is very important at this point.

Two BLOCKS Parts

First notice that the program in Example 6-4 has two parts to its BLOCK. There is the declaration of variables in line 1, and a BEGIN . . . END operation between line 2 and line 27. Of course, the PROGRAM ends with a period in line 27.

The BEGIN . . . END portion of the major BLOCK operation is made up of a series of five statements: WRITE statements in lines 3 and 4, a READ statement in line 5, and IF . . . THEN . . . ELSE statement occupying lines 6 through 25, and a final WRITE statement in line 26. Notice that each of these five BLOCK statements are separated from one another by semicolons: lines 3, 4 and 5 end with a semicolon, the IF . . . THEN . . . ELSE statement ends with a semicolon in line 25, and line 26 does also.

Are you beginning to appreciate the systematic structure of Pascal programming? The program BLOCK ends with a period, there are two major sections in the block, and the block is divided into a sequence of STATEMENT operations—five of them in this case.

From the viewpoint of Pascal structure, the major WRITE and READ statements are rather straightforward. They include some tricks not yet introduced in this book, but that has nothing to do with the program structure.

Conditionals

As far as the structure is concerned, the major IF . . . THEN . . . ELSE statement calls for a lot of discussion. Note that the consequences of satisfying either part of the IF . . . THEN . . . ELSE statement are rather extensive and, in fact, call for the use of their own BEGIN . . . END formats.

If the conditional in line 6 is satisfied and, indeed, variable PROG is equal to 89 (the ASCII code for the letter Y), the system executes the series of statements enclosed between BEGIN and END, between lines 7 and 14.

If, on the other hand, the conditional in line 6 is *not* satisfied, the system jumps down to the ELSE clause in line 15. That line tests variable PROG for a value of 78 (the ASCII code for the letter N). And if PROG=78, the system executes the BEGIN . . . END block of operations between lines 16 and 25.

But if neither conditional is satisfied (PROG equals something other than 89 or 78), the system defaults to the major statement following the IF . . . THEN . . . ELSE statement. That happens to be the WRITE statement in line 26.

Sub-blocks

Returning now to the subblock between lines 7 and 14, you will find that it contains six statements of its own: four WRITE statements and two READ statements, each separated from the others by semicolons. So this little block within a statement follows the same syntax rules as statements within the major block of operations do.

There is nothing else of structural importance in that block between lines 7 and 14, so consider the block, the BEGIN . . . END sequence between lines 16 and 25. The subblock between lines 16 and 25 contains seven statements: 4 WRITE statements, two READ statements, and a single IF . . . THEN statement. This is a Pascal BLOCK in its own right, and can certainly contain an IF . . . THEN statement of its own. That secondary conditional appears in line 23. If it is satisfied, the system goes to line 24 and does a WRITE operation. If that conditional in line 23 is *not* satisfied, the system defaults to the next statement in the block, END in line 25.

You ought to be seeing the distinctive Pascal programming structure by now. There are expressions within statements, blocks within statements, and statements within blocks. All follow their respective syntax rules.

Questions and Answers

Here are a few questions and answers that are intended to bring home the Pascal structure/syntax in Example 6-4.

Why does END in line 27 conclude with a period, while the END in line 25 concludes with a semicolon? The END in line 27 belongs to the BEGIN in line 2; since the entire Pascal program lies between lines 2 and 27, the syntax rules for PROGRAM dictate that it conclude with a period.

The END in line 25, however, happens to rest at the end of a long, single IF . . . THEN . . . ELSE statement. That statement has to be separated from the next one (the WRITE statement in line 26) by a semicolon. That's what the semicolon is for in line 25. The fact that it follows an END is coincidental as far as structure is concerned.

Why is there no punctuation at all after the END in line 14? The END delimiter in line 13 merely marks the conclusion of a BEGIN . . . END block of statements that begin at line 7. You will not find any syntax rules that say a block of statements has to end with any sort of punctuation. Statements are separated by a semicolon; but line 14 does not mark the end of the IF . . . THEN . . . ELSE statement that encompasses it. Hence, no punctuation.

These questions about punctuation after an END can be important to Pascal novices. There seems to be a natural sort of feeling that every END delimiter must be concluded with some punctuation. There is, however, no necessary relationships between END and some punctuation. The punctuation is often there, but for entirely different reasons, namely to separate statements that happen to end with END, or to conclude an entire program.

Why do some of the WRITE statements in Example 6-4 end with a semicolon while others do not? Those ending with a semicolon you see, are immediately followed by another statement. Semicolons, from a structural viewpoint, are used only to separate statements.

The WRITE statement in line 13 does not conclude with a semicolon because the END delimiter following it is *not* a statement. It is a delimiter that signals the end of a BEGIN . . . END block of statements.

At this point in your experience with Pascal programming, it is far more important to understand the structural characteristics of Example 6-4 than any of its other features. Certainly it is appropriate to discuss some of the other features in a moment. Until you grasp the careful, systematic and distinctive structure of Pascal, though, the other nice little features aren't going to do you much good.

Features Unrelated to Pascal Syntax

Now consider some of the features of Example 6-4 that aren't directly related to Pascal structure and syntax. The first point of interest is the READ(PROG) statement in line 5. It is the point where you are supposed to designate whether or not you want to see the remainder of a division operation. This is done by assigning a value to variable PROG from the keyboard. The important point is that PROG is not followed by a pound sign or a percent sign. In other words, PROG is assigned a value that is neither a decimal nor a hexadecimal value. So what kind of value is it?

Whenever you do a READ(variable) statement, the system looks for you to strike any key on the keyboard. Upon striking the key, the variable immediately takes on a value equal to the ASCII code for that key. Strike any key, and the READ (variable) statement is immediately executed. There is no waiting around for you to strike the ENTER key. You should have noticed that when you ran the program yourself.

Line 5 thus forces variable PROG to take on a number that is equal to the ASCII code for any key you happen to strike. Line 6 then tests that value, and the line is satisfied if PROG happens to equal 89. What is the significance of 89? Well, it is the ASCII code for keyboard character Y. If you struck the Y key in response to line 5, PROG has a value of 89 and the conditional in line 6 is satisfied. As a result the system executes the block of statements between lines 7 and 14.

But if PROG does not equal 89, the system skips down to the corresponding ELSE clause in line 15. Here the value of PROG is tested for 78. Of course, 78 is the ASCII code for the keyboard character N. So if you hit the N key in response to the READ(PROG) statement in line 5, the condition in line 15 is satisfied. The system executes the block of statements between lines 16 and 25.

Finally, you might strike some key other than Y or N in response to line 5. PROG will not be 89 or 78, so neither condition (line 6 and line 15) is satisfied. In that case, the system passes through the IF . . . THEN . . . ELSE statement without doing any of the operations for one block of statements or another. It also covers for keyboard goofs on the part of the operator. It responds to an operator error by immediately doing four line feed/carriage returns in succession, printing ENTER R TO DO AGAIN and concluding the program.

I don't think you will find anything especially puzzling about the operations in lines 7 through 14. Just note that the two READ statements specify a variable followed by a pound sign. In both of those instances, the system accepts integers in decimal form and waits for you to strike the ENTER key before moving to the next step in the program.

More on WRITE Statements

But do compare the WRITE statements in lines 13 and 22. Both do the same task, but in different ways. Specifically, line 13 prints out the / and = as string constants. The same two characters are printed by line 22, but they are called in a different fashion. Instead of calling a slash symbol by specifying it as a string constant, the WRITE statement in line 22 calls that same symbol as an ASCII character. Check the listing of ASCII character codes in the Appendix, and you will see that decimal 42 represents the slash character. By the same token, the string specifier for the equal sign in line 13 is replaced by the ASCII-call version in line 22—code number 61.

When it comes to printing keyboard symbols on the screen, you always have the choice of specifying them as a string constant or calling them via an ASCII code number. Take your pick. You'll find both techniques used in this book.

Along the same line of thinking, what is the significance of the WRITE (32, 43) statement in line 24? Code 32, according to the Appendix, simply calls a space operation. Code 43, however, is the ASCII designator for a plus sign. Provided the conditional in line 23 is satisfied, the system responds by doing a space, followed by a plus sign. That's the point in the program where you see a + whenever a remainder is supposed to follow a division operation.

Now here is something new. Notice the (X DIV Y)# expression appearing at the end of the WRITE statements in lines 13 and 22. The syntax diagrams in this chapter show that it is altogether possible to build an EXPRESSION within a WRITE statement that consists of math terms and factors. In these instances X is divided by Y as part of the WRITE statements that embody them.

Certainly it is possible to solve the division problem as a separate program statement, doing something such as Z:=X DIV Y. After that, include a Z# expression within a WRITE statement. That approach would mean adding another variable to line 1 and including two assignment statements.

The only problem with doing math operations within WRITE statements is that the math operation must conclude with a pound sign, if, of course, the "answer" is to be printed out in decimal form. In our particular case here, the pound sign must apply to the entire math operation. It is thus necessary to enclose the operation within parentheses to make sure the pound sign applies to the overall operation, and not just part of it. You should be able to analyze all other features of the program in Example 6-4 on your own.

DOING LOGIC WITH AND, OR AND NOT

Tiny Pascal includes three Boolean operators that can be quite helpful when it comes to making program control decisions. The following discussion assumes you already have some understanding of the technical meanings of the AND, OR and NOT operators. If that isn't the case, you can find the necessary definitions in any number of books on computer logic, digital electronics and even general encyclopedias.

First, here are a few examples of IF . . . THEN statements that include the Boolean logical operators:

IF (A=10) AND (B=2) THEN

or

IF (A>B) OR (A=24) THEN

or

IF (A*2<=C) AND (C>100) OR (A=2) THEN

or

IF NOT ((A=10) OR (B*2>12)) THEN

You should be able to justify the syntax in all these examples by referring to the summary of syntax diagrams at the end of this chapter. In order to understand them in an unambiguous fashion, however, you must know that the AND operator takes precedence over OR. In the third example, then, the system first deals with the AND relationship between (A*2<=C) and (C>100) before it tests the OR relationship with A=2. Using parentheses to clarify the precedence in that third example, it reads:

IF ((A*2<=C) AND (C>100) OR (A=2) THEN

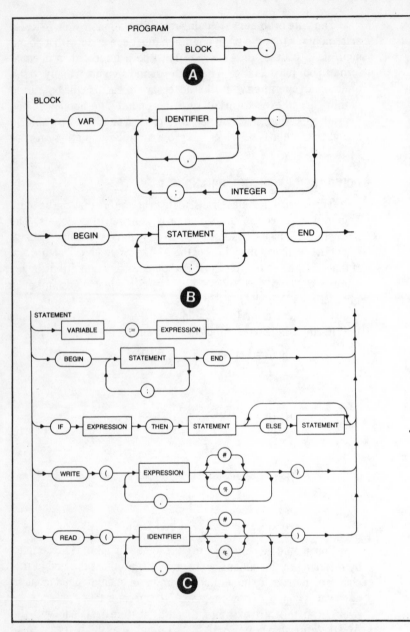

Fig. 6-5. Composite syntax diagrams for all material described so far in the book. (A) PROGRAM diagram. (B) BLOCK diagram. (C) STATEMENT diagram. (D) EXPRESSION diagram. (E) SIMPLE EXPRESSION diagram. (F) TERM diagram. (G) FACTOR diagram. (H) CONSTANT diagram.

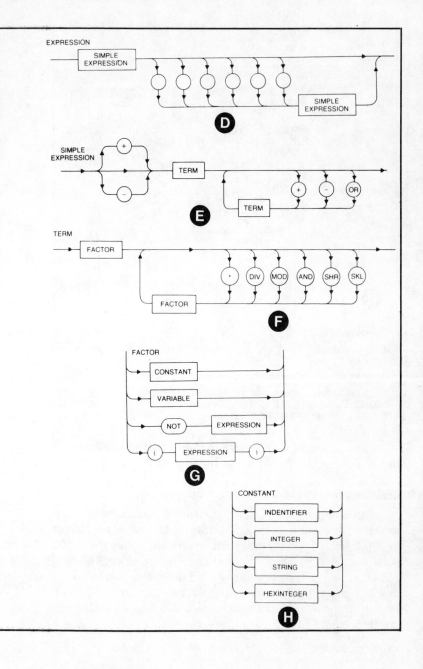

EXPRESSION

SIMPLE EXPRESSION

D

SIMPLE EXPRESSION

+

−

TERM

TERM

+ − OR

E

TERM

FACTOR

FACTOR

· DIV MOD AND SHR SKL

F

FACTOR

CONSTANT

VARIABLE

NOT EXPRESSION

(EXPRESSION)

G

CONSTANT

INDENTIFIER

INTEGER

STRING

HEXINTEGER

H

91

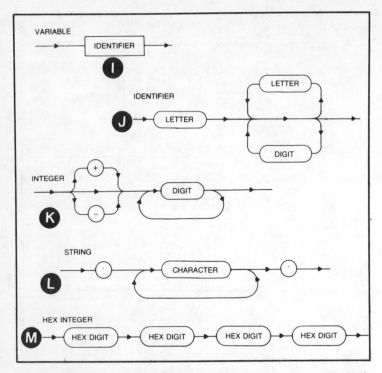

Fig. 6-5. Composite syntax diagrams for all material described so far in the book. (I) VARIABLE diagram. (J) IDENTIFIER diagram. (K) INTEGER diagram. (L) STRING diagram. (M) HEX INTEGER diagram.

Numerous examples through the remainder of this book will illustrate the application of these Boolean operators for you.

SUMMARY OF SYNTAX DIAGRAMS USED

The diagrams in Fig. 6-5 represent the syntax rules for all blocks, statements, expressions, terms and factors described thus far in this book. Follow their evolution carefully, making sure you know what is happening or can happen anywhere along the way.

If you are really conscientious about the matter, you will come up with some program combinations you haven't seen in this book yet. Try programming them for yourself. You should be able to do that by now.

Chapter 7
Applications of
REPEAT . . . UNTIL Loops

At last! It is time to begin working with a Pascal repetitive, or looping, statement. It might have seemed to you that the discussions through Chapter 6 were getting a bit tedious and boring, and maybe they were. The most interesting kinds of programs generally contain at least one repetitive operation; and it has been getting difficult to devise fun examples without being able to do that. Now things really get rolling.

This chapter features the Pascal REPEAT . . . UNTIL statement, which is one of three possible repetitive statements. This one is perhaps the most commonly used of them all.

SYNTAX RULES FOR REPEAT . . . UNTIL

Figure 7-1 shows the syntax diagram for the REPEAT . . . UNTIL repetitive statement. It consists of the word REPEAT, followed by any number of program statements. There can be any number of STATEMENT lines, just as long as they are separated by semicolons (as usual).

After the STATEMENT lines comes the word UNTIL, followed by any legal Pascal EXPRESSION. Refer back to Fig. 6-5 if you need some reminders about the definitions of STATEMENT and EXPRESSION.

Thus, a REPEAT . . . UNTIL statement generally takes this kind of form:

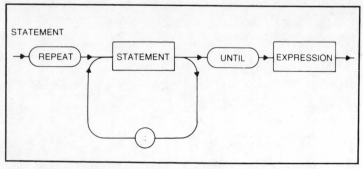

Fig. 7-1. Syntax diagram for the REPEAT...UNTIL statement.

> REPEAT
>> statement;
>> statement;
>> statement
>
> UNTIL expression

The operation of the REPEAT . . . UNTIL statement is conceptually simple. All it does is REPEAT the list of specified STATEMENTs UNTIL the conditions specified in EXPRESSION are met. Here's an example:

> REPEAT
>> N:=N+1
>
> UNTIL N=10

That example repeats the N:=N+1 operation, incrementing the value of N until it is equal to 10.

Now things are really beginning to take shape. Try these two programs:

Example 7-1A

```
VAR N:INTEGER;
BEGIN
WRITE (28, 31);
N:=0;
REPEAT
       WRITE(N#, 32);
       N:=N+1
UNTIL N=10
END.
```

Example 7-1A counts for you, printing numerals 0 through 9 horizontally across the screen. The value of N is initialized at zero by the assignment statement in the fourth line of the program. After that the program repeats two statements, printing the current value of N and then incrementing N, until N is equal to 10. Then the program ends.

Example 7-1B does the same sort of task, but counts by fives from zero through 50. You will find that the numerals are listed vertically this time. Which statement caused the change in the direction of the printing?

Example 7-1B

```
VAR N:INTEGER
BEGIN
WRITE(28, 31);
N:=0;
REPEAT
        WRITE (N#, 13);
        N:=N+5
UNTIL N>50
END.
```

COUNTING EVENTS WITH REPEAT. . .UNTIL

While one of the other Pascal repetitive statements is sometimes easier to use for counting applications, REPEAT. . .UNTIL can do the jobs quite nicely, too. The following programming examples illustrate some of the different ways REPEAT. . .UNTIL counting can be used.

Example 7-2

```
VAR SPOTZ:INTEGER;
BEGIN
WRITE(28, 31);
SPOTZ:=0;
REPEAT
        WRITE(42);
        SPOTZ:=SPOTZ+1
UNTIL SPOTZ>63
END.
```

The program in Example 7-2 prints a string of 64 asterisks along the top line of the screen. The statement WRITE(42) is the one responsible for calling the asterisk character in ASCII. Try substituting some other ASCII character codes in that particular statement, maybe question mark (ASCII 63) or a dollar sign (ASCII 36).

Example 7-3

```
VAR FIG, LINE:INTEGER;
BEGIN
WRITE(28, 31);
FIG:=0; LINE:=0;
REPEAT
        WRITE(13);
        LINE:=LINE+1
UNTIL LINE>8;
REPEAT
        WRITE(42);
        FIG:=FIG+1
UNTIL FIG>63
END.
```

The program in Example 7-3 prints a string of 64 asterisks across the middle line on the screen. It takes two REPEAT . . .UNTIL statements to do the job. The first one, working with variable LINE, does a series of eight line feed/carriage returns (the WRITE(13) statement) to carry the cursor to the middle line on the screen. The second REPEAT. . .UNTIL statement uses variable FIG and WRITE(42) to print the line of asterisks.

Notice that the two variables in Example 7-3 happen to be initialized to 0 on the same line. That is a 2-statement line that reflects the fact that the two operations have identical meanings. Writing the two statements on the same line is purely a matter of personal taste, however.

Nesting Statements

The next programming example, Example 7-4, is built around a sequence of three REPEAT. . .UNTIL statements. The second one, itself, contains yet another REPEAT . . .UNTIL. These repetitive statements, in other words, can be nested, one serving as a valid statement within another.

Example 7-4

```
VAR TOP, BOT, SIDES, SKIP:INTEGER;
BEGIN
WRITE(28, 31);
TOP:=0;
REPEAT
        WRITE(176);
        TOP:=TOP+1
```

```
        UNTIL TOP>62;
        WRITE(13);
        SIDES:=Ø;
        REPEAT
              WRITE(149);
              SKIP:=Ø;
              REPEAT
                    WRITE(32);
                    SKIP:=SKIP+1
              UNTIL SKIP>6Ø;
              WRITE(17Ø, 13);
              SIDES:=SIDES+1
        UNTIL SIDES>12;
        BOT:=Ø;
        REPEAT
              WRITE(131);
              BOT:=BOT+1
        UNTIL BOT>62
        END.
```

From an operator's point of view, the program in Example 7-4 simply clears the screen and draws a neat rectangle that virtually fills the screen. From a programmer's point of view, the important things are the nesting of a REPEAT . . . UNTIL statement and the use of some TRS-80 graphics symbols.

The names of the variables declared in the first line are rather descriptive of the roles they play in the rectangle drawing task. TOP is used for drawing the top edge, SIDES draws the sides, and BOT is used for drawing the bottom edge of the rectangle figure.

As mentioned earlier, the program is built around three major REPEAT. . .UNTIL loops. The first uses variable TOP and graphics code number 176 to draw the top edge, while the last loop uses variable BOT and graphics code 131 to draw the bottom line.

The most important point is the fact that the middle REPEAT. . .UNTIL loop first draws graphics code 149, and then uses another REPEAT. . .UNTIL loop to move the cursor to the right-hand side of the screen. SKIP counts the number of spaces (ASCII control code 32) the cursor should move between drawing an element of the left side and right side of the figure.

Study that side drawing, nested loop operation carefully. It represents one of the most useful and powerful Pascal structures.

Example 7-4, incidentally, could be improved significantly, using fewer variables and statements. It is presented in the present form for the sake of clarity, but you already possess the know-how to reduce the number of variables to two and cut the number of statements by about one-third. Try it.

Counting Keyboard Operations

In an entirely different vein, REPEAT. . . UNTIL can be used for counting keyboard operations. The next example illustrates this particular point.

Example 7-5

```
VAR SUM, ENTRY, NUMBER:INTEGER;
BEGIN
WRITE(28, 31);
SUM:=∅;ENTRY:=∅;
REPEAT
      ENTRY:=ENTRY+1;
      WRITE('ENTRY NUMBER', ENTRY#, 'OF 1∅');
      READ(NUMBER#);
      SUM:=SUM+NUMBER;
UNTIL ENTRY=1∅;
WRITE(28, 31, 'THE SUM IS', SUM#)
END.
```

This program asks you to enter 10 different integers, one at a time. It keeps track of the number of integers you've entered. And when you have entered the 10th integer, as determined by the ENTRY variable, it clears the screen and prints the sum of your 10 numbers.

USING REPEAT. . .UNTIL FOR TIMING OPERATIONS

A number of programming situations call for building timing or time delay loops. The lightning-fast character is not a positive attribute under all possible conditions; things have to be slowed down sometimes. The short program in Example 7-6 represents a Pascal timing operation.

Example 7-6

```
VAR TIME:INTEGER;
BEGIN
WRITE(28, 31, 'TIMING NOW');
TIME:=∅;
REPEAT
      TIME:=TIME+1
```

```
UNTIL TIME=1000;
WRITE(28, 31, 'TIMING DONE')
END.
```

Upon running the program in Example 7-6, you see the screen clear and the message TIMING NOW in the upper left-hand corner. That message remains there for almost exactly 1 second; then it is replaced with TIME DONE.

REPEAT. . .UNTIL statement handles the 1-second timing operation, using variable TIME as a counter. Essentially, the loop counts from zero to 1000; since TRS-80 Tiny Pascal executes the loop in about 1 millisecond, it figures that 1000 loopings will add up to a 1-second delay. Change the UNTIL expression to read TIME=5000, and you will find the delay interval increased to about 5 seconds.

Time Bomb Program

Example 7-7 is a novel little program that illustrates some important structural features. You might want to run it before attempting to analyze it.

Example 7-7

```
VAR INT, TIME:INTEGER;
BEGIN
TIME:=1;
REPEAT
      WRITE(28, 31, 'TICK');
      INT:=0;
      REPEAT
            INT:=INT+1;
      UNTIL INT=1000;
      WRITE(28, 31, 'TOCK');
      INT:=0;
      REPEAT
            INT:=INT+1;
      UNTIL INT=1000;
      TIME:=TIME+1;
UNTIL TIME=10;
WRITE(28, 31, 'BOOM !!!')
END.
```

The "time bomb" program in Example 7-7 prints the words TICK and TOCK alternately on the screen. Each of the two messages appears for 1 second, and they run that way for 10 cycles.

The total time delay—before seeing BOOM !!! written on the screen—is about 20 seconds.

The major REPEAT. . .UNTIL loop uses the TIME variable to count the number of TICK/TOCK cycles. That loop begins on line 4 and ends at the third line from the bottom.

Now the major REPEAT. . .UNTIL loop, among other things, includes a sequence of two more REPEAT. . .UNTIL loops. These two "inner" loops are responsible for timing the TICK and TOCK intervals.

The program in Example 7-7 is thus built around a sequential pair of REPEAT. . .UNTIL timing loops that are fit into a larger REPEAT. . .UNTIL loop that does a counting job.

Real time bombs, however, ought to have provisions for presetting the time delay interval. You should not be restricted to the fixed 20-second interval inherent in the last example. Here is a somewhat better "time bomb" that lets you input the desired time delay (number of TICK/TOCK cycles):

Example 7-8

```
VAR INT, TIME, DELAY:INTEGER;
BEGIN
WRITE(28, 31, 'HOW MUCH TIME DELAY—IN SEC-
    ONDS');
READ(DELAY#);
TIME:=1;
REPEAT
    WRITE(28, 31, 'TICK');
    INT:=∅;
    REPEAT
        INT:=INT+1;
    UNTIL INT=5∅∅;
    WRITE(28, 31, 'TOCK');
    INT:=∅;
    REPEAT
        INT:=INT+1;
    UNTIL INT=5∅∅;
    TIME:=TIME+1;
UNTIL DELAY=DELAY;
WRITE(28, 31, 'BOOM!!!')
END.
```

Stopwatch Program

The next example shows how to use REPEAT. . .UNTIL loops to make a computerized stopwatch. In this case, the display shows the passage of seconds and tenths of seconds from 0:0 to 99:9. Does this one give you any ideas about building a Pascal program for a real-time clock?

Example 7-9

```
VAR SEC, TENTH, DEL:INTEGER;
BEGIN
SEC:=0;
REPEAT
        TENTH:=0;
        REPEAT
                DEL:=0;
                REPEAT
                        DEL:=DEL+1
                UNTIL DEL=99;
                WRITE(28, 31, SEC#, ':', TENTH#);
                TENTH:=TENTH+);
        UNTIL TENTH=9
        WRITE(28, 31, SEC#, ':', TENTH#);
        SEC:=SEC+1
UNTIL SEC=100
END.
```

Example 7-9 does its job by means of three nested REPEAT . . . UNTIL repetitive statements. The innermost of the three uses variable DEL to create a time delay interval of about one-tenth of a second. Each time that loop is satisfied, the middle loop increments the value of variable TENTH. TENTH is thus incremented at one-tenth of a second intervals.

The counting range for TENTH is set by that middle loop to zero through 9. And when TENTH is restarted at zero, the outermost counting loop—the one using variables SEC—is incremented.

The counting range for the outer loop is between zero and 100. Since the last WRITE operation prints the value of SEC before SEC is incremented again, the counter actually counts up to 99:9. Loops within loops within loops—it all fits the Pascal structure quite nicely.

See if you can modify Example 7-9 to work as a rocket launching counter. Make it count backwards from 99:9 to 0:0 seconds. All the assignment statements have to be changed.

WRITING UNENDING LOOPS

If you have any experience with writing BASIC programs, you have most likely run into the sort of panicky situation where you accidentally write a program having an unending loop. It is very easy to write unending loops in BASIC. Pascal, however, doesn't allows such accidents to occur easily.

In fact, you generally have to work carefully to build an endless loop on purpose. It can be done, though. As an example, suppose you want a program that counts by ones from zero to infinity.

Sorry, but Tiny Pascal cannot handle numbers larger than 32767. So you cannot count to infinity. But you can structure a loop that will cycle endlessly through the range of numbers available in Tiny Pascal. Here it is:

Example 7-10

```
VAR N:INTEGER;
BEGIN
N:=0;
REPEAT
        WRITE(N#, 13);
        N:=N+1
UNTIL N<>N
END.
```

What? REPEAT UNTIL N doesn't equal N? That doesn't make any sense. A number is always equal to itself. How can the UNTIL expression ever be satisfied? Well, it can't. That's the trick to building endless loops in Pascal. Just set up an expression that is logically impossible to satisfy.

That example, incidentally, counts through the entire range of Tiny Pascal numbers. It begins at zero and increments to 32767. After that the counting switches to negative integers, counting from -32767 to -1. Then it starts all over from zero again. That is an incidental point right now, but you ought to file it away in your memory for possible future reference.

Example 7-10 illustrates the operation of an endless Pascal loop, but the program isn't really a very practical one. The next example shows how to use an endless loop for more realistic purposes.

Example 7-11

```
VAR NUM, ACC, CYC:INTEGER;
BEGIN
ACC:=0;
WRITE(28, 31);
REPEAT
```

```
        WRITE('NEW NUMBER');
        READ(NUM#);
        ACC:=ACC+NUM;
        WRITE(13, 'SUM IS', ACC#, 13)
    UNTIL CYC<>CYC
    END.
```

Example 7-11 works like a calculator that sums signed integers. It asks you to enter a number; then it sums that number with a subtotal already assigned to variable ACC. Then it writes the accumulated sum and asks for the next number.

The program runs without end, because the UNTIL expression CYC<>CYC can never be satisfied. The only way to get out of the program is by striking the BREAK key twice in succession.

In this case, variable CYC is used as a "dummy" variable. It is never initialized, and it is only used as part of the impossible UNTIL expression. There is really no need to introduce such a dummy variable; ACC<>ACC or NUM<>NUM would do the job just as well. Using the dummy is just one of those stylistic features some programmers like to employ for clarity.

Although the program in Example 7-11 can handle any number of entries (because of the endless loop feature), it isn't always desirable to break out of the loop by terminating the entire program. The operations in Example 7-11. for instance, might be followed by more programming. If the only way to end the summing phase is by breaking out of the program, you'll never get to the operations that follow it.

Here is one way to handle the situation:

Example 7-12
```
    VAR NUM, ACC, CYC:INTEGER;
    BEGIN
    WRITE(28, 31);
    ACC:=Ø; CYC:=Ø;
    REPEAT
        WRITE('NEW NUMBER');
        READ(NUM#);
        ACC:=ACC+NUM;
        WRITE(13, 'SUM IS', ACC#, 13, 'STRIKE + KEY
            TO ADD ANOTHER', 13);
        READ (CYC)
    UNTIL CYC<>43;
    WRITE('DONE ---- GRAND TOTAL IS', ACC#)
    END.
```

This program does the same calculator-type adding as Example 7-11, but CYC is no longer a simple dummy variable. Its value is read as an ASCII character code in the READ(CYC) statement; and the UNTIL expression, CYC<>43, allows the REPEAT. . .UNTIL cycle to loop around until CYC happens to read a value of 43. If you refer to the listing of ASCII codes in the Appendix, you will find that 43 is the ASCII code for the plus sign. So the loop repeats until you strike (no ENTER is necessary) something other than the + key.

Run the program in Example 7-12. You will see that you can keep on adding numbers as long as you answer the STRIKE + KEY TO ADD ANOTHER message by striking something other than the + key. The ENTER key works nicely in this case. When you answer the message by striking something other than the + key the UNTIL expression is satisfied. The system breaks out of the loop and goes to the next statement.

GOOF-PROOFING ENTRIES WITH REPEAT. . .UNTIL

Programs that make it necessary for an operator to enter information from the keyboard are susceptible to operator errors. Some programs are more sensitive to operator errors than others. It is always a good idea to include some provisions for prompting an error-prone operator, making that individual repeat an input operation until it is done right.

Example 7-13 does little more than demand a certain kind of input. It can be used just about anywhere in a larger program that calls for operator goof-proofing.

Example 7-13
```
VAR NUMBER:INTEGER;
BEGIN
REPEAT
        WRITE(28, 31, 'ENTER AN INTEGER BETWEEN
            Ø AND 9');
        READ(NUMBER#)
UNTIL(NUMBER>=Ø) AND (NUMBER<=9);
WRITE(13, NUMBER#, 'IS FINE.')
END.
```

The program in Example 7-13 simply asks you to enter an integer between 0 and 9 inclusively, and the system remains in the REPEAT. . .UNTIL loop until you answer that request properly. The UNTIL expression, you see, is not satisfied until the NUMBER variable is *both* greater than or equal to zero (a positive integer) *and* less than or equal to 9.

The UNTIL expression dictates the terms of the entry. Until the operator meets those standards, the system continues asking for the number. The program will finally print the number and message, IS FINE, when the operator manages to enter an integer that is indeed between 0 and 9. It isn't a very exciting little program, but it makes the point.

A number of program schemes call for prompting the operator to answer a question by entering YES or NO. Unless there are some provisions for goof-proofing this kind of operation, there is always the chance that the program will whip off into some unwanted parts of the program memory. Here is a Y/N scheme that uses ASCII-character codes to satisfy the REPEAT. . .UNTIL goof-proofing loop:

Example 7-14

```
VAR RESPO, FIELD, NUMBER:INTEGER;
BEGIN
WRITE(28, 31);
REPEAT
    WRITE('DO YOU WANT TO SEE ME DO MY
        THING — Y OR N');
    READ(RESPO)
UNTIL (RESPO=89) OR (RESPO=78);
IF RESPO=89 THEN
    BEGIN
    WRITE(28, 31);
    FIELD:=0;
    REPEAT
        WRITE(92, 13);
        FIELD:=FIELD+1
    UNTIL FIELD>8;
    NUMBER:=0;
    REPEAT
        WRITE(NUMBER#, 32);
        NUMBER:=NUMBER+1
    UNTIL NUMBER>9
    END
ELSE WRITE(28, 31, 'OK, JUST WAIT UNTIL YOU WANT
TO SHOW OFF!!')
END.
```

This program latches into the first REPEAT. . .UNTIL loop until the operator strikes either the Y or N keys, ASCII 89 or 78 respectively. Then, and only then, will the program proceed. While the remainder of the program has no direct bearing on the subject of goof-proofing, it is nevertheless worthy of some study in its own right. For instance, see if you can completely justify the syntax of the rather extensive IF. . . THEN. . .ELSE expressions.

A FOUR-FUNCTION CALCULATOR PROGRAM

The following program illustrates the application of many principles described in Chapters 6 and 7, including a bit of operator goof-proofing discussed in the previous section of this chapter.

Example 7-15
```
    VAR SGN, NUM, ACC, REM:INTEGER;
    BEGIN
    REPEAT
        REPEAT
                WRITE(28, 31, ACC#);
                IF REM<>∅ THEN
                        WRITE(32, 'REMAINDER OF', REM#);
                WRITE(13, 13, 13, 13, 'TO ENTER
                    ANOTHER NUMBER:', 13, 2∅∅);
                WRITE('TYPE OPERATOR (+, −, * OR /)
                    AND ENTER NUMBER;);
                WRITE (13, 13, 'TO ENT EH PROGRAM:;
                    13, 2∅∅);
                WRITE('TYPE = AND ENTER ∅', 13);
                REM:=∅;
                READ(SGN, NUM#)
        UNTIL (SGN=43) OR (SGN=45) OR (SGN=42)
            OR (SGN=47) OR (SGN=61);
        IF SGN=43 THEN ACC:=ACC+NUM
        ELSE IF SGN=45 THEN ACC:=ACC−NUM
        ELSE IF SGN=42 THEN ACC:=ACC*NUM
        ELSE IF SGN=47 THEN
                BEGIN
                REM:=ACC MOD NUM;
                ACC:=ACC DIV NUM
                END;
    UNTIL SGN=61;
    WRITE(28, 31, ACC#);
    IF REM<>∅ THEN WRITE (32, 'REMAINDER OF',
        REM#)
    END.
```

Upon running this calculator program, you first see this set of messages on the screen:

Ø
TO ENTER ANOTHER NUMBER:
        TYPE OPERATOR (+, −, * OR /) AND
        ENTER NUMBER
TO END THE PROGRAM:
        TYPE = AND ENTER Ø

The zero appearing in the upper left-hand corner of the screen is the current subtotal. At the beginning of the process, that value is zero as it should be. According to the instructions on the screen, you should next specify an arithmetic operation (add, subtract, multiply or divide), and then type some number, followed by striking the ENTER key.

The system responds immediately whenever you strike the operator symbol. The operator is entered into the system as an ASCII character code and assigned to variable SGN. See the READ(SGN, NUM#) statement. The system responds by printing a question mark that indicates it is time to type the first number and strike the ENTER key. You have to strike the ENTER key in this case because the number value is assigned to variable NUM; that variable is taken as a decimal value by the READ(SGN, NUM#) statement.

The REPEAT. . .UNTIL statement that encloses the main message writing and READ(SGN, NUM#) statements makes up a goof-proofing loop. It does not allow the program to proceed until the operator enters a valid math symbol. Note the ASCII codes in the UNTIL expression: UNTIL (SGN=43) OR (SGN=45), etc. The system loops through this part of the program until the operator enters a valid math symbol and a number.

The remainder of the program executes the designated math operations, prints the result in the upper left-hand corner of the screen, and repeats the operator/number message writing sequence. You can continue doing calculator-type operations until you enter an equal sign as a math operator, followed by entering 0. That kind of operation satisfies the major REPEAT. . .UNTIL loop that ends with UNTIL SGN=61. Sure enough, entering an equal sign (ASCII code number 61) gets the system out of its main loop and brings things to a close. As is the case with most of the examples in this book, you will be better off attempting to justify the syntax of this example than simply playing with the program and taking the syntax for granted.

Chapter 8
Two More
Looping Statements:
WHILE...DO And FOR...DO

While the REPEAT...UNTIL loop might be the most commonly used repetitive statement in Pascal, there are two others that make up for some shortcomings inherent in REPEAT...UNTIL. This chapter first points out the essential characteristics of WHILE...DO and FOR...DO loops, and compares them with RE-PEAT...UNTIL. After making those important contrasts and comparisons, you will have a chance to use them in some demonstration programs.

THE SYNTAX RULES

Figure 8-1 shows the syntax diagrams for all three of Pascal's repetitive loop statements, including the REPEAT...UNTIL loop you studied in the previous chapter of this book.

A WHILE...DO statement takes this general form:

WHILE expression DO
    statement

If you want to make some variable increment from zero to 9, using a WHILE...DO loop, you can use this sort of sequence within a program:

NUMBER:=∅;
WHILE NUMBER<1∅ DO
    NUMBER:=NUMBER+1;

In essence, the program says to increment variable NUMBER WHILE, or as long as, NUMBER is less than 10. In other words, WHILE...DO executes its *statement* as long as its *expression* is satisfied. If the value of NUMBER were intialized to 20, or any other number equal to or larger than 10, the WHILE...DO loop in this instance would be skipped altogether.

WHILE...DO Statement Features

Comparing the syntax diagrams for WHILE...DO and RE-PEAT...UNTIL, you should be able to see two important differences. For one, the WHILE... DO statement allows only one statement to be executed within it. Unlike the statement for RE-PEAT...UNTIL, there are no provisions for executing multiple statements separated by semicolons.

Does that mean that a WHILE...DO statement is good for running just one statement? The syntax diagram would seem to imply that. But if you refer back to Fig. 6-5C, you will see that BEGIN...END is a legitimate Pascal statement as well as one of the major block operations.

So the single STATEMENT in WHILE...DO can be occupied by a BEGIN...END sequence. Thus, you often see statements with this sort of form:

```
NUMBER:=Ø;
WHILE NUMBER<1Ø DO
        BEGIN
        WRITE(NUMBER#);
        NUMBER:=NUMBER+1
        END;
    .
    .
    .
```

In practice, it is thus possible to construct WHILE...DO loops that encompass any number of statements just as long as those statements are, in turn, encompassed by a single BEGIN...END statement. The most practical form of a WHILE...DO loop is more like this:

```
WHILE expression DO
        BEGIN
        expression
        expression
        .
        .
        .
        END;
```

A second feature of WHILE...DO is the fact that its STATE-MENT is not executed if its EXPRESSION is not satisfied. Be-

cause the value of variable NUMBER is set to 10 before the
WHILE…DO loop is encountered, the loop in this next example is
never executed:

```
NUMBER:=15
WHILE NUMBER<1Ø DO
    BEGIN
    WRITE(NUMBER#);
    NUMBER:=NUMBER+1
    END;
```

The fact that the computer does not have to execute the
STATEMENT portion of a WHILE…DO loop might seem obvious
and trivial, but not after comparing it with REPEAT…UNTIL.

The statements encompassed by a REPEAT…UNTIL loop
must be executed at least one time. The statement within a
WHILE…DO loop need not be executed at all. Here is what makes
the difference.

In a REPEAT…UNTIL loop, the condition for breaking out of
the loop is specified *after* the statement listings. The computer
must execute the list of statements before it knows whether or not
it should break out of the loop.

In a WHILE…DO loop, the condition for breaking out of the
loop is specified *ahead of* its statement listing. The computer thus
knows in advance whether or not it should execute the statement
that follows.

FOR…DO Statement Features

The FOR…DO repetitive statement is used whenever a given
set of statements is to be executed a predetermined number of
times. It is so much like BASIC's FOR…NEXT loop that some
comparisons are inevitable. According to the syntax diagram in
Fig. 8-1, FOR…DO statements take this general form:

```
FOR identifier := expression TO expression DO
    statement
```

More specifically:

```
FOR NUMBER:=1 TO 9 DO
    WRITE(NUMBER#);
```

That one prints number 1 through 9 for you. Each time
FOR…DO executes its accompanying statement, the value of
IDENTIFIER is incremented by one, beginning with the first
number and ending with the second number in the EXPRESSION

part. In that particular example, the value of variable NUMBER is incremented between 1 and 9, writing the value of the number each time. It works just like this BASIC sequence:

line number   FOR N=1 TO 9
line number   PRINT N
line number   NEXT N

The FOR...DO syntax diagram also shows that it is possible to count backwards. Look at this example:

FOR NUMBER:= 9 DOWNTO Ø
       WRITE(NUMBER#);

That one writes numbers backwards from 9 to 0. You've probably figured out the difference for yourself. A TO delimiter causes the FOR...DO variable to increment upward, while the DOWNTO delimiter causes it to decrement or count backwards by ones.

As in the case of the UNTIL...DO statement, FOR...DO allows only one STATEMENT to be executed within the context of its syntax diagram. As you have already seen in the case of UNTIL...DO, it is possible to "cheat" the system by using a BEGIN...END statement which, itself, can be made up of any number of individual statements.

SOME APPLICATIONS OF WHILE...DO

Example 8-1 uses the WHILE...DO repetitive statement to list numbers zero through 9.

Example 8-1

VAR NUM:INTEGER;
BEGIN
NUM:=Ø;

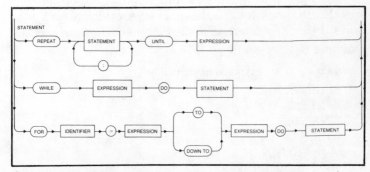

Fig. 8-1. Syntax diagram for Pascal's three repetitive statements.

```
WHILE NUM<10 DO
        BEGIN
        WRITE(NUM#,32);
        NUM:=NUM+1
        END;
WRITE(13,'DONE')
END.
```

Then Example 8-2 shows the application of a sequence of WHILE...DO statements and some cursor graphics:

Example 8-2

```
VAR CHAR,NUM:INTEGER;
BEGIN
WRITE(28,31,'WHAT CHARACTER');
READ(CHAR);
WRITE(28,31);
NUM:=0;
WHILE NUM<9 DO
        BEGIN
        WRITE(13);
        NUM:=NUM+1
        END;
NUM:=0;
WHILE NUM<64 DO
        BEGIN
        WRITE(CHAR);
        NUM:=NUM+1
        END;
END.
```

Application Of Nested WHILE...DO Loops

Example 8-3 illustrates the application of nested WHILE...DO loops. Run it and then see if you can figure out how it works. Pay special attention to the Pascal structure and syntax.

Example 8-3

```
VAR SPACE, LINE:INTEGER;
BEGIN
WRITE(28,31);
LINE:=0;
WHILE LINE<8 DO
        BEGIN
        SPACE:=0;
        WHILE SPACE<32 DO
```

112

```
                BEGIN
                WRITE(32);
                SPACE:=SPACE+1
                END;
        WRITE(191,13);
        LINE:=LINE+1
SPACE:=-1;
WHILE SPACE<63 DO
        BEGIN
        IF SPACE=31 THEN
            WRITE(191)
        ELSE WRITE(131);
        SPACE:=SPACE+1
        END;
LINE:=LINE+1;
WHILE LINE < 14 DO
        BEGIN
        SPACE:=0
        WHILE SPACE<32 DO
                BEGIN
                WRITE(32);
                SPACE:=SPACE+1
                END;
        WRITE(191,13);
        LINE:=LINE+
        END;
WRITE('2-DIMENSIONAL COORDINATES')
END.
```

Frankly, the program in Example 8-3 could do its job in a somewhat simpler fashion, using one of the tab code numbers for placing the vertical coordinate. This particular approach, however, shows the construction of nested WHILE...DO loops.

Timing Programs Around WHILE...DO Statements

Of course, it is entirely possible to make up timing programs around the WHILE...DO statement. Example 8-4 shows how such a scheme can be applied, but you will find in the section following this one that FOR...DO statements make the most efficient sorts of timing loops.

Example 8-4

```
    VAR TIME,INT:INTEGER;
    BEGIN
```

```
WRITE(28,31,'SPECIFY DELAY INTERVAL IN MIL-
LISECONDS');
READ(TIME#);
WRITE(28,31,'TIMING NOW');
INT:=0
WHILE INT<TIME DO
      INT:=INT+1;
WRITE(28,31,'BOOM !!',13,13,'TIMING DONE')
END.
```

And here is a slowed-down counter:

Example 8-5

```
VAR NUMBER,TIME, INT:INTEGER;
BEGIN
WRITE(28,31,'HOW HIGH DO YOU WANT TO COUNT');
READ(TIME#);
NUMBER: =0;
WHILE NUMBER<=TIME DO
      BEGIN
      WRITE(28,31,NUMBER#);
      INT:=0
      WHILE INT <500 DO
          INT:=INT+1;
      NUMBER:=NUMBER+1
      END;
WRITE(13,13,'DONE')
END.
```

How would you go about making up an unending loop with the
WHILE . . . DO statement? Just set up some impossible conditions, such as:

```
WHILE FIX<>FIX DO
      statement
```

That one uses a dummy variable you have to specify in the variable
declaration line, but it executes its statement forever, or until you
do a BREAK from the keyboard.

It is a bit easier to build an unending loop accidentally when
fooling around with WHILE...DO. Back in Example 8-3, delete one
of the LINE:=LINE+1 statements. Pretend you forgot to put it in,
and watch that program draw one section of the coordinates from
here to eternity. By failing to increment the value of variable
LINE, you will never reach the logical specifications for breaking
out of a LINE loop.

114

WHILE...DO Approach To Goof Proofing

Here is how WHILE...DO can be used for goof-proofing keyboard information:

Example 8-6A

```
VAR X:INTEGER;
BEGIN
X:=100;
WHILE (X<10) OR (X> 10) DO
        BEGIN
        WRITE(28,31,'ENTER AN INTEGER BETWEEN
        0 and 10');
        READ(X#)
        END;
WRITE(28,31,'GOOD JOB. X=',X#)
END.
```

Using this particular approach to goof-proofing (making certain the operator enters an integer that is indeed between 0 and 10), it is necessary to initialize variable X to some value that does not meet the WHILE...DO criteria. If, for example, you initialized X at 0, the WHILE...DO loop would never be executed. Try it.

Comparison With REPEAT...UNTIL Version

Now compare that example with this REPEAT...UNTIL version of the same thing:

Example 8-6B

```
VAR X:INTEGER;
BEGIN
REPEAT
        WRITE(28,31,'ENTER AN INTEGER BETWEEN
        0 and 10');
        READ(X#)
UNTIL (X<=0) AND<∝=10);
WRITE(28,31,'GOOD JOB.  X=',X#)
END.
```

The fact that a REPEAT...UNTIL sequence of statements is run one time before the results are tested makes that version seem simpler than the WHILE...DO version in Example 8-6A. The point is that the WHILE...DO repetitive statement, as nice as it might be under some circumstances, is not always the most effective choice. Of course, the same is true for the REPEAT...UNTIL statement.

In Examples 8-6A and 8-6B, it so happens that the RE-PEAT...UNTIL wins out.

SOME APPLICATIONS OF FOR...DO

The FOR...DO statement is most appropriate whenever you want to execute a block of statements a specific, well-defined number times. The nice thing about this statement, compared with the other two, is that the incrementing or decrementing operations are automatic. Compare these:

Example 8-7A

```
VAR X:INTEGER
BEGIN
X:=0;
REPEAT
        WRITE(X#,32);
        X:=X+1
UNTIL X>9;
END.
```

Example 8-7B

```
VAR X:INTEGER;
BEGIN
X:=0;
WHILE X<10 DO
    BEGIN
    WRITE(X#,32);
    X:=X+1
    END;
END.
```

Example 8-7C

```
VAR X:INTEGER;
BEGIN
FOR X:=0 TO 9 DO
        WRITE(X#,32)
END.
```

All three of these examples do the same thing. They print numerals 0 through 9, with spaces inserted between them. It's quite apparent from looking at the examples that the FOR...DO scheme is easier to program. Remember, it is built for counting.

Time delays are even simpler with FOR...DO:

Example 8-8

```
VAR TIME, INT:INTEGER;
BEGIN
```

```
WRITE (28,31, 'ENTER   TIME   DELAY   IN   MIL-
LISECONDS');
READ(TIME#);
WRITE(28,31, 'NOW TIMING');
FOR INT:=0 TO TIME DO;
WRITE(28,31, 'BOOM !! TIMING IS DONE')
END.
```

Timing and Counter Loops

The entire timing operation in Example 8-8 is handled by the
line, FOR INT:=0 TO TIME DO;. Does that look like a proper sort
of Pascal FOR...DO statement? Where is the STATEMENT part
of it?

Well, Pascal can handle something call *null statements* that
don't do anything. The fact that a 1-line timing statement concludes
with a semicolon implies that a do-nothing statement is inserted
between the word DO and the semicolon. In other words, the
statement calls for incrementing the value of INT from 0 to TIME,
and doing nothing else in the meantime.

It's hard to imagine a timing loop that is any easier to imple-
ment than that one is. Don't forget that FOR...DO loops can count
backwards, too.

Example 8-9

```
VAR TIM,INT:INTEGER;
BEGIN
WRITE(28,31, 'ROCKET LAUNCH DEMO');
FOR TIM:=0 TO 2500 DO;
FOR TIM:=10 DOWNTO 0 DO
      BEGIN
      WRITE(28,31,TIM#);
      FOR INT:=0 TO 1000DO;
      END;
WRITE(13, 'BLAST OFF!!')
END.
```

Example 8-9 includes two upward-counting timing loops and a
down-counting counter loop. The first timing loop, made up of FOR
TIM:=0 TO 2500, gives the operator about 2.5 seconds to view the
title of the program, ROCKET LAUNCH DEMO. TIM is the
incrementing variable for that one. The second upward-counting
timing loop uses variable INT, and provides a 1-second delay
between each of the down-counting intervals.

The statement TIM:=10 DOWNTO 0 DO is the one that generates the figures you see on the screen. The DOWNTO portion is responsible for making the thing count backwards for you.

Another Digital Stopwatch

As you might imagine by now, FOR...DO loops are great for clock and timekeeping operations. Here is a FOR...DO version of the "digital stopwatch" already featured in Example 7-9 of Chapter 7:

Example 8-10
```
VAR SEC,TENTH,DEL:INTEGER;
BEGIN
WRITE(28,31);
FOR SEC:=0 TO 99 DO
      FOR TENTH:=0 TO 9 DO
          BEGIN
          FOR DEL:=0 TO 100 DO;
          WRITE(28,31,SEC#,':',TENTH#)
          END
END.
```

Now isn't that a lot simpler than Example 7-9? FOR...DO loops really come to the forefront when it is necessary to count through a specific number of steps.

Here's a question of syntax regarding Example 8-10. Why isn't the FOR SEC:=0 TO 99 DO statement immediately followed by a BEGIN...END sequence? The FOR TENTH:=0 TO 9 DO statement is.

The first FOR...DO is not followed by a BEGIN for the simple reason that the rest of the program comprises one statement. A FOR...DO statement can be followed by just one statement, as illustrated in Fig. 8-1. Through most of the examples cited so far, it has been necessary to follow a FOR...DO statement with more than one other statement. That's where the BEGIN...END comes into the picture. A BEGIN...END fakes the FOR...DO into thinking it is just working with one statement. The fact that BE-GIN...END, itself, contains more than one statement is perfectly okay.

As far as Pascal structure is concerned, FOR SEC:=0 TO 99 DO is followed by just one statement, another FOR...DO. The fact that the second FOR...DO contains more than one statement (as allowed by BEGIN...END) is incidental.

Chapter 9
A Miscellany Of Pascal
And Tiny Pascal Operation

Pascal, and Tiny Pascal for TRS-80 in particular, include some operations that are generally rather simple. Few of the operations described in this chapter fit very well into any of the preceding discussions, so they're brought together here for the sake of tying up some loose ends.

Most of these operations are quite useful, and some are vital under certain programming situations. So while this is something of a catch-all chapter, study the ideas as carefully as you would any others.

REMARKS FOR PASCAL

In BASIC, REM statements give you a chance to write out some commentary in any program. Such statements are never acted upon by the computer, but merely serve as convenient ways to write explanatory notes or labels in the program listing itself.

The Pascal counterpart of BASIC's REM statement is any string of characters or comment enclosed within the 2-character form, (* and *). Standard Pascal calls for enclosing remarks within curly brackets. Since very few personal computers have those symbols on the keyboard, Tiny Pascal substitutes the 2-character combinations cited here.

Pascal remarks can be inserted anywhere in the program, anywhere on a separate line, or right on the same line with some regular program text. Here are a few examples:

```
VAR FUN,SILLY,DOIT:INTEGER; (* DECLARE THE
VARIABLES *)
```

or

```
BEGIN
(* INITIALIZE THE VARIABLES *)
FUN:=Ø;
```

or

```
(* LINE 1 *)   BEGIN
(* LINE 2 *)   FUN:=Ø;
```

While many programmers object strongly to the prospect of using too many remarks in a program, the statements are indeed very helpful when it comes to designating the beginning of different kinds of operations. There isn't much else of practical value to be explained. Pascal remarks are simple to use. From now on, you will find a lot of them in programming examples.

DECLARING CONSTANTS IN PASCAL

It is possible to dream up a number of instances where it would be nice to call some long numbers by means of an identifier, rather than having to write out the number each time it is to be used. Suppose, for instance, you have to begin some counting operations from 15360 a number of different times within a given program. Rather than writing out that number every time you need it, you can assign it to an identifier and then simply call that identifier whenever you need the number.

Constants are declared at the beginning of a Pascal program in much the same way variables are. Figure 9-1 shows the syntax diagram for CONST.

To declare a constant, begin by writing CONST, followed by an IDENTIFIER, an equal sign and the desired CONSTANT value. If you want to declare more than one constant, simply separate them with a semicolon. In any event, be sure to end the operation with a semicolon.

Here are a couple of examples:

```
CONST HCOUNT=1536Ø;
      HEND=1666Ø;
```

CONST BLINKS=1234;

Aside from using the proper syntax rules, the important thing about declaring constants is that you write the CONST line *before anything else* in Tiny Pascal. The constants must be declared even before the variables are.

Example 9-1

```
CONST STOP=63;      (* DECLARE THE CONSTANT *)
VAR HCOUNT:         (* DECLARE THE VARIABLE *)
INTEGER;
BEGIN
WRITE(28,31);       (* CLEAR THE SCREEN AND *)
                    (* HOME THE CURSOR      *)

FOR HCOUNT:=0 TO
STOP DO
     WRITE(42);     (* PRINT ASTERISKS      *)
END.
```

The constant in Example 9-1 is identified, or declared, as STOP, and it is evaluated at decimal 63. It is called later in the program to set the limit on the number of asterisks this thing prints.

SORTING STATEMENTS WITH CASE...OF

Now here is a more powerful sort of Pascal operation. It bears some resemblance to BASIC's ON...GOTO statement, letting the system select one of any number of lines according to the value of some number.

It is the relative complexity of the syntax, rather than its basic idea, that makes the CASE...OF statement a bit tricky to use at first. Start out by looking at its syntax diagram in Fig. 9-2.

Days Of The Week Program

If that diagram blows your mind, run the program in Example 9-2, compare its listing with the syntax diagram, and see if you can begin figuring it out from there.

Example 9-2

(* DAYS OF THE WEEK *)
VAR DAY:INTEGER;

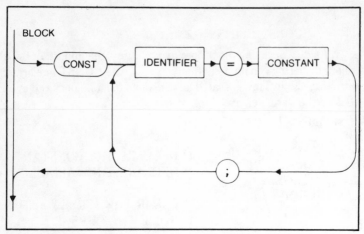

Fig. 9-1. Syntax diagram for declaring constants with CONST.

```
BEGIN
WRITE(28,31,'ENTER A DAY NUMBER BETWEEN 1
AND 7', 13);
READ(DAY#);
WRITE(13,13,'DAY ',DAY#,' OF THE WEEK IS:',13,200);
CASE DAY OF

    1: WRITE('SUNDAY');
    2: WRITE('MONDAY');
    3: WRITE('TUESDAY');
    4: WRITE('WEDNESDAY');
    5: WRITE('THURSDAY');
    6: WRITE('FRIDAY');
    7: WRITE('SATURDAY')

ELSE WRITE('WHAT?? THERE IS NO SUCH DAY!!')
END
END.
```

The program in Example 9-2 asks you to enter a number for DAY between 1 and 7 inclusively. The CASE...OF statement then translates that number into the name of a day, printing it out on the screen for you. If you mess up the entry and put in a number that is not between 1 and 7, the ELSE portion of the CASE...OF statement informs you of your lack of cooperation.

The numbers preceding the colons and WRITE statements represent the possible integer values of variable DAY. Once that value is entered via the READ statement, the CASE...OF statement searches its own list for a matching number. Upon finding a match, it executes the statement following it. Then it skips down to the END part of CASE...OF to get on with the rest of the program. In this case, however, there is no programming left.

Compare the listing in Example 9-2 with the specifications in the syntax diagram in Fig. 9-2. See if you can justify the whole CASE...OF operation.

School Test Program

The next example demonstrates a nice feature of CASE...OF, doing a set of operations under more than one numerical condition.

Example 9-3

```
(* SIMPLE Q&A *)
VAR ANS:INTEGER;
BEGIN
WRITE(28,31,'QUESTION:');
WRITE(13,13,'WHO IS BURIED IN GRANT',39,'S
TOUMB?'13,13);
WRITE(200,'(1) A. LINCOLN',13);
WRITE(200,'(2) B. BUNNY',13);
WRITE(200,'(3) G. WASHINGTON',13);
WRITE(200,'(4) U.S. GRANT',13);
WRITE(200,'(5) NONE OF THE ABOVE',13);
READ(ANS#);
CASE ANS OF
    1,2,3,5: WRITE('WRONG!! RUN AGAIN');
    4: WRITE('RIGHT!!SMART, AREN',39,'T YOU?')
END(* OF CASE *)
END.
```

Example 9-3 is one of those school-type, multiple-choice questions. The operator is supposed to respond to one of the five choices by entering a number between 1 and 5. The CASE...OF statement then sorts out the right answer, writing appropriate messages.

The point of this illustration is to show how more than one number designation can be assigned to a single case statement.

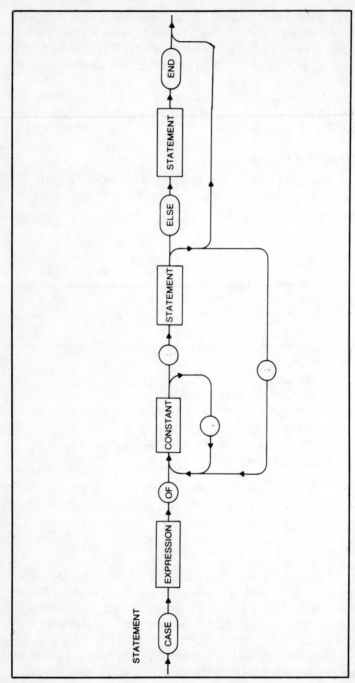

Fig. 9-2. Syntax diagram for CASE...OF.

Answers 1,2,3 and 5, for instance, are assigned to the first case—the one printing out the WRONG!! message. Answer number 4, however, is assigned to the second case statement.

The values of the constants in CASE statements can be scrambled any way you want, there is no practical limit on the number of case constants you can use, and you can use integers of any size. The only thing to bear in mind is that one particular case constant should be specified just one time. If you happen to specifiy the same case constant more than once, the computer responds only to the first one.

Example 9-3, incidentally, contains no ELSE clause. So if the operator enters a number not included in the list of case constants, the program simply comes to an end. The ELSE clause in a CASE...OF statement is optional, but it is usually very handy.

Playing Card Program

Example 9-4 shows how CASE...OF is handy for translating or decoding numbers.

Example 9-4

```
(* CARDS *)
VAR VALUE:INTEGER;
BEGIN
WRITE(28,31);
FOR VALUE:=2 TO 14 DO
      BEGIN
      CASE VALUE OF
            2,3,4,5,6,7,8,9,10:WRITE(VALUE#);
            11:   WRITE('JACK');
            12:   WRITE('QUEEN');
            13:   WRITE('KING');
            14:   WRITE('ACE')
      END;   (* OF CASE *)
      WRITE(32)
      END    (* OF COUNTING *)
END.
```

The program in Example 9-4 uses a FOR...DO counting loop to generate integers between 2 and 14. Those integers are translated by CASE...OF into playing card values. Upon running this program, here is what you should see on the screen:

2 3 4 5 6 7 8 9 10 JACK QUEEN KING ACE

Does that little example give you any ideas about Pascal games you might want to devise in the future?

Program Consisting Of Three Smaller Programs

There are two more features of the CASE...OF statement that are worthy of special note at this time. First, consider the EXPRESSION part of the statement. In all of the examples cited so far, EXPRESSION has been nothing more than a particular variable identifier. It can, however, be any sort of mathematical expression. The CONSTANT values in CASE...OF can, in other words, be scaled according to some sort of mathematical operation.

The second remaining point is that the operations performed within a CASE...OF statement need not be 1-line WRITE statements (as in all the foregoing examples). The syntax diagram in Fig. 9-1 show that each CONSTANT value must be followed by a single STATEMENT. You should recall from the previous chapter that BEGIN...END comprises a "single" statement, and that such a statement can, itself, be made up of a whole lot of others. Example 9-5 illustrates both of these points.

Example 9-5

```
(* HAIRY CASE DEMO *)
VAR VAL,SPACE,LINE:INTEGER;
BEGIN   (* THE PROGRAM *)
WRITE(28,31,'ENTER AN INTEGER BETWEEN 0 AND 2',13);
READ(VAL#);
WRITE(28,31);
CASE VAL+1 OF
  1:FOR LINE:=1 TO 4 DO
    BEGIN  (* LINE OPS *)
    FOR SPACE:=1 TO 21 DO
      WRITE(42);
    WRITE(13)
    END;  (* OF LINE OPS *)
  2:BEGIN  (* OPS FOR CASE #2 *)
    FOR LINE:=1 TO 4 DO
      WRITE(13);
    FOR LINE:=1 TO 4 DO
      BEGIN  (* LINE OPS *)
      FOR SPACE:=1 TO 21 DO
        WRITE(32);
      FOR SPACE:=1 TO 21 DO
        WRITE(42);
      WRITE(13)
      END  (* OF LINE OPS *)
    END;  (* OF OPS FOR CASE #2 *)
   3:BEGIN (* OPS FOR CASE #3 *)
    FOR LINE:=1 TO 8 DO
      WRITE(13);
    FOR LINE:=1 TO 4 DO
```

```
      BEGIN   (* LINE OPS *)
      FOR SPACE:=1 TO 42 DO
        WRITE(32);
      FOR SPACE:=1 TO 21 DO
        WRITE(42);
      WRITE(13)
      END   (* OF LINE OPS *)
    END      (* OF OPS FOR CASE #3 *)
  ELSE WRITE('ENTRY NOT BETWEEN 0 AND 2 ... RUN AGAIN')
  END   (* OF CASE STATEMENT  *)
END.  (* OF PROGRAM *)
```

The program in Example 9-5 is made up of three different smaller programs, each selected according to the CASE...OF statement. The operator is first asked to input a number between 0 and 2. The value is then assigned to variable VAL.

At the beginning of the CASE...OF statement, VAL is incremented by 1 to yield case constants of 1, 2 and 3, instead of 0, 1 and 2. This is done merely for purposes of illustration to show that case values can be scaled.

At any rate, the value of VAR+1 determines which one of the three case programs is executed . Actually all three programs do the same sort of thing, printing a 21 x 4 rectangle made up of asterisks. Case 1, however, places the rectangle in the upper left-hand corner of the screen. Case 2 puts it near the middle of the screen. Case 3 places the rectangle near the lower right-hand corner.

Granted, this isn't an especially exciting program. There are probably easier ways to go about doing it. The point, though, is to show how the statements within a case statement can be complete little Pascal programs in their own right. As you might imagine, the whole thing can get rather complex, even more complex than the program in Example 9-5.

This example also shows some nice Pascal structuring as well as some tricky little bits of syntax. Justify as many of the operations, structural qualities and syntax features as you can. You get an "A" for the chapter if you can see a reason why everything is done(or not done).

Do you see any reason why CASE...OF statements cannot be nested? Can you think of why you might want to put some CASE...OF statements within a CASE...OF statement? Think about it. Better yet, back up your thinking by trying it.

TWO MATH EXPRESSIONS PECULIAR TO TINY PASCAL

Supersoft's version of Tiny Pascal includes two math expressions that do not appear in Standard Pascal. The ABS(expression) returns the absolute value of any expression enclosed within the parentheses. The SQR(expression) returns the square of any expression enclosed within the parentheses.

Both expressions perform the same functions as their counterparts in BASIC. Actually they are FUNCTION identifiers. Since you have not encountered FUNCTION blocks in this book yet, the fact probably has little significance. For the time being, you can be content to use these functions in a straightforward fashion. For instance:

Example 9-6

```
VAR NUM:INTEGER;
BEGIN
WRITE(28,31,'ENTER AN INTEGER',13);
READ(NUM#);
NUM:=ABS(NUM);
WRITE(13,13,NUM#)
END.
```

Example 9-6 requests any integer from the keyboard, assigns the value to variable NUM, and then works out the absolute value of the number. Of course, the whole program doesn't have much meaning until you decide to enter some negative numbers.

Example 9-7

```
VAR NUM:INTEGER;
BEGIN
WRITE(28,31,'ENTER AN INTEGER',13);
READ(NUM#);
NUM:=SQR(NUM);
WRITE(13,13,NUM#)
END.
```

Example 9-7 figures the square of whatever number you enter from the keyboard. It's as simple as that.

TRS-80 "SET/RESET" GRAPHICS WITH PASCAL PLOT

The unique character of TRS-80 plotting graphics can be handled with Tiny Pascal PLOT statements. This one statement, properly handled, does the job of two in BASIC—SET (expression, expression) and RESET(expression, expression).

Recall that your TRS-80 screen can, for graphics purposes, be divided up into a 127 x 47 coordinate system. You can set a spot of light on the screen, at any desired point, by doing a SET(x,y), where x is the horizontal coordinate (between 0 and 127) and y is the vertical coordinate (between 0 and 47). By the same token, you can erase any such spot on the screen by doing a RESET(x,y).

The statement for doing the same sort of thing in TRS-80 Tiny Pascal is PLOT(x,y,z). The x and y terms represent constant values or expressions for the x and y coordinates, respectively. The z is fixed at a value of 1 or 0. If it is set to 1, the statement does a SET operation and places a point of light on the screen. If z=0, the statement does a RESET for you.

Actually the z in PLOT(x,y,z) can be any expression. If the result is an odd-numbered value, the statement sets the point of light. If the z expression turns out to be even-valued (or 0), it resets the point of light.

The following program first fills the screen with light by doing a SET-type operation for all coordinate positions on the screen. Then when you respond to the question mark by striking the ENTER key, the program RESETs all the points.

Example 9-8 .

```
VAR X,Y,MORE:INTEGER;
BEGIN
FOR Y:=0 TO 47 DO
        FOR X:=0 TO 127 DO
             PLOT(X,Y,1);
WRITE('?');
READ(MORE);
FOR Y:= 47 DOWNTO 0 DO
        FOR X:=127 DOWNTO 0 DO
             PLOT(XY,0)
END.
```

Then try it again with a new wrinkle:

Example 9-9

```
VAR X,Y,Z:INTEGER;
BEGIN
FORY:=0 TO 47 DO
        BEGIN
        IF Y THEN Z:=0
        ELSE Z:=1;
        FOR X:=0 TO 127 DO
             PLOT(X,Y,X+Z)
    END
END.
```

Example 9-9 draws a finely graded checkerboard on the screen. But notice the statement IF Y THEN Z:=∅. Its meaning isn't obvious according to anything you have studied thus far, so here's some explanation. That sort of statement is saying: IF the value of variable Y is *odd*, THEN assign 0 to variable Z. Such a statement is responsive to odd-numbered values.

It is tempting to begin playing around with some exciting graphics at this point. Do so if you wish; but you will find a lot of graphics worked out for you in the latter sections of this book. For the moment, there are some special statements of importance.

TRS-80 BASIC has a POINT(x,y) function that works in conjunction with its SET and RESET statements. In TRS-80 graphics, POINT looks at the coordinates specified by x and y, and returns a value of 1 or 0, depending upon whether that point is SET or RESET. The same kind of statement is included in Supersoft Tiny Pascal for the TRS-80. It is the POINT(x,y,) statement.

How about that! You have just seen the one and only statement that is absolutely common to both TRS-80 BASIC and Tiny Pascal. Read about POINT(x,y) in your BASIC manual, and you will know how to use it in Tiny Pascal.

THE MEM STATEMENT

You have probably heard a lot of talk about how Pascal runs faster than BASIC. If you base your own opinion of the matter on the programs in Examples 9-8 and 9-9, you might have some serious reservations about the high-speed reputation of Pascal. Frankly, those two graphics operations are quite slow.

To ally your fears about the capabilities of your Tiny Pascal, give this next example a try.

Example 9-10

```
VAR PLACE:INTEGER
BEGIN
FOR PLACE:=15360 TO 16383 DO
     MEM(PLACE):=191
END.
```

Now that's a lot better. This program fills the screen with light, just as Example 9-8 does, but this one does it a lot faster. The key to higher speeds is the MEM statement.

A MEM STATEMENT takes this general form:

MEM (expression):=expression

And it is about the same thing as TRS-80 BASIC's POKE (expression) statement. The expression in parentheses designates a memory address, and the assignment expression specifies the data to be written into that memory address.

As in the case of POKE statements in BASIC, you have to be careful about MEM-ing around in your computer's memory. One little miscalculation, and you can wipe out the entire program, and maybe even the Tiny Pascal editor/compiler.

Graphics Operations

The program in Example 9-10 increments through memory addresses 15360 through 16383, depositing a code 191 in each place. What does that mean? Well, on your TRS-80, addresses 15360 through 16383 are devoted to the video memory. Any intelligible data inserted into that section of memory will create a character or graphic element on the screen. Code 191, the code being fed into all the video memory, represents a graphic that fills the entire character space. See the Appendix.

Of course you can substitute other character codes for the 191 in Example 9-10, and come up with a screen full of other things. Dollar signs are nice.

Modify Example 9-10 as shown next, and you'll find the graphics running even faster. Why? The computer works in hexadecimal right from the start, and there is no need to do any decimal-to-hexadecimal conversions (for the benefit of those who haven't gotten around to learning the hex system yet).

Example 9-11

```
VAR PLACE:INTEGER;
BEGIN
FOR PLACE:=%3C00 TO %3FFF DO
        MEM(PLACE):=191
END.
```

It's the same idea, and the same program, with a different counting format and a higher speed. The percent signs appearing ahead of the hex numbers designate the numbers as hex integers. Using no percent prefix, as has been done everywhere before in this book, implies a decimal format.

It is entirely possible to turn around the MEM statement you have been using here, and create the effect of a TRS-80 BASIC PEEK statement:

```
        identifier:=MEM(expression)
```

This statement assigns to an identifier the data stored in memory address expression.

If you want to snoop around in your system's memory, just do a bunch of these operations:

Example 9-12

```
VAR PLACE:INTEGER;
BEGIN
WRITE('WHAT ADDRESS—IN DECIMAL',13);
READ(PLACE#)
PLACE:=MEM(PLACE);
WRITE(13,PLACE#)
END.
```

Other Uses

The MEM expression is good for doing things other than graphics operations. You can, for instance, write machine language programs, storing hex codes in portions of memory you choose for yourself. And then there is this intriguing possibility:

$$MEM(expression):=MEM(expression)$$

That's something you can use to transfer a byte of information from one place to another in the system's memory.

Tiny Pascal does not have arrays. But the MEM statement comes to the rescue, providing a 1-dimensional array of any desired length. You will find an entire section devoted to Tiny Pascal arrays later in the book.

It is difficult to overestimate the usefulness and power of the MEM statement in Tiny Pascal. The only problem for some people is that one must know their system pretty well to get the full benefit.

THE INKEY STATEMENT

The INKEY function in Tiny Pascal works very much like its TRS-80 BASIC counterpart, the INKEY$ function. This function causes the computer to scan the keyboard and pick up the ASCII code for any key that happens to be depressed at the moment. If no keys are depressed during the INKEY keyboard scanning operation, the INKEY function returns ASCII code number 0.

While INKEY does indeed allow the operator to assign values from the keyboard, its function is quite different from the READ statement. The main difference is that a READ statement forces the program to stop until there is some response from the operator.

On the other hand, an INKEY statement does not necessarily halt the program execution.

Perhaps the features of the INKEY statement are better demonstrated than explained in words. So here it goes:

Example 9-13

```
BEGIN
WHILE INKEY<>13 DO;
END.
```

Example 9-13 certainly appears to be a very simple program. And it is. Literally, it says, "Until the operator strikes the ENTER key (13 is the ASCII code number assigned to the ENTER KEY), do nothing." So the program does nothing until the operator strikes the enter key. Then the program simply ends. While the program is running, you can depress any other key you want and nothing happens. The program is sensitive only to the ENTER key by virtue of the fact that the WHILE...DO statement is no longer satisfied when that key is hit.

Consult the table of ASCII codes in the Appendix. Replace the number 13 in Example 9-13 with codes representing other keys.

Escape Route

Repetitive operations built around INKEY functions must have a well defined means of "escape." When you run the program in Example 9-13, you will find you cannot get out of the loop by striking the BREAK key. INKEY functions override the BREAK operation; if you enter a program that has no possible way to end, you can end the program only by doing a manual RESET. Doing a manual reset on your TRS-80 returns it to BASIC. The Tiny Pascal routine is completely lost, and you have to load the Pascal system tape all over again.

Here is an example of how you can mess yourself up with the INKEY function, use WHILE INKEY<>1ØØØ DO in Example 9-13. There is no code number 1ØØØ for the keyboard, so the program will not end until you RESET or turn off the computer.

Here is a more interesting application of the INKEY function:

Example 9-14

```
VAR X:INTEGER;
BEGIN
REPEAT
    REPEAT
```

133

```
                X:=INKEY
            UNTIL X(>∅;
            WRITE(X#,32,X%,32,X)
         UNTIL X=32
         END.
```

The program in Example 9-14 scans the keyboard until you strike one of the keys. It then writes a line showing the decimal and hexadecimal codes for the ASCII character as well as the character figure itself. The program's "escape route" is through ASCII code 32, the space bar.

Striking the space bar, in other words, ends the program. It is a program that is quite helpful to users who want to learn their way around the ASCII keyboard a little better.

Example 9-15

```
(* INKEY CONTROL DEMO *)
VAR X,NUM: INTEGER;
BEGIN
WRITE(28,31,'STRIKE THE ENTER KEY TO START');
REPEAT
    WHILE INKEY<>13 DO;
    FOR NUM:=∅ TO 9 DO WRITE(NUM,32);
    WRITE(13,13,'STRIKE ENTER KEY TO DO AGAIN');
    WRITE(13,'STRIKE SPACE BAR TO END THE
    PROGRAM);
    REPEAT
            X:=INKEY
    UNTIL (X=13) OR (X=32);
    WRITE(28,31)
UNTIL X=32
END.
```

Writing Integers

Upon running this program, you are greeted with the heading message, STRIKE THE ENTER KEY TO START. The program then repeats the WHILE INKEY 13 DO statement until you strike the ENTER key. Continuing the program is thus contingent upon striking the ENTER key at that point.

Then the program simply writes out integers 0 through 9. After that, the program offers two alternatives, either STRIKE THE ENTER KEY TO DO AGAIN or STRIKE SPACE BAR TO END THE PROGRAM.

At that point, the system repeats the X:=INKEY operation until you strike one of those two keys. If you strike the ENTER key, X is assigned ASCII number 13. The system repeats the counting operation. But if you strike the SPACE BAR, X takes on the ASCII code number 32. The major REPEAT...UNTIL loop is satisfied. As a result, the program ends. You will find other applications of the INKEY statement in numerous program examples throughout the remainder of this book.

Chapter 10
Procedure, Function
and Array Operations

The three operations featured in this chapter conclude the list of Pascal operations that are included in Tiny Pascal. The fact that they are presented last is certainly no reflection on their importance; nor is it really any indication of their difficulty. The only reason for introducing procedures and functions at the end of the list is so the examples can incorporate principles described in earlier chapters of this book. The array operation is offered here only because it is the only command left in Tiny Pascal. It didn't seem to fit in anywhere else.

SIMPLE PROCEDURES

A procedure operation is Pascal's idea of a program subroutine. It is a little program, often complete in itself, that can be called from a master or mainline program. BASIC has its GOSUB and RETURN commands for working with subroutines, and Pascal has its PROC command.

Just to make certain you understand some of the reasons for using subroutines in the first place, compare the programs in Examples 10-1A and 10-1B. Example 10-1A is written without the benefit of a procedure, while Example 10-1B does the same job, but with the help of a procedure operation.

The basic idea of the program in this example is to first print a string of asterisks across the top of the screen, and then show a timed sequence of numbers from 0 through 9. The screen is cleared and a string of plus signs appears across the top. The timed counting sequence occurs again. Finally, the program shows a string of commas, followed by that same sequence of numbers.

The practical significance of such a program is certainly questionable. But the point is to illustrate the vast differences between programs written with procedures and those that are written without procedures.

Example 10-1A

```
VAR FIG, TIME, LINE:INTEGER;
BEGIN
WRITE(28, 31);
FOR LINE:=0 TO 63 DO WRITE(42);        (* PRINT AS-
                                          TERISKS *)
FIG:=0;                         (* COUNT SEQUENCE *)
WHILE FIG<10 DO
        BEGIN
        FOR TIME:=0 TO 500 DO;
        WRITE(FIG#, 32);
        FIG:=FIG+1
        END;
WRITE(28, 31);
FOR LINE:=0 TO 63 DO WRITE(43); (*PRINT PLUS
                                    SIGNS *)
FIG:=0;                         (* COUNT SEQUENCE *)
WHILE FIG<10 DO
        BEGIN
        FOR TIME:=0 TO 500 DO;
        WRITE(FIG#, 32);
        FIG:=FIG+1
        END;
WRITE(28, 31);
FOR LINE:=0 TO 63 DO WRITE(44); (*PRINT COMMAS *)
FIG:=0;                         (* COUNT SEQUENCE *)
WHILE FIG<10 DO
        BEGIN
        FOR TIME:=0 TO 500 DO;
        WRITE(FIG#, 32);
        FIG:=FIG+1
        END
END.
```

Note in Example 10-1A that the COUNT SEQUENCE of operations has to be reproduced three different times. Why write a

137

certain sequence of operations again and again, when they can be represented by a single PROC operation? See the next example.

Example 10-1B

```
    VAR LINE:INTEGER;
    PROC COUNT;
            VAR TIME, FIG:INTEGER;
            BEGIN
            FIG:=0;
            WHILE FIG<10 DO
                    BEGIN
                    FOR TIME:=0 TO 500 DO;
                    WRITE(FIG#, 32);
                    FIG:=FIG+1
                    END
        END;
    BEGIN
    WRITE(28, 31);
    FOR LINE:=0 TO 63 DO WRITE(42);      (* PRINT AS-
                                             TERISKS *)
    COUNT;                          (* COUNT SEQUENCE *)
    WRITE(28, 31);
    FOR LINE:=0 TO 63 DO  WRITE(43); (* PRINT PLUS
                                           SIGNS *)
    COUNT;                          (* COUNT SEQUENCE *)
    WRITE(28, 31);
    FOR LINE:=0 TO 63 DO WRITE(44); (*PRINT COMMAS *)
    COUNT                           (* COUNT SEQUENCE *)
    END.
```

Examples 10-1A and 10-1B do exactly the same job, but in entirely different ways. An operator would never know the difference, but someone setting up the program certainly would. The COUNT SEQUENCE operations have to be written out three times in Example 10-1A. But in Example 10-1B, the same sequence is given a name of its own (COUNT) and specified just one time as a procedure. Calling the counting sequence is a simple matter of specifying COUNT as a Pascal statement, a new statement that is custom defined.

Defining a Procedure

Figure 10-1 shows the syntax diagram for simple PROC operations. They are called "simple" here to distinguish them from a

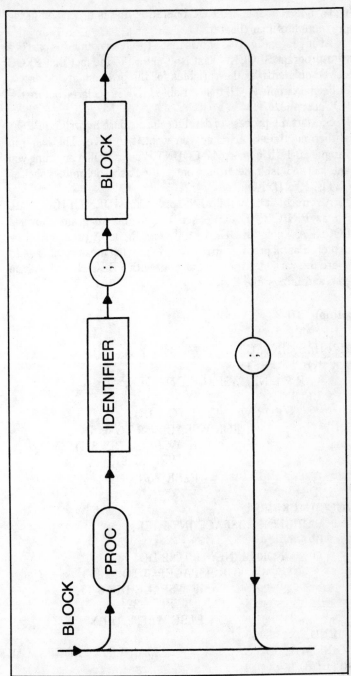

Fig. 10-1. Syntax diagram for a simple procedure.

slightly different sort of PROC operation that is described in the next section of this chapter.

At any rate, Fig. 10-1 shows that a PROC is defined as part of a larger program BLOCK. What isn't shown is the fact that PROC must be defined *after* the variables for the program are declared. Notice in Example 10-1B that variable LINE is declared before the PROCedure is.

So start the process of defining a procedure by writing PROC and then any identifier name you want it to have. The name in Example 10-1B happens to be COUNT. You can call it anything you want, just so it isn't identical to one of the Pascal delimiters such as WRITE, READ, FOR, etc.

A semicolon must follow the procedure IDENTIFIER name, such as PROC COUNT;. Then the syntax diagram shows a BLOCK. A whole BLOCK of its own? Right! A procedure is a complete Pascal program in its own right. That means you have to declare the variables it uses, start out with a BEGIN, end with an END, and things like that.

Example 10-2
```
(* CHECKER *)
VAR PHASE:INTEGER;
PROC WHITEFIRST;
        VAR WLINE, WSPACE:INTEGER;
        BEGIN
                FOR WLINE:=1 TO 2 DO
                        FOR WSPACE:=0 TO 63 DO
                                IF WSPACE DIV 8 THEN
                                        WRITE(191)
                                ELSE WRITE(32)
        END;
PROC BLACKFIRST;
        VAR BLINE, BSPACE:INTEGER;
        BEGIN
                FOR BLINE:=1 TO 2 DO
                        FOR BSPACE:=0 TO 63 DO
                                IF WSPACE DIV 8 THEN
                                        WRITE(32)
                                ELSE WRITE (191)
        END;
BEGIN                              (* MAINLINE PROGRAM *)
WRITE(28);
```

```
FOR PHASE:=1 TO 4 DO
    BEGIN
    WHITEFIRST;
    BLACKFIRST;
    END
END.
```

Checkerboard Pattern

Example 10-2 uses a series of two procedure subroutines, named WHITEFIRST and BLACKFIRST, to build a nice checkerboard pattern on the screen. The mainline program is relatively simple, calling the two procedures alternately, four times in succession.

Notice that WHITEFIRST and BLACKFIRST are practically identical. The only difference is that WHITEFIRST prints a line of alternate black and white spaces, beginning with a white space. BLACKFIRST, on the other hand, begins the same sort of operation with a black square instead of a white one. By alternating these two operations in the mainline program, the overall effect is that of a checkerboard pattern.

A Pascal program can contain just about any desired number of different procedures. Just bear in mind that they are Pascal's version of subroutines, and carry with them the same reasons for using them in the first place.

You have seen in Example 10-1B that procedures are handy whenever a certain set of operations has to be performed a number of different times. They save both a lot of programming time and memory space. Then in Example 10-2 you can see how easy it would be to alter the size of the checkerboard pattern without having to overhaul the entire program. This particular advantage of using procedures makes it quite easy to expand and modify existing Pascal programs.

All that, plus the ability to nest procedures—inserting procedures within procedures. Supersoft Tiny Pascal allows you to nest up to 7 deep. Just remember one rule. When nesting procedures, any procedure that is called must be written into the program listing ahead of the one that calls it.

The need for nesting procedures arises only when working with rather complex programs or attempting to make drastic modifications of existing ones. For this reason, specific examples of nested procedures aren't appropriate at this time. However, you will find some nested procedures in the latter chapters of this book.

PROCEDURES WITH VALUE PARAMETERS

The examples of procedures presented so far in this chapter are wholly independent of any variable values established in the mainline program. The "simple" procedures are simply called to do a specific task that has no particular relevance to any values in the mainline program.

It is often necessary, however, to run a procedure, using some numerical value established during the course of the mainline program. The value of some variable must be passed to the procedure before it knows exactly what it is supposed to do. Procedures that are capable of accepting numerical values from the mainline program, or other procedures, are called *value parameter procedures*.

Suppose, for example, you want a program that accepts an integer value from the keyboard and then draws a horizontal line having a length proportional to the value of that number. The idea is to use a value parameter procedure to draw the line; in order to do the job properly, the procedure must know how long the line is supposed to be. And that value is passed to the value parameter procedure. Simple procedures cannot accept variable values from outside itself.

Figure 10-2 shows the syntax diagram for both simple and value parameter procedures. Simple procedures bypass the need for writing any parentheses and identifiers, while value parameter procedures must use them.

LENGTH Variable

Here is a program that uses a value parameter procedure:

Example 10-3

```
VAR LENGTH:INTEGER;      (* DECLARE VARIABLE FOR
                            MAINLINE *)
PROC DRAW (LENGTH);      (* DEFINE VALUE PARAME-
                            TER PROCEDURE *)
   VAR SPACE:INTEGER; (* DECLARE PROC VARIABLE *)
   BEGIN
   FOR SPACE:=0 TO LENGTH DO WRITE(42)
   END;
BEGIN                    (* BEGIN MAINLINE PROGRAM *)
WRITE(28, 31);
REPEAT
```

```
        WRITE('ENTER Ø TO 63', 32);
        READ(LENGTH#);      (* SET THE VALUE OF LENGTH
                                VARIABLE *)
        DRAW (LENGTH); (* CALL THE DRAW PROCEDURE *)
        WRITE(13)
UNTIL LENGTH<>LENGTH
END.
```

The value parameter in Example 10-3 is LENGTH. Notice that it is declared as a variable for the mainline program in the first line, and then it is cited again as a procedure parameter in the second line. Declaring it as a mainline program variable makes it possible to fool around with the value of LENGTH in the mainline part of the program. Citing it as a parameter in procedure DRAW lets the numerical value of that same variable be carried into the DRAW operations.

The whole idea of the program, itself, is to print some designated number of asterisks along a line on the screen. In the process, the LENGTH variable carries the number of asterisks to be printed to the DRAW procedure where it is needed most. A simple procedure wouldn't have the foggiest idea what LENGTH means. Give Example 10-3 a try on your own machine.

INCHWORM Program

Example 10-4 is a little animation demonstration program that uses a set of three value parameter procedures. All three happen to use the same parameter variable, PLACE, but it just turned out that way. Pascal programs having more than one value parameter procedure quite often use different variables for each one. The

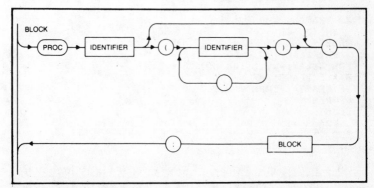

Fig. 10-2. Syntax diagram for simple and value parameter procedures.

program in Example 10-4 is called INCHWORM, and you have to see its animation effects first hand to appreciate it fully. What you will see is the figure of a little worm that moves across the screen by first bunching itself up and then stretching out.

Example 10-4

```
(* INCHWORM *)
VAR PLACE,FRAME,DELAY:INTEGER;
PROC FR1(PLACE);
  BEGIN
  MEM(PLACE):=176;
  MEM(PLACE+1):=176;
  MEM(PLACE+2):=191;
  MEM(PLACE+3):=131;
  MEM(PLACE+4):=191;
  MEM(PLACE+5):=176;
  MEM(PLACE+6):=176;
  MEM(PLACE+7):=188;
  MEM(PLACE+8):=188
  END;
PROC FR2(PLACE);
  VAR DX:INTEGER;
  BEGIN
  FOR DX:=0 TO 9 DO
    MEM(PLACE+DX):=176;
  MEM(PLACE+10):=188;
  MEM(PLACE+11):=188
  END;
PROC ERASE(PLACE);
  VAR DX:INTEGER;
  BEGIN
  FOR DX:=0 TO 11 DO
    MEM(PLACE+DX):=32
  END;
(* BEGIN MAINLINE PROGRAM *)
BEGIN
WRITE(28,31);
FOR PLACE:=15424 TO 16242 DO
  BEGIN
  IF FRAME=1 THEN
    FR1(PLACE)
  ELSE
    FR2(PLACE);
  FOR DELAY:=0 TO 100 DO;
  ERASE(PLACE);
  IF FRAME=1 THEN
    FRAME:=2
  ELSE
    FRAME:=1
  END
END.
```

The INCHWORM program in Example 10-4 uses three value parameter procedures: FR1(PLACE), FR2(PLACE) and

ERASE(PLACE). Procedure FR1(PLACE) draws the inchworm figure in its bunched-up position, while FR2(PLACE) draws the worm in its stretched-out position.

Animation Sequence

The animation sequence thus consists of two frames. One frame ought to be erased before the other is drawn. It is necessary to use an erasing operation, ERASE(PLACE).

The animation sequence is controlled by the mainline program. The mainline program calls the frame drawing and erasing procedures in the appropriate sequence. The main program also increments the worm's position on the screen. Variable PLACE is the position counter for the worm figure. As that variable increases in value (by means of a FOR. . .TO statement), the positions for drawing the frames and erasing them changes as well.

You will find value parameter procedures specified in nearly all the animation sequences described later in this book. Many of those procedures will work according to more than one value parameter. An animation frame such as B1FRAME(BPLACE, PHASE, FNO) might draw one or more slightly different figures, depending on the value of FNO from the mainline program. It draws those figures at a place determined by value parameter BPLACE and perhaps erases part of the figure, depending on the value of the PHASE variable. Value parameter procedures are indeed powerful tools in the world of Pascal programming.

Variable Parameter Procedures

Before going to the subject of Pascal functions, you should become aware of the fact that Standard Pascal has a third type of procedure called a *variable parameter procedure*. This one not only accepts values from the mainline program, but can pass values back to the mainline. The practical significance is that a variable parameter procedure can do some operations that alter the values of variables used within the program that calls it. *Value parameter procedures cannot pass values back to the calling program.*

That is one of the little shortcomings, one of the tradeoffs, necessary for making Tiny Pascal workable in relatively small personal computer systems. There is a way, however, to do some mathematical operations and pass the result back to the mainline or calling program. The trick is to use Pascal's function operation.

THE FUNCTION OPERATION

In the course of devising real programs, it is often necessary to perform a particular mathematical operation a number of different times at different places in the program. Tiny Pascal offers a number of useful math functions: ABS(X), SQR(X), A DIV B, etc. It is possible, though, to make up such functions of your own and use them in the same sort of way.

Devising your own function commands is a matter of applying the FUNC statement. The function statement, like procedures, must be declared and defined in the early part of the Pascal program. Normally it is declared and defined before any of the procedures are. Figure 10-3 is the syntax diagram for FUNC.

Declaration and Definition

When declaring and defining the function, first write FUNC, followed by an IDENTIFIER. After that you have the option of simply entering an semicolon and a BLOCK of operations that define the function, or preceding the semicolon and BLOCK with a set of one or more variable identifiers.

Actually, a function is declared and defined exactly as procedures are. The only difference is that the initial delimiter is FUNC instead of PROC.

Here is a very simple function block:

```
FUNC CUBE(X);
    BEGIN
    CUBE:=X*X*X
    END;
```

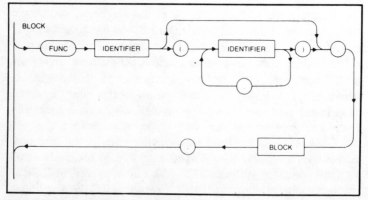

Fig. 10-3. Syntax diagram for FUNCtion.

This one picks up a value of X from the calling program, and then sets the value of variable CUBE to the cube of X (3 Xs multiplied together). The value of CUBE is then passed back to the calling program.

Maybe the calling program, at least a portion of it, looks like this:

```
FOR X:=0 TO 9 DO
        BEGIN
        CUBE(X);
        WRITE(X#, 32, CUBE(X)#, 13)
        END;
```

As the FOR. . .TO statement increments the value of variable X, the program calls function CUBE(X) just as though it is a math function already built into the Pascal system. The program writes each value of X, followed by its cube.

The complete program could look like this:

Example 10-5

```
(* CUBES *)
VAR X:INTEGER;
FUNC CUBE(X);
        BEGIN
        CUBE:=X*X*X
        END;
BEGIN
WRITE(28, 31);
FOR X:=0 TO 9 DO
        BEGIN
        WRITE(X#, 32, CUBE(X)#, 13)
        END
END.
```

Random Number Generating Process

In Example 10-5, function CUBE(X) is called as an expression within a WRITE statement. You can treat functions you define yourself as you would most other functions in Pascal.

You are well aware of the fact that Tiny Pascal does not include a random number generator. If you weren't fully aware of that bit of news, you are enlightened now. A random number generating process, however, lends itself quite nicely to being done as a Pascal function. Here it is. Mark this place in the book, because you will most likely want to refer to it whenever you begin writing game programs of your own.

Example 10-6

```
FUNC RND(RLOW, RHIGH);
      VAR M,P:INTEGER;
      BEGIN
      REPEAT
        M:=N*3125;
        IF M<Ø THEN M:=ABS(M);
        N:=M;P:=M;
        P:=P MOD RHIGH
   UNTIL (P>=RLOW) AND (P<=RHIGH);
   RND:=P
   END;
```

The theory behind the operation of this particular random number generating algorithm is described in some detail in Chapter 11. It is sufficient for now to realize that this function generates random numbers between the values specified for RLOW and RHIGH.

Just for the sake of demonstrating the use of this custom-made random function, try the program in Example 10-7. It simply prints out a list of random numbers between 1 and 9, but you can alter the range by changing the values (RLOW and RHIGH) carried to the function as values.

Example 10-7

```
(* RANDOM LIST *)
VAR LINE, N:INTEGER;
FUNC RND(RLOW, RHIGH);
      VAR M,P:INTEGER;
      BEGIN
      REPEAT
              M:=N*3125;
              IF M Ø THEN M:=ABS(M);
              N:=M;P:=M;
              P:=P MOD RLOW
      UNTIL (P = RLOW) AND (P =RHIGH);
      RND:=P
      END;
BEGIN
WRITE(28, 31, 'ENTER A SEED NUMBER BETWEEN 999
```

```
    AND 9999', 13);
READ(N#);
WRITE(28, 31);
FOR LINE:=1 TO 10 DO
    WRITE(RND(1,9), 13)
END.
```

By calling function RND (1, 9) in the WRITE statement, the values of RLOW and RHIGH are preset to 1 and 9 respectively. The function responds by returning random numbers between those two extremes.

TINY PASCAL'S ONE-DIMENSIONAL ARRAY

Tiny Pascal allows one-dimensional arrays, and they are applied just as they are in BASIC. Like procedures, variables, constants and functions must be declared as defined before they can be called from the program, as must the arrays.

Figure 10-4 is the syntax diagram for declaring an array. Arrays are fairly simple to use in Pascal, but the syntax for declaring them is rather cumbersome. Here is the general form.

VAR identifier: ARRAY(constant) OF INTEGER;

Constant is an integer representing the largest subscript in the array and identifier is the name of the array you want to assign.

By way of a specific example, suppose you want to create an array called BUGGER and allow subscripts 0 through 9. The array declaration line then looks like this:

VAR BUGGER: ARRAY(9) OF INTEGER;

In other parts of the program, then, you have access to BUGGER(0), BUGGER(1), BUGGER(2)...BUGGER(9). All are variables you can use at will.

Example 10-8 is a simple program intended to demonstrate some of the features fo Tiny Pascal's array.

Example 10-8
```
(* ARRAY DEMO *)
VAR NUM:INTEGER;
VAR MULTI:ARRAY(9) OF INTEGER;
BEGIN
WRITE(28, 31);
FOR NUM:=0 TO 9 DO
    MULT(NUM):=10*NUM;
FOR NUM:=0 TO 9 DO
```

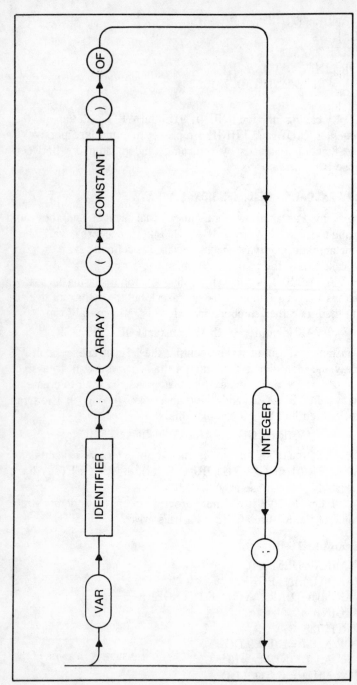

Fig. 10-4. Syntax diagram for declaring an ARRAY.

```
        WRITE(MULT(NUM)#, 13);
END.
```

Upon running this program, you will see a simple listing of numbers 0 through 90 in increments of 10. The *how* of the matter is far more important that the *what* in this case.

Example 10-8 defines a 10-element array (subscripts 0 through 9) as MULT. That takes place in the array declaration line, VAR MULT:ARRAY(9) OF INTEGER.

After that, the mainline part of the program uses variable NUM and a FOR. . .TO statement to set the values of the array elements to 10 times the value of NUM. That's the statement, FOR NUM:=∅ TO 9 DO MULT(NUM):=1∅*NUM. As a result of this operation, the elements of the array take on this form:

```
MULT(∅)=∅
MULT(1)=1∅
MULT(2)=2∅
MULT(3)=3∅
MULT(4)=4∅
MULT(5)=5∅
MULT(6)=6∅
MULT(7)=7∅
MULT(8)=8∅
MULT(9)=9∅
```

Finally, the mainline program asks the system to write out the contents of the array, one element at a time. As NUM is again incremented from ∅ through 9 by a second FOR. . .TO operation, the contents of the array is written out on the screen.

Even though Tiny Pascal is limited to 1-dimensional arrays, it is possible to use a number of different arrays. The only limitation on the number of arrays and number of elements in each array is the size of your memory. Declaring an array, you see, sets aside a portion of working memory for the array data. The more array elements you declare, the less memory you have available for the program.

The fact that it is possible to use any number of 1-dimensional arrays brings up the possiblity of synthesizing multi-dimensional arrays. You can, in other words, "fake" the behavior of multi-dimensional arrays by a clever application of two or more 1-dimensional arrays. That technique, however, is beyond the scope of this book. Watch for articles on the subject in some of the more popular personal computing magazines.

Chapter 11
Games of Chance

It is virtually impossible to put together a single book that describes all possible Pascal programming situations and techniques. Even Tiny Pascal is so rich in possibilities that general discussions of programming techniques would turn out to be just about endless and, worst of all, rather dull.

There is, however, a way to keep things brief and yet meaningful and exciting. This chapter marks the beginning of such a phase of your Pascal learning experience.

WORK THROUGH ALL PROGRAMS

Instead of dealing with general programming ideas, the procedure through the remainder of this book is to show you a particular Tiny Pascal program (usually a game), describe how it runs from an operator's point of view, and then analyze the program, itself, to see how it works.

It is absolutely essential you work with every one of these programs, whether you happen to be interested in playing the games or not. The reason it is important to work with *all* the games is that each one includes at least one important Pascal programming principle which you might not encounter anywhere else in the book.

The first game presented in this chapter, for instance, is a rather simple heads/tails coin toss game. You might not have a whole lot of interest in playing such a game on your computer, but you should work with it anyhow. Why? It introduces two notions you might find important later in this book and in your future experiences with the Pascal language.

You should work through the programs in the order you find them here. The reasoning is straightforward. The explanation of how one particular program works might be based upon things you should have learned from an earlier program.

In short, you ought to prepare yourself to work all the programs remaining in this book, and work them in the order they are presented. Study each one carefully, but have some fun with them, too.

If you study the programs conscientiously, and refer back to the technical discussions in the first 10 chapters as necessary, I can promise you will soon be a competent Pascal programmer.

COIN TOSS GAME

The COIN TOSS game presented here is a computerized version of the old heads/tails game. See Fig. 11-1 for the flow chart. The program gives you a chance to call HEADS or TAILS. It then "flips" the coin for you and tells you whether or not there is a match. You have a 50/50 chance of being right; and if you call it right, you win. If you don't call it right, you lose.

That's a simple idea. Here is how it works on the screen. Upon running the program, you will see this:

COIN TOSS
CALL IT—HEADS OR TAILS

You should respond by striking either the *H* key (for selecting HEADS) or the *T* key (for calling TAILS. You don't have to do an ENTER because, as you will see in the analysis of the program, the system is using an INKEY function to pick up your call.

Suppose, for the sake of this discussion, you call HEADS and lose. The actual toss turns up TAILS. In such a situation, the display on the screen looks like this:

COIN TOSS

CALL IT—HEADS OR TAILS
     YOUR CHOICE WAS HEADS   THE TOSS IS TAILS
SORRY . . . YOU LOSE

ENTER TO DO AGAIN?_

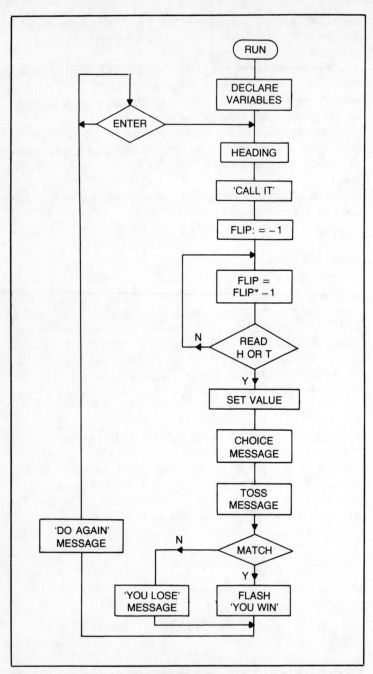

Fig. 11-1. Flow chart for COIN TOSS program.

To play again, all you have to do is strike the ENTER key. That action brings up the original CALL IT message, and you're in business again.

Whenever you manage to call the toss right, the SORRY . . . YOU LOSE message is replaced by YOU MATCHED IT!! One of the game's programming features is that the winning message flashed on and off five times.

The game continues until you strike the BREAK key twice in succession. Then you can rerun the program, dump it onto tape or do whatever else you want with it.

Program

Here is the COIN TOSS program:

```
(* COIN TOSS *)
VAR FLIP,VALUE,LINE,SPACE:INTEGER;
BEGIN
REPEAT
  WRITE(28,31,220,'COIN TOSS');
  WRITE(13,13,'CALL IT -- HEADS OR TAILS',13,13);
  FLIP:=-1;
  REPEAT
    FLIP:=FLIP*(-1);
    VALUE:=INKEY
  UNTIL (VALUE=72) OR (VALUE=84);
  WRITE(200,'YOUR CHOICE WAS  ');
  IF VALUE=72 THEN WRITE('HEADS')
    ELSE IF VALUE=84 THEN WRITE('TAILS');
  WRITE(200,'THE TOSS IS  ');
  IF FLIP=1 THEN WRITE('HEADS')
    ELSE IF FLIP=-1 THEN WRITE('TAILS');
  WRITE(13,13);
  IF ((FLIP=1) AND (VALUE=72)) OR ((FLIP=-1)
    AND (VALUE=84)) THEN
    BEGIN
    SPACE:=0;
    REPEAT
      WRITE(215,'YOU MATHCED IT!!');
      FOR LINE:=0 TO 250 DO;
      WRITE(29,30);
      FOR LINE:=0 TO 100 DO;
      SPACE:=SPACE+1
    UNTIL SPACE>5;
    END
  ELSE WRITE('SORRY ... YOU LOSE');
  FOR LINE:=1 TO 6 DO WRITE(13);
  WRITE('ENTER TO DO AGAIN');
  READ(SPACE#)
UNTIL LINE<>LINE
END.
```

Variables

The variable declaration line specifies four variables: FLIP, VALUE, LINE and SPACE. FLIP is assigned to the coin itself. The

155

program "flips" the coin for you, and the result is saved as variable FLIP. You will find that FLIP is equal to either 1 or −1, 1 representing a HEADS flip and −1 representing TAILS. One of the important Pascal "tricks" introduced in this program is the way FLIP varies between integers 1 and −1 in a quasi-random fashion. More about that shortly.

Variable VALUE is assigned to the HEADS or TAILS designation you "call." You can see from the program that VALUE is read from the keyboard as either 72 or 84, the ASCII codes for H and T respectively. So if you select HEADS by striking the H key, VALUE takes on a value of 72. Striking the T key to call TAILS gives VALUE a value of 84.

Variables LINE and SPACE are used in a couple of different ways. As its name implies, LINE is used for setting up the vertical position of some of the text on the screen. It is also used for timing the flashing YOU MATCHED IT!! message and building an endless game playing loop. Variable SPACE is used to set the duration of the flashing MATCHED message and serve as a dummy variable for repeating the game when the player strikes the ENTER key.

Causing some variables in a program to serve more than one purpose does little more than reduce the number of variables required for doing the program. Such a trick is bound to cause some confusion for the unwary student, however. The "trick" of using multiple-purpose variables is used here, and indeed through the rest of this book, in order to get you out of the "unwary student" class as effectively as possible. The program's major BEGIN . . . END block starts directly after the variable declaration line, and concludes with END. on the last line.

Structure

In a structural sense, the program is just one big REPEAT . . . UNTIL loop. The REPEAT part of the statement appears on the line following BEGIN, and concludes with UNTIL LINE LINE in the next to last line of the program. Since it is logically impossible to satisfy the LINE LINE condition, it follows that the program will loop indefinitely. In other words, you can do as many coin tosses as you want.

The first two WRITE statements in the program set up the CLIN TOSS heading and the CALL IT, HEADS OR TAILS message. Directly after that, variable FLIP is initialized at −1. The coin is always tossed with TAILS showing initially.

After the FLIP: = −1 assignment statement comes a brief REPEAT . . . UNTIL statement. Within that repetitive statement you find an assignment FLIP:=FLIP*−1. Since the value of FLIP is initially set to −1, it figures that FLIP alternates between 1 and −1 each time this repetitive loop is executed.

How many "flips" of this sort take place? The VALUE:=IN-KEY statement has a lot to do with the answer to that question. Until the operator depresses one of the keys on the keyboard, INKEY (and, hence, VALUE) will be equal to 0. But VALUE will take on a different value the instant the operator strikes a key.

If that key happens to be an *H* or *T*, VALUE will be set to either 72 or 84, the ASCII codes for H and T. Under either of those conditions, the UNTIL condition is satisfied and the repetitive loop is broken. The important thing is that FLIP takes on a 1 or −1 value, depending upon whether the loop is executed an odd or even number of times.

The loop is executed so rapidly that the player has no way of reckoning whether the loop will be ending with a 1 or −1 assigned to FLIP. For all practical purposes, the scheme makes up a 1 or −1 random number generator.

Upon leaving the REPEAT . . . UNTIL loop that follows the FLIP:=−1 statement, the operational part of the game is over. FLIP has a value indicating what the coin is showing, and VALUE carries the player's call. The rest of the program is devoted to testing for a MATCH and printing out the appropriate messages.

A good MATCH is detected by the compound logic statement: IF ((FLIP=1) AND (VALUE=72)) OR ((FLIP=−1) AND (VALUE=84)) THEN. The first part of the statement detects successful HEADS matches while the second part detects successful TAILS matches. If either case is satisfied, the player wins and the system goes through a short routine that flashes the YOU MATCHED IT!! message.

If the logic statement is not satisfied, there is a mismatch between FLIP and VALUE. The system executes the ELSE part of the statement, writing the message SORRY . . . YOU LOSE. Whether the player calls a MATCH or not, the program does a series of six WRITE(13) statements to carry the cursor near the bottom of the screen where it prints the invitation to play the game again.

Message Flashing Technique

The message flashing technique calls for further explanation here. That particular operation is initialized with the assignment statement, SPACE:=∅, and then it is built around a sequence of REPEAT . . . UNTIL statements.

WRITE (215, 'YOU MATCHED IT!!') situates that particular message near the horizontal center of the screen. The tab 215 part of the statement takes care of that positioning operation. FOR LINE:=0 TO 250 DO; actually does nothing while variable line is incremented to 250. It is a timing operation that lasts about ¼ of a second.

The next statement WRITE (29, 30) is a command operation that returns the cursor to the beginning of the current line—the one carrying the YOU MATCHED IT!! message—and then clears it. In other words, that particular WRITE statement erases the YOU MATCHED IT!! message, but nothing else on the screen is affected.

After that you find another time delay operation built around FOR LINE:=0 TO 100;. This is a 1/10 of a second time delay.

Putting together these operations, the system writes the YOU MATCHED IT!! messages and displays it for about ¼ of a second. Then it erases the message for about 1/10 of a second. Since these operations are enclosed within a REPEAT loop, the timing operations are executed until variable SPACE is incremented beyond a value of 5.

SPACE is initialized at 0, and then increments (by SPACE:=SPACE+1) each time the message timing operations are performed. The overall effect is that YOU MATCHED IT!! flashes on and off five times.

Play the COIN TOSS game a few times, run through the program to make sure you see how it works, and then see if you can justify all the syntax. If you can manage that, you are really getting somewhere with this business of understanding Pascal programming.

Now the important thing about the COIN TOSS program is not the game itself. Sure, it's fun to play, but the essential thing is the programming features it demonstrates. As shown in the next game program, these same principles can be applied to generate what appears to be an entirely different game.

RUSSIAN ROULETTE GAME

Russian roulette is a nasty little life-or-death game that can be played in a harmless fashion on your personal computer. You have a six-round revolver, and insert one live round into a chamber of your choosing. Give the cylinder a spin and pull the trigger. If you "win," you hear just a clicking sound and you live to try a stupid thing like that again some other day. If you lose, you might hear a loud BANG!! Whether or not you actually hear the sound is purely academic. You're dead in any case.

Your chances of coming out alive are 5 out of 6. It figures, then, that your chances of losing are 1 out of 6. The program is flow charted in Fig. 11-2.

Upon running the program, you get some messages on the screen that look something like this:

RUSSIAN ROULETTE

WHICH CHAMBER WILL HAVE THE LIVE ROUND?
(ENTER A NUMBER BETWEEN 1 AND 6)
?_

Do that; ENTER a number between 1 and 6. If you goof up and try entering a number outside that range, the system politely requests you to do it again.

After entering a number between 1 and 6, you see this sort of message on the screen:

FIRST PLAYER

ENTER TO PULL THE TRIGGER . . . _

It takes at least two people to make Russian Roulette exciting. This message asks the first of two players to do their thing and pull the trigger.

Suppose you started the game by inserting the live round into chamber 4. If the first player doesn't happen to pull the trigger at chamber 4, he or she lives. Upon doing the ENTER TO PULL THE TRIGGER, the screen shows this:

CLICK!! YOU'RE SAFE . . .

THAT WAS CHAMBER 2

That informative little message appears for about 2.5 seconds. Then the screen clears and the second player is invited to pull the trigger. Actually the cylinder is spun again, too, so the next chamber isn't necessarily the one that comes up next.

The screen shows:

SECOND PLAYER

ENTER TO PULL THE TRIGGER . . . _

And the second player is supposed to do an ENTER. The odds are still 5 out of 6 in favor of the player, but suppose he or she loses. In that case you see:

BANG!!

YOU'RE DEAD

The game is over. The message, ENTER R TO PLAY AGAIN, appears near the lower left-hand corner of the screen. If you elect to play again, the program starts from the beginning, requesting a chamber number and so on.

Program

From a programming point of view, one of the more interesting features is the way in which the play alternates between two players until one of them loses. That part of the program is a repetitive loop. It ends only when one of the players happens to turn up a random number that matches the one entered from the keyboard at the beginning of the game. Unlike the COIN TOSS game, this one is not automatically repeated from beginning to end. Telling the operator to ENTER R TO PLAY AGAIN is just a tricky way to say the whole program should be run from the start.

```
(* RUSSIAN ROULETTE *)
VAR LINE,ROUND,FIRE,PLAY:INTEGER;
BEGIN
WRITE(28,31,215,'RUSSIAN ROULETTE');
FOR LINE:=1 TO 8 DO WRITE(13);
REPEAT
  WRITE('WHICH CHAMBER WILL HAVE THE LIVE ROUND?',13);
  WRITE('(ENTER A NUMBER BETWEEN 1 AND 6)',13);
  READ(ROUND#)
UNTIL (ROUND>=1) AND (ROUND<=6);
PLAY:=1;
REPEAT
  WRITE(28,31,215);
  CASE PLAY OF
    1:WRITE('** FIRST PLAYER **');
    -1:WRITE('** SECOND PLAYER **')
  END;
  WRITE(13,13,'ENTER TO PULL THE TRIGGER...');
  FIRE:=1;
  WHILE INKEY<>13 DO
    BEGIN
    FIRE:=FIRE+1;
    IF FIRE>6 THEN FIRE:=1
    END;
  IF FIRE<>ROUND THEN
    BEGIN
    FOR LINE:=1 TO 8 DO WRITE(13);
    WRITE(220,'CLICK!!  YOU',39,'RE SAFE...');
    WRITE(13,13,'THAT WAS CHAMBER ',FIRE#);
```

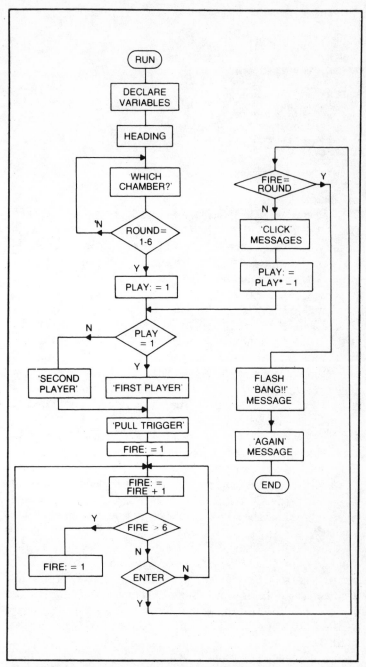

Fig. 11-2. Flow chart for RUSSIAN ROULETTE program.

```
          FOR LINE:=0 TO 2500 DO
          END;
      PLAY:=PLAY*(-1);
UNTIL FIRE=ROUND;
FOR LINE:=1 TO 4 DO WRITE(13);
WRITE(210,'BANG!!',13,13);
FIRE:=0;
REPEAT
      WRITE(220,'YOU',39,'RE DEAD');
      FOR LINE:=0 TO 100 DO;
      WRITE(29,30);
      FOR LINE:=0 TO 50 DO;
      FIRE:=FIRE+1
UNTIL FIRE>10;
WRITE(13,13,'ENTER R TO PLAY AGAIN')
END.
```

Variables

The variable declaration line specifies variables LINE, ROUND, FIRE and PLAY. ROUND is used exclusively for carrying the value of the chamber that has a live round in it. That value is read from the keyboard at the statement, READ(ROUND#), and it carries that value until one of the players gets a BANG!! and the game is started again from scratch.

Variable PLAY is used only for designating FIRST PLAYER or SECOND PLAYER. It does its job by employing the multiply-by-minus one trick introduced in the COIN TOSS game. PLAY is initially assigned a value of 1 to indicate it's up to FIRST PLAYER to pull the trigger. After the playing sequence for the first player is done (assuming he or she gets a CLICK!!), you can find a PLAY:=PLAY*(−1) statement. That changes the value of PLAY to −1, indicating a playing phase for SECOND PLAYER.

PLAY thus alternates between values of 1 and −1 until someone gets a BANG!! That's how the system alternates between cycles for two different players.

You've seen that same programming trick used for a different purpose in the COIN TOSS game. Now that you have seen it used twice, there should be no need to explain it in such detail whenever it is applied in any of the games to follow.

Variables FIRE and LINE are both used for a couple of different purposes. One of the most critical applications of FIRE is to pick a quasi-random number between 1 and 6, a number representing the chamber that is in place when a player pulls the trigger. The player gets a BANG!! whenever it turns out that FIRE is equal to ROUND. If a player gets a CLICK!!, it means FIRE is not equal to ROUND.

Every time a player pulls the trigger, the program generates a randomly selected value for FIRE. After a player gets a BANG!!, however, there is no need to save the current value of FIRE. It is used for an entirely different purpose, to time the interval that the flashing BANG! message appears on the screen.

Variable LINE is used for both setting the vertical position of some messages on the screen and timing the durations of the on and off phases of the flashing BANG!! message. So much for defining the purposes of the variables.

Structure

Now look at the first REPEAT . . . UNTIL loop, which invites the player to enter a number between 1 and 6. The purpose of this loop is to make certain that variable ROUND does indeed get a value between 1 and 6 inclusively. It is a goof-proofing loop that can repeat its request until you enter the right sort of number. The game cannot proceed until you enter a value for ROUND that is both equal to or greater than 1 and, at the same time, less then or equal to 6. Those conditions are spelled out in the UNTIL portion of that first REPEAT . . . UNTIL statement.

You have already seen how the value of PLAY alternates between − 1 and 1, depending upon which player is supposed to pull the trigger next. The next important idea is to see how these two numbers are translated into text that is more meaningful to the players. The job in this instance is done with a CASE...OF statement. Specifically, it's done with a CASE PLAY OF statement.

According to that statement in the program, the system prints ** FIRST PLAYER ** whenever PLAY is set at 1, and writes ** SECOND PLAYER ** whenever PLAY is equal to − 1. Tiny Pascal cannot handle complex strings as variables, so it is necessary to do this sort of translation between integer values and string writing operations. Standard Pascal can handle strings as variables, but Tiny Pascal cannot.

The moment a player is invited to pull the trigger, the program goes into a cyclic counting loop that very rapidly cycles between 1 and 6, assigning the values to FIRE as it goes along. This loop is controlled by the statement, WHILE INKEY<>13 DO, and the counting operations are those encompassed by that repetitive statement.

To put it bluntly, FIRE counts like a bat between 1 and 6 until the player strikes the ENTER key and INKEY is indeed set to 13 as a result. Look at the control codes in the Appendix, and you will see that line feed/carriage return—doing ENTER—is code 13. There is no way that a player can interrupt the counting cycle at some desired number. So, in effect, the loop is a tricky way to come up with a random number between 1 and 6.

The statement, IF FIRE<>ROUND THEN, begins a comparison operation. If FIRE does not equal ROUND, the system prints the CLICK!! message, informs the player which FIRE value was "randomly" selected, and flips the value of PLAY. When it turns out that FIRE=ROUND, the whole CLICK!! routine is bypassed and operations pick up at the line, FOR LINE:=1 TO 4 DO WRITE(13). The REPEAT...UNTIL statement following that line holds a number of statements that flash the BANG!! and write out YOU'RE DEAD.

See if you can figure out for yourself how the program can write the apostrophe in the contraction, YOU'RE. Remember, you cannot simply insert an apostrophe character into a string statement without the system thinking it is the end of the string.

NUMERIC DICE ROLL GAME

Rolling dice is generally something better done with real dice than by means of a computer simulation. The programming involved in simulating dice rolls includes some procedures that can be quite useful in other kinds of situations, so you will find two different kinds of dice rolling simulation programs presented here. See Fig. 11-3 for the flow chart.

The dice rolling game demonstrated in this section allows the user to select the number of dice to be rolled. It is possible to select a single dice or a thousand of them. While the latter might be far beyond the realm of practical necessity, the game nevertheless illustrates the operation of a nice pseudo-random number generator.

When this program is first run, the player sees these messages:

NUMERIC DICE GAME

HOW MANY DICE? _

Respond by entering any number you want. For the sake of this discussion, choose a common number of dice, say, two of them. Remember the game runs exactly the same way, no matter how many dice you specify at this point.

After entering the number of dice, the ENTER TO START message appears on the screen. Responding by striking the ENTER key, you get something like this:

1,3

ENTER TO ROLL AGAIN
STRIKE SPACE BAR TO END _

The 1,3 combination represents the dice values "thrown" by the first roll. At that point, the player has the option of rolling the dice again by striking the ENTER key or ending the whole thing by striking the space bar.

Striking the ENTER key at this point simply brings up another set of values for the two dice and reprints the messages just described. The dice can be rolled any number of times by simply striking the ENTER key.

The only way to change the number of dice being rolled is to respond to the messages by striking the space bar. That terminates the program. It can then be run again, and the HOW MANY DICE?__ inquiry will appear. Maybe you ENTER a 5 this time. The system will then print the values for five dice every time you strike the ENTER key. The display might look something like this:

2,5,4,4,3

ENTER TO ROLL AGAIN

STRIKE SPACE BAR TO END—

Program

This program is fun to run for a short while. Since it has no scorekeeping features, though, it can get tiresome. The real meat of the thing is in the programming itself.

```
(* NUMERIC DICE ROLL *)
VAR DINO,SEED,M,N,P,NUM:INTEGER;
BEGIN
        (* HEADING *)
WRITE(28,31,215,'NUMERIC DICE ROLL');
WRITE(13,13,'HOW MANY DICE');
READ(DINO#);
WRITE(13,13,'ENTER TO START');
        (* SYSTEM PICKS SEED NUMBER *)
WHILE INKEY<>13 DO
  BEGIN
  SEED:=SEED+1;
  IF (SEED<99) OR (SEED>999) THEN SEED:=99;
  END;
N:=SEED;
        (* RUN DICE SELECT *)
REPEAT
  WRITE(28,31);
  NUM:=1;
  REPEAT
    REPEAT
    M:=N*125;
    IF M<0 THEN M:=ABS(M);
    N:=M;P:=M;
    P:=P MOD 7+1
```

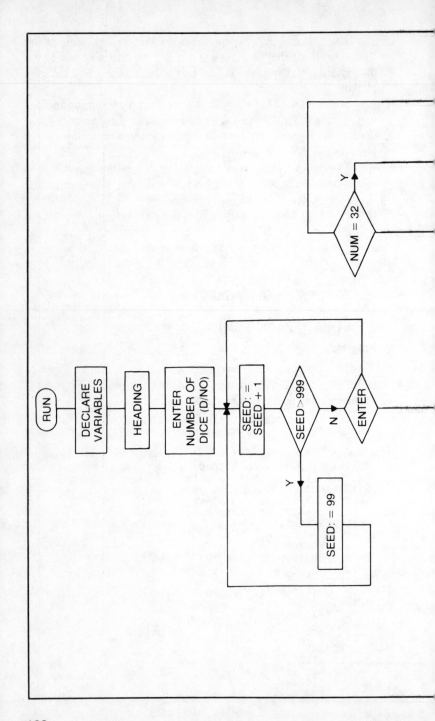

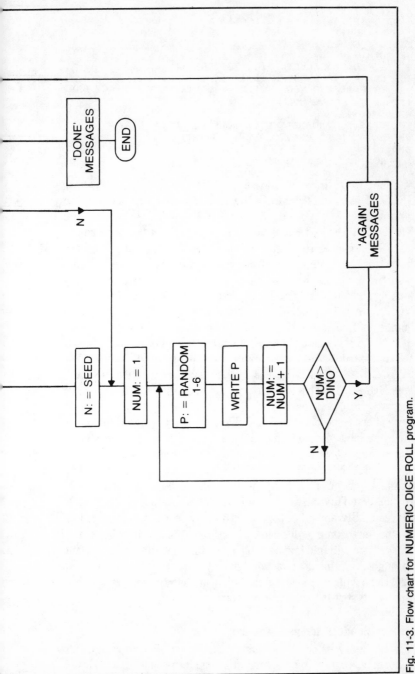

Fig. 11-3. Flow chart for NUMERIC DICE ROLL program.

```
  UNTIL P<>7;
  WRITE(P#,44);
  NUM:=NUM+1
UNTIL NUM>DINO;
WRITE(8);
      (* DICE SELECT/PRINT IS DONE *)
FOR NUM:=1 TO 8 DO WRITE(13);
WRITE('ENTER TO ROLL AGAIN',13,'STRIKE THE SPACE BAR
TO END');   READ(NUM);
UNTIL NUM=32;
WRITE(28,31,'NUMERIC DICE ROLL IS DONE');
WRITE(13,'DO A RUN TO START AGAIN')
END.
```

Variables

The variables declared in this program are DINO, SEED,M,N,P and NUM. DINO is a variable that carries the number of dice you want to roll. Its value is set at the READ(DINO#) statement near the beginning of the program.

NUM serves two different purposes. Its main purpose is to keep track of the number of die values the machine has actually selected for you. The system, as you will see shortly, continues picking random die values and printing them on the screen until NUM is equal to DINO—until the system picks and prints a number of figures equal to the number of them you want to see.

NUM plays a secondary role near the end of the program. If the user strikes the space bar in response to the STRIKE THE SPACE BAR TO END message, the statement, READ(NUM), sets NUM to 32. That situation breaks a repetitive loop and brings the program to a close.

There is no direct relationship between the two roles of the NUM variable. Using it in two different situations simply reduces the number of variables required for writing the program.

SEED, N,M and P are all used as part of a psuedo-random number generator. If you haven't noticed by now, you should realize that Tiny Pascal does not include a handy RANDOM function as BASIC and other languages do. Give some special attention to the forthcoming description of how this random generator works. You will find it appearing in a number of different programs through the remainder of this book. Wherever it is feasible, the programs will use the same variable names to remind you that it is this same sort of generator at work.

Pseudo-Random Number Generator

In theory, there is no such thing as a true random number generator program. The algorithms used for producing a series of random numbers will always repeat themselves after a while. The idea is to get the series of numbers as long as possible before that cycle starts all over again.

There is no point in going into the theory of this sort of psuedo-random number generator in great detail. It is sufficient to point out some general ideas that will not only explain how the algorithm works in these programs, but let you build custom versions for your own games in the future.

The very heart of the psuedo-random generator begins with the statement M:=N*125. Variable N is a number selected earlier in the program, and we will have more to say about its origin later on. For now, consider it a noncritical integer value between 99 and 999. So that first statement line assigns a value of N time 125 to variable M.

Where does that 125 come from? As a rule of thumb, that number has to be an odd power of 5. The power in this case is 3, $5^3=125$. It could be 3125 (5^5) or 3125(5^7) as well; but 125 is the smallest and most easily remembered number in that power series. So the previously selected "mystery" number N is multiplied by an odd power of 5.

The result of the multiplication is sometimes a negative number. It turns out that negative numbers are quite undesirable here, so the next statement simply makes sure M is positive. M:=ABS(M) always returns a positive value for M.

Two assignment statements in succession give the value of M to variables N and P. N is no longer a "mystery" number. Variable P is then, itself, used in the modulus expression: P:=P MOD 7+1.

The overall result is that P turns out to be a number between 1 and, sometimes, 7. It's usually a number between 1 and 6, exactly the range for a die. The UNTIL<>7 works in conjunction with the preceding REPEAT statement to eliminate those 7s that sometimes pop out of the algorithm. If P turns out to be equal to 7, the whole random number algorithm runs again to get a number within the range of 1 to 6 inclusively. Incidentally, without adding 1 to the 7 in the modulo statement, the system would come up with 0 now and then.

What remains to be done is to explain the origin of the variable N. That number is technically called the SEED for the pseudo-random number generator. That number determines where the cycle of numbers begins. It turns out that the randomness of the numbers is even better if the SEED is, itself, randomly generated. The value of SEED is selected by one of those INKEY-interrupted, fast-as-a-bat counters featured in the COIN TOSS and RUSSIAN ROULETTE games.

WHILE INKEY 13, SEED counts like mad between 99 and 999. There's no telling where that count will be when the operator strikes the ENTER key to make INKEY equal to control code number 13. That's how the system picks up the SEED number for the pseudo-random number algorithm.

If you want to see this number generator do its work, run the dice game and specify a 100 dice or so. It will print out 100 numbers that are pretty well scrambled. See if you can find a repeating sequence.

To get more technical information about this process, consult a more academic text for the topic, multiplicative-congruential method of generating pseudo-random numbers. Or maybe you'd just like to see that it works for yourself. It's easier to remember how to do it than to remember what it's called.

So the dice roll program picks up a SEED number and uses it as a basis for generating and printing randomly distributed numbers between 1 and 6. This sequence loops around until the number of die values equals the number you want to see.

The remainder of the program is fairly straightforward. The only thing different from the things done thus far is the option of rolling again by striking the ENTER key or ending the program by striking the space bar.

Advantage Of The Algorithm

Before moving to the next dice roll game, consider this question. Why use such a complicated number generating process (a multiplicative-congruential method of generating pseudo-random numbers) when the simple, INKEY-interrupted fast counter method works so well in the COIN TOSS and RUSSIAN ROULETTE games?

The problem here is that the INKEY-interrupted counter method relies on a random number of milliseconds between the presentation of a message and the operator striking the ENTER key. That means the scheme must include one key operation for each random number required. If you want to roll two dice, using this INKEY-interrupt method, you'd have to strike the ENTER key twice in succession. That can get awkward.

The SEED-and-algorithm technique can be repeated any number of times based on a single SEED number. In the COIN TOSS and RUSSIAN ROULETTE games, it was necessary to get just one randomly generated number for each play. The INKEY-interrupt method works quite nicely. But the dice game calls for more than one random number; Hence, there is a desirability for the more complex, but easier to use algorithm.

GRAPHIC DICE ROLL GAME

This program is also a dice roll simulation. Instead of simply showing some numerals that indicate the value of the rolls, the actual die patterns appear near the center of the screen. It's a cute effect that I have been wanting to do on my TRS-80 for quite some time. It seemed too much trouble using BASIC, but Tiny Pascal makes it a lot easier.

The only tradeoff is that this program displays just two dice, no more and no less. But it's still fun to watch. See Fig. 11-4.

There are no fancy player controls built into the program. The graphics part is extensive enough for an elementary Pascal program. When you begin running the program, you see a heading near the center and top of the screen, GRAPHIC DICE ROLL. A couple of lines below that you see the instruction, ENTER TO START.

Striking the ENTER key at that point, the screen clears and you can see the outline of two dice emerging near the middle of the screen. The outline is filled with the distinctive die pattern of 1 to 6 dots. Then another message, ENTER TO ROLL AGAIN, appears on the screen.

You can strike the ENTER key to roll the dice as many times as you choose. It is possible to break out of the program and end the matter by either striking the BREAK key twice in succession or striking the space bar when the program requests another roll.

As mentioned earlier, this program emphasizes the graphics angle. You will find that most of the graphics is done by means of procedures, Pascal's version of subroutines. For the sake of clarity, the procedures are flow charted separately in Figs. 11-6 and 11-7. The mainline part of the program is flow charted for you in Fig. 11-5.

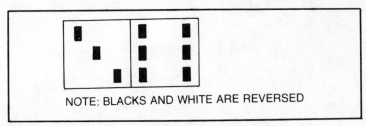

NOTE: BLACKS AND WHITE ARE REVERSED

Fig. 11-4. Graphic format for GRAPHIC DICE ROLL GAME.

171

Program

The program is presented here as it is to be entered into your computer. In order to understand what is going on at any point in the program, you'll have to consult the appropriate flow chart. If you start feeling lost, just remember that Pascal works according to a very well-defined structure. Once you can sort out the structure, you can see exactly how it all works. First, the program:

```
  (* DRAW DICE GAME *)
VAR D1,D2,DIENO,SEED,M,N,P:INTEGER;
  (* DICE OUTLINE DRAWING PROCEDURES *)
PROC HDRAW(DX,DY);
  BEGIN
  PLOT(DX,DY,1);
  PLOT(DX,DY+11,1)
  END;
PROC VDRAW(DX,DY);
  BEGIN
  PLOT(DX,DY,1);
  PLOT(DX+1,DY,1)
  END;
PROC DIEDRAW;
  VAR DX,DY:INTEGER;
  BEGIN
  WRITE(28,31);
  FOR DX:=34 TO 61 DO HDRAW(DX,18);
  FOR DX:=66 TO 92 DO HDRAW(DX,18);
  FOR DY:=18 TO 29 DO
    BEGIN
    VDRAW(34,DY);
    VDRAW(60,DY);
    VDRAW(66,DY);
    VDRAW(92,DY)
    END
  END;
  (* DICE VALUE DRAWING PROCEDURES *)
PROC MIDDOT(DIENO);
  VAR DY,DX:INTEGER;
  BEGIN
  FOR DY:=23 TO 24 DO
    FOR DX:=47+DIENO TO 48+DIENO DO
      PLOT(DX,DY,1)
  END;
PROC ULLRDOT(DIENO);
  VAR DY,DX:INTEGER;
  BEGIN
  FOR DY:=20 TO 21 DO
    FOR DX:=40+DIENO TO 41+DIENO DO
      PLOT(DX,DY,1);
  FOR DY:=26 TO 27 DO
    FOR DX:=54+DIENO TO 55+DIENO DO
      PLOT(DX,DY,1)
  END;
PROC LLURDOT(DIENO);
  VAR DY,DX:INTEGER;
```

172

```
    BEGIN
    FOR DY:=26 TO 27 DO
      FOR DX:=40+DIENTO TO 41+DIENO DO
        PLOT(DX,DY,1);
    FOR DY:=20 TO 21 DO
      FOR DX:=54+DIENO TO 55+DIENO DO
        PLOT(DX,DY,1)
    END;
  PROC LRDOT(DIENO);
    VAR DY,DX:INTEGER;
    BEGIN
    FOR DY:=23 TO 24 DO
      BEGIN
      FOR DX:=40+DIENO TO 41+DIENO DO
        PLOT(DX,DY,1);
      FOR DX:=54+DIENO TO 55+DIENO DO
        PLOT(DX,DY,1)
      END
    END;
  PROC VALDRAW(DIENO,VAL);
    BEGIN
    CASE VAL OF
      1:MIDDOT(DIENO);
      2:ULLRDOT(DIENO);
      3:BEGIN
        MIDDOT(DIENO);
        ULLRDOT(DIENO)
        END;
      4:BEGIN
        ULLRDOT(DIENO);
        LLURDOT(DIENO)
        END;
      5:BEGIN
        MIDDOT(DIENO);
        ULLRDOT(DIENO);
        LLURDOT(DIENO)
        END;
      6:BEGIN
        ULLRDOT(DIENO);
        LLURDOT(DIENO);
        LRDOT(DIENO)
        END   (* OF CASE #6 *)
      END   (* OF ENTIRE CASE STATEMENT *)
    END;   (* OF PROCEDURE *)
  (* BEGINNING OF MAINLINE PROGRAM *)
  BEGIN
  WRITE(28,31,'GRAPHIC DICE ROLL');
  WRITE(13,13,'ENTER TO START');
  (* PICK SEED VALUE *)
  WHILE INKEY <> 13 DO
    BEGIN
    SEED:=SEED+1;
    IF (SEED<99) OR (SEED>999) THEN SEED:=99
    END;
  N:=SEED;
  (* PICK RANDOM NUMBERS BETWEEN 1 AND 6 *)
  REPEAT
    DIENO:=0;
```

173

```
  WHILE DIENO<=32 DO
    BEGIN
    REPEAT
      M:=N*125;
      IF M<0 THEN M:=ABS(M);
      N:=M;P:=M;
      P:=P MOD 7
    UNTIL (P>=1) AND (P<=6);
    IF DIENO=0 THEN D1:=P
      ELSE IF DIENO=32 THEN D2:=P;
    DIENO:=DIENO+32
    END;
  DIEDRAW;
  VALDRAW(0,D1);
  VALDRAW(32,D2);
  WRITE('ENTER TO ROLL AGAIN');
  READ(D1);
UNTIL D1=32
END.
```

Mainline Flow Chart

So much for the program itself. Now begin comparing the program with the flow charts in Figs. 11-5 through 11-7.

The flow chart for the mainline program (Fig. 11-5) ought to appear somewhat familiar. It is much the same as the program for NUMERIC DICE ROLL. See Fig. 11-3.

Those two flow charts look much alike because they do much the same job. They pick random numbers between 1 and 6 for some dice values.

Running through the mainline flow chart in Fig. 11-5, you can see that the program first writes out an appropriate heading, and then gets down to the job of selecting a SEED value for the pseudo-random number generator. The SEED value is chosen by letting a SEED counter "buzz" between 99 and 999 until the operator depresses the ENTER key. Whatever value SEED happens to have at that moment is then assigned to variable N.

This graphic dice game has only two dice, so DIENO (the dice counter) is initially set to 0. See the block DIENO:=∅ in Fig. 11-5. Then the program picks a random number between 1 and 6, using the same technique described in some detail in the previous section of this chapter.

After picking a randomly generated number between 1 and 6, the system wants to know if DIENO is still equal to 0. Well, DIENO was set to 0 a few steps before, and nothing has happened to change that fact, not yet, anyway. So DIENO is equal to 0 and, as a result, variable D1 is set to the value pulled from the random number generator. D1 represents the value to be printed on the first die figure.

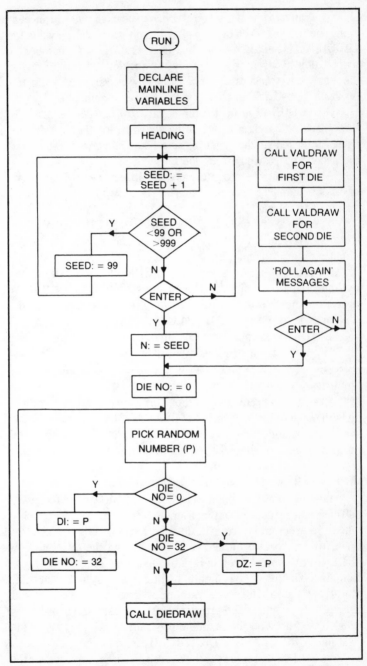

Fig. 11-5. Flow chart for the mainline program of GRAPHIC DICE ROLL.

The random number generator has to be used twice in succession, one time for each die. So after the program picks a value for D1, DIENO is set to 32. Just why the program uses the number 32 will become apparent when you see how the dots are printed on the die figures. At any rate, DIENO is now equal to 32, and the program loops back up to pick a second random number.

Since DIENO is no longer equal to 0 but 32 instead, the flow chart shows variable D2 being set to P. In other words, the value of the second die is set to the random number picked during the second pass through this loop.

At this point, the program has done little more than pick a pair of random numbers between 1 and 6. Those two values have been assigned to D1 and D2.

The program then calls a procedure named DIEDRAW. Then it calls procedure VALDRAW twice in succession, but under slightly different conditions.

As you will see in a moment, DIEDRAW simply draws the outlines of the two dice figures on the screen. The VALDRAW procedure then fills in those die figures with spots representing the die patterns for numbers D1 and D2.

DIEDRAW is called just one time. There is no need to draw the outlines of the die figures more than once. VALDRAW, however, is called twice—first to draw the spots for die value D1, and then again to draw the spots for die value D2.

After the program does all those drawing procedures, it ends up with some of the usual sorts of PLAY AGAIN messages. When the player decides to play again (by striking the ENTER key), the program picks up where DIENO is initialized to 0. The program picks two more random die values, draws the die figures and fills them with the appropriate spot patterns.

There is really no need to pick a new SEED value for every roll of the dice. It turns out that a single SEED value, selected only when the program is first run, is good for hundreds of rolls.

Now that you've worked your way through the mainline flow chart, it is time to correlate it with the actual Tiny Pascal programming. The mainline program might not be easy to find at first. Recall that the variables for a mainline program must be declared at the very beginning of the program. After that, all the procedures must be defined. So the mainline program actually begins at the first line of the GRAPHIC DICE ROLL program, but then doesn't resume until the latter part of the overall program. Just look for the comment line, BEGINNING OF MAINLINE PROGRAM.

After that comment line, you will find things picking up with the heading and ENTER TO START message. The program then follows the flow chart in Fig. 11-5 very closely to the end.

DIEDRAW, HDRAW and VDRAW Procedures

The first procedure called from the mainline program is DIEDRAW. Remember, that is the one that simply draws the outline of the two dice figures on the screen. That procedure is flow charted for you in Fig. 11-6.

According to the DIEDRAW flow chart, things begin by declaring the variables used in that particular procedure. Right after that, the program clears the screen. The screen clearing operation is important at this stage because it wipes out the die values drawn on the screen during any previous rolls.

But then DIEDRAW calls another procedure, HDRAW. You bet. The system is using nested procedures. HDRAW is responsible for drawing the horizontal components of the die outlines, tops and bottoms, in other words. You can see the top and bottom drawing operations specified in the little HDRAW flow chart in Fig. 11-6A.

The game uses two dice, so DIEDRAW has to call HDRAW twice in succession, once for the first die and then again for the second one. When you get a chance to study the actual programming for DIEDRAW and HDRAW, you will see that DIEDRAW passes variable values DX and DY to HDRAW. Those values determine where the horizontal lines will be actually drawn.

To complete the die figures, the system has to draw four vertical lines, one for each of the two sides of the two dice. That is why you see procedure VDRAW called four times in succession. VDRAW, flow charted in Fig. 11-6C, simply draws two vertical lines right beside each other. The system has to draw two adjacent lines in order to give the vertical lines the same width as the horizontal ones.

So DIEDRAW calls VDRAW four times, passing variables DX and DY to tell VDRAW exactly where the lines are to be drawn. Procedure DIEDRAW and its own procedures, HDRAW and VDRAW, appear very early in the GRAPHIC DICE ROLL program. Just look for the comment line, DICE OUTLINE DRAWING PROCEDURES. The first procedure you see after that comment line is HDRAW. After that comes VDRAW, and finally there is DIEDRAW.

Since DIEDRAW calls procedures HDRAW and VDRAW, Pascal structure requires that the called procedures be specified

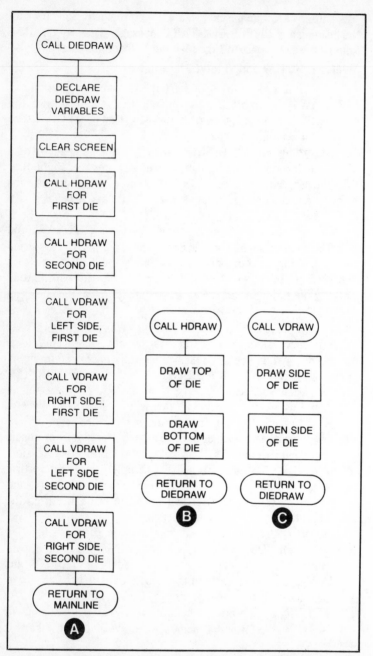

Fig. 11-6. Flow charts for GRAPHIC DICE ROLL procedures. (A) DIEDRAW procedure. (B) HDRAW procedure. (C) VDRAW procedure.

before the calling procedure is. Just as you have to declare all variables before a program that uses them can be run, you must specify all procedures before any other procedure or program that calls them. Hence, HDRAW and VDRAW are specified ahead of DIEDRAW in the program; DIEDRAW is, in turn, specified ahead of the program that calls it, the mainline program.

To this point in the discussion, you've seen how the mainline program selects randomly generated values for the dice and then gets into the graphics end of the matter by drawing the outlines of the two dice. Now it's time to see how the dice values are translated into little patterns of spots within the dice figures.

VALDRAW Procedure

The spot drawing procedure, VALDRAW, is flow charted in Fig. 11-7. That might appear to be a rather extensive flow chart at first sight, but it really isn't very difficult to understand.

When VALDRAW is called from the mainline program, it knows the value of the die being drawn on the screen. Values D1 and D2 are carried to VALDRAW by variable VAL. According to that flow chart, the value of variable VAL determines which one of six kinds of operations will take place.

If, for example, VAL is equal to 1, the VAL=1 conditional is satisfied and the system calls procedure MIDDOT. More procedures within procedures? You bet. And what does procedure MIDDOT do? Look at the four little squares at the bottom of Fig. 11-7, and you will see what all the subprocedures do. MIDDOT places a dot in the center of the die figure being drawn at the moment.

When VAL is equal to 1, then, the system calls MIDDOT. MIDDOT puts a dot in the center of the appropriate die figure. That's what a "1" die value is supposed to look like.

When VAL is equal to 2, the flow chart shows that VALDRAW calls another procedure named ULLRDOT. According to the figures at the bottom of Fig. 11-7, ULLRDOT places spots in the upper-left and lower-right corners of the die figure.

Consider just one more example. Suppose VAL is equal to 3 when the mainline program calls VALDRAW. In that case, conditional VAL=3 is satisfied. VALDRAW calls two different procedures in succession, first MIDDOT and then ULLRDOT. If you put those two spot drawing operations together in this fashion, you end up with a die figure having 3 spots running diagonally, from upper left to lower right. Sure enough, that makes it look like you rolled a "3" on the die.

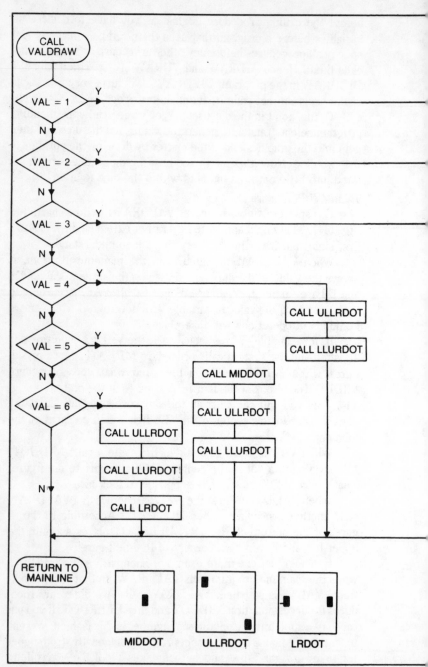

Fig. 11-7. Flow chart for VALDRAW procedure, GRAPHIC DICE ROLL GAME.

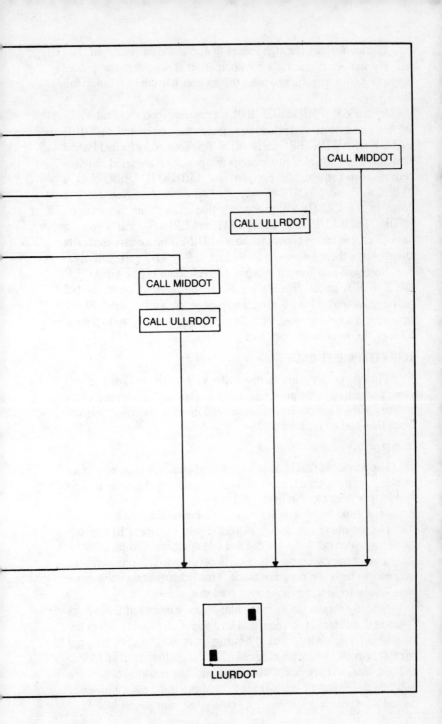

CALL MIDDOT

CALL ULLRDOT

CALL MIDDOT

CALL ULLRDOT

LLURDOT

181

Work your way through values of 4, 5 and 6 on your own. You will see that each one calls a combination of spot drawing procedures that work together to paint the appropriate set of spots on the die figure.

In the GRAPHIC DICE ROLL program, you can find VALDRAW and its 4 nested procedures under the comment line, DICE VALUE DRAWING PROCEDURES. As dictated by formal Pascal structure, the "inside" procedures are specified ahead of the procedure that calls them. So you see MIDDOT, ULLURDOT, LLURDOT and LRDOT clearly spelled out before you can get down to the VALDRAW procedure that calls them. So you see MIDDOT, ULLURDOT, LLURDOT and LRDOT clearly spelled out before you can get down to the VALDRAW procedure that calls them. All of them follow the flow chart in Fig. 11-7 quite closely.

So there you have a complete breakdown of the GRAPHIC DICE ROLL game. There is a lot to be learned about nested procedures and TRS-80 graphics guised as Tiny Pascal PLOT graphics. To get the most from this program, you'll have to dig out a lot of the details on your own.

ROULETTE WHEEL GAME

This game program is not quite as graphic as the dice roll game presented in the previous section. This one, however, incorporates some user control schemes and number-to-string translations that add to its interest.

Format

The format is that of a roulette wheel game. A sequence of 32 numbers, 0 through 31, flashes in the middle of the screen. The flashing is rather rapid at first, but then it gradually slows down to a stop. The final number is, of course, the winning number.

The numbers are assigned red or black colors. In half the cases, the even numbers are red and odd numbers are black. In the other half of the cases the situation is reversed. The odd numbers are red and the even ones are black. That scheme makes the game come close to looking like a real roulette wheel.

Actually this game is more like a real game than the others described thus far in this chapter. Here you are invited to select the type of bet you want to make, betting on an odd or even winning number, a red or black winning color, or a combination of odd/even and red/black. Your odds of winning in the first two kind of bets are 1:2, and the payoff (if you win) is 2:1. In the third case, however, the odds of winning are just 1:4. Of course, the payoff is 4:1.

Upon running this program, you first see this text on the screen:

** ROULETTE WHEEL BET TYPES **

SELECT ONE BY NUMBER:

1—COLOR (2:1 PAYOFF)
2—ODD/EVEN (2:1 PAYOFF)
3—COLOR AND ODD/EVEN (4:1 PAYOFF)

ENTER CHOICE (1, 2 OR 3) . . . ?—

You respond by entering one of those three numbers. Upon doing so, the screen text changes according to the type of bet you selected. If you selected bet type 1, the next thing you see is a request for a color:

COLOR: RED OR BLACK
—

But if you picked number 2, you see:

ODD OR EVEN
—

Selecting bet type 3, you get two requests in succession:
COLOR: RED OR BLACK
—

After you reply to that request you get:

ODD OR EVEN
—

So you first get a choice of three kinds of bets. Then the system asks for the appropriate betting details: color, odd/even or both.

When you have entered your betting detail, the screen clears and you see your bet rewritten for you at the upper left-hand corner of the screen. The message ENTER TO SPIN THE WHEEL appears at the middle of the screen.

Striking the ENTER key then begins the spinning action. You see the sequence of wheel numbers and their corresponding colors flashing near the center of the screen. As mentioned earlier in this section, the numbers and their colors flash by rather rapidly at first, but then eventually slow down to a halt. The action is simulating that of a real roulette wheel.

When the "wheel" finally comes to a stop, the program informs you of your level of success or failure. If you have picked a

183

winner, you see one of the following, depending on the type of bet you originally made.

YOU WIN AT 2:1 PAYOFF!!

or

YOU WIN AT 4:1 PAYOFF!!

In the event you fail to pick a winner (which happens most of the time as roulette wheels always favor the house), you see:

SORRY . . . YOU LOSE YOUR BET

In any event, the program prints ENTER TO PLAY AGAIN. You get a chance to select another kind of bet and betting details after than. Then the whole program repeats itself.

Program

Here is the program, presented exactly as it should be entered into your system:

```
(* ROULETTE WHEEL GAME *)
VAR LINE,SPACE,TYPE,PCOLOR,POE,NUM,GCOLOR,GOE,TIME:
  INTEGER;
BEGIN
REPEAT (* ENTIRE GAME *)
  REPEAT (* BET TYPE SELECTION *)
    WRITE(28,31,210,'** ROULETTE WHEEL BET TYPES **');
    WRITE(13,13,'SELECT ONE BY NUMBER:');
    WRITE(13,13,200,'1 -- COLOR (2:1 PAYOFF)');
    WRITE(13,200,'2 -- ODD/EVEN (2:1 PAYOFF)');
    WRITE(13,200,'3 -- COLOR AND ODD/EVEN(4:1 PAYOFF)');
    FOR LINE:=1 TO 6 DO WRITE(13);
    WRITE('ENTER CHOICE (1,2 OR 3)...');
    READ(TYPE#)
  UNTIL (TYPE>=1) AND (TYPE<=3);
  WRITE(28,31,210,'** ROULETTE WHEEL BETTING DETAIL
    **',13,13);
  CASE TYPE OF
    1:REPEAT
        WRITE('COLOR:  RED OR BLACK',13);
        READ(PCOLOR)
      UNTIL (PCOLOR=82) OR (PCOLOR=66);
    2:REPEAT
        WRITE('ODD OR EVEN');
        READ(POE)
      UNTIL (POE=79) OR (POE=69);
    3:BEGIN
      REPEAT
        WRITE('COLOR: RED OR BLACK',13);
        READ(PCOLOR)
      UNTIL (PCOLOR=82) OR (PCOLOR=66);
      REPEAT
```

```
        WRITE(13,'ODD OR EVEN');
        READ(POE)
      UNTIL (POE=79) OR (POE=69)
    END  (* OF CASE #3 *)
  END;  (* OF ENTIRE CASE STATEMENT *)
  WRITE(28,31,'YOUR BET IS: ');
  CASE TYPE OF
    1,3:IF PCOLOR=82 THEN WRITE ('RED')
        ELSE IF PCOLOR=66 THEN WRITE ('BLACK');
    2:  IF POE=79 THEN WRITE('ODD')
        ELSE IF POE=69 THEN WRITE('EVEN')
  END;  (* OF CASE STATEMENT *)
  IF (TYPE=3) AND (POE=79) THEN WRITE('--ODD')
  ELSE IF (TYPE=3) AND (POE=69) THEN WRITE('--EVEN');
  FOR LINE:=1 TO 7 DO WRITE(13);
  WRITE('ENTER TO SPIN THE WHEEL');
(* SPINNING AND DECODING SEQUENCE *)
  WHILE INKEY<>13 DO
    BEGIN
    NUM:=NUM+1;
    IF NUM>31 THEN NUM:=0
    END;
  TIME:=1000;
  REPEAT
    WRITE(29,30,220,NUM#);
    IF ((NUM>=0) AND (NUM<=7)) OR((NUM>=16)AND (NUM<=23))
      THEN LINE:=1
      ELSE LINE:=2;
    CASE LINE OF
      1:IF NUM MOD 2=0 THEN
          BEGIN
          GCOLOR:=82;
          WRITE('--RED');
          GOE:=69
          END
        ELSE
          BEGIN
          GCOLOR:=66;
          WRITE('--BLACK');
          GOE:=79
          END;
      2:IF NUM MOD 2=0 THEN
          BEGIN
          GCOLOR:=66;
          WRITE('--BLACK');
          GOE:=69
          END
        ELSE
          BEGIN
          GCOLOR:=82;
          WRITE('--RED');
          GOE:=79
          END    (* OF CASE #2 *)
    END;  (* OF ENTIRE CASE STATEMENT *)
    FOR SPACE:=TIME TO 1000 DO;
    TIME:=TIME-10;
    NUM:=NUM+1;
    IF NUM>31 THEN NUM:=0
```

185

```
    UNTIL TIME=400;
    FOR LINE:=1 TO 4 DO WRITE(13);
(* SHOW RESULTS SEQUENCE *)
    CASE TYPE OF
      1:IF PCOLOR=GCOLOR THEN
            WRITE('YOU WIN  AT 2:1 PAYOFF!!')
            ELSE WRITE('SORRY ... YOU LOSE YOUR BET');
      2:IF POE=GOE THEN
            WRITE('YOU WIN AT 2:1 PAYOFF!!')
            ELSE WRITE('SORRY ... YOU LOSE YOUR BET');
      3:IF (PCOLOR=GCOLOR) AND (POE=GOE) THEN
            WRITE('YOU WIN AT 4:1 PAYOFF!!')
            ELSE WRITE('SORRY ... YOU LOSE YOUR BET')
      END;      (* OF CASE *)
    WRITE(13,220,'ENTER TO PLAY AGAIN');
    READ(SPACE);
UNTIL SPACE<>SPACE
END.
```

Disadvantages

The flow charts for this ROULETTE WHEEL GAME program occupy Figs. 11-8 through 11-11. The analysis is somewhat simplified by the fact that this program contains no formal procedures. At the same time, it is made to appear rather complicated because of the need to translate between numerical and string expressions a number of different times. Sigh! I wish Tiny Pascal could handle extended string variables.

While on the subject of Tiny Pascal's few shortcomings, this program very clearly shows the disadvantages of not being able to carry variable values from a procedure to a mainline program. As a result of this little problem, you will see some operations repeated several times throughout the listing. Double sigh!

Don't feel too badly about your Tiny Pascal, though. It just so happens that this particular program brings together the disadvantaged under one heading. That, of course, tends to make things seem worse than they really are. So much for the bad stuff. It should be pointed out, but not dwelled upon.

Detail Phase Flow Chart

Figure 11-8 is a flow chart of the opening part of the program. You can see that it first calls for declaring the variables. Directly after than it writes out the BET TYPE listing illustrated earlier. The system expects a value for variable TYPE at that point, and that should be a number 1, 2 or 3 from the keyboard. Recall that entering a 1 at this point sets up the betting on color, 2 sets up things for betting on an odd/even win, and 3 establishes a bet that combines color and odd/even.

186

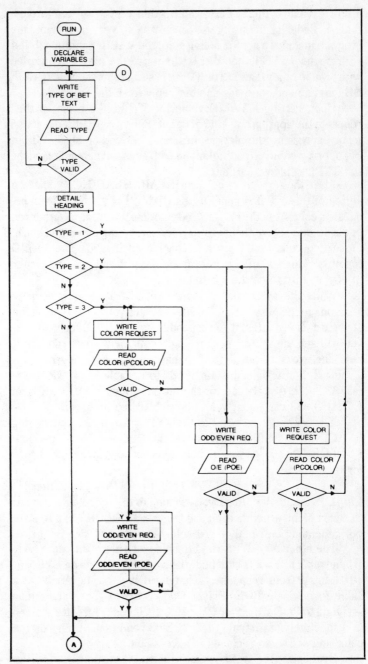

Fig. 11-8. Flow chart for detail phase of the ROULETTE WHEEL program.

The value of the TYPE variable is thus very important through the remainder of the program. Since it is so very important, the program includes a goof-proofing step, the VALID conditional. If it so happens TYPE is not VALID (because the player responded with a value other than 1, 2 or 3), the system repeats the TYPE OF BET listing and waits for another reply from the keyboard.

Upon getting a VALID value for TYPE, the program then requests the appropriate kind of detail. Specifically, it looks for an input expressing the player's desire to bet red or black, odd or even, or a combination of color and odd/even, all depending on the bet TYPE selected earlier.

After the flow chart block, 'DETAIL' HEADING, you see a series of three TYPE conditionals. If TYPE= 1, the system requests a color from the player. The color must be read as either red or black. If the player happens to enter something other than one of those two colors, the input is considered invalid. The VALID conditional then returns to repeat the request and give the player an opportunity to do the job right.

While the system does indeed request a color, it actually responds to the first letter of whatever color you try to type on the keyboard. If you attempt to respond by typing RED, for instance, you will see the system responding the moment you strike the R key. The two remaining letters in that word are not relevant at all. Typing R then assigns the number 82 to variable PCOLOR. Decimal 82 is the ASCII code for the letter R, and PCOLOR (Player COLOR) will carry that value throughout the program.

If you want to respond to the TYPE=1 request by entering BLACK, the system will assign the number 66 to variable PCOLOR. That 66, as you might imagine by now, is the ASCII code for the letter B.

So if you first select a TYPE 1 bet, the TYPE=1 conditional in Fig. 11-8 is satisfied. After you respond to the request for a color, this part of the program is concluded with PCOLOR equal to 82 or 66, depending on whether you selected red or black.

The other two TYPE conditionals work much the same way. Whenever TYPE=2 is satisfied, the system requests an EVEN or ODD entry. Your response, assuming it is valid, is carried as a value for variable POE (Player Odd or Even). The values thus assigned to POE are either 69 or 79, ASCII codes for letters E and O respectively. Satisfying the TYPE=3 conditional brings up the color and odd/even requests in succession.

By the time the system gets to the end of the flow chart in Fig. 11-8, variable TYPE is carrying a number representing the type of

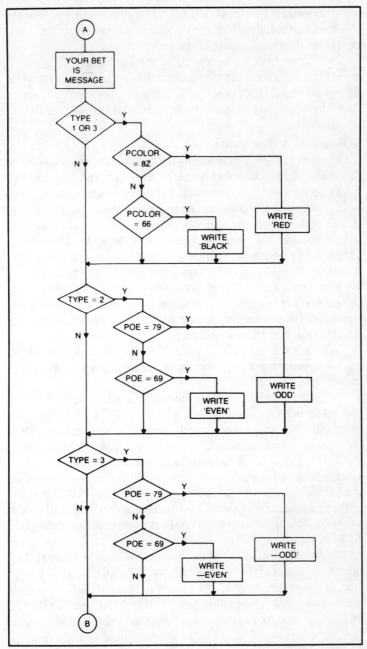

Fig. 11-9. Flow chart for bet message phase of the ROULETTE WHEEL program.

bet you've made. Variable PCOLOR is carrying a color code you've selected, and variable POE carries your odd/even selection. That concludes the opening part of the program.

Referring back to the program, the flow chart in Fig. 8-11 covers the lines from the beginning and down to the line carrying the comment, OF ENTIRE CASE. See if you can see a correspondence between the blocks on the flow chart and the lines of Pascal programming.

Betting Details Flow Chart

In the excitement of watching the roulette wheel spin, players sometimes forget the exact details of their bet. The flow chart in Fig. 11-9 represents a portion of the program that reconstructs and writes out the betting details near the top of the screen. Those details remain there through the remainder of the program.

"Reconstructs" is an important word here. In the opening phase of the program, the player's inputs were translated into ASCII numbers. That was necessary because Tiny Pascal cannot work with string expressions, just integers. In this second phase of the program, you want to see string expressions, plain English words, on the screen. That means it is necessary to translate from integer values to strings again.

The process begins by writing, YOU BET IS, and then it ends up "filling in the blank" with a verbal description of your bet. Here's how it does the job.

The messages depends on which TYPE of bet you've made. If you made bet type 1 or 3, the conditional, TYPE=1 OR 3, is satisfied. The system then checks the color you entered. That color, you recall, is carried as an ASCII number by variable PCOLOR. If PCOLOR happens to be equal to 82 (letter R), the system "fills in the blank" by writing out RED. The full message at the top of the screen would then be YOUR BET IS RED. If you are betting on black, PCOLOR=82 is *not* satisfied but PCOLOR=66 is satisfied. The system then completes the sentence by printing out BLACK instead of RED.

Satisfying the TYPE=2 conditional calls up the same sort of operations, but they are oriented toward the ODD/EVEN selection. If you selected bet TYPE 3, the flow chart in Fig. 11-9 shows you would satisfy two conditionals, TYPE=1 OR 3 and TYPE=3. In the first case, the system would print out your color choice. In the second, it would print out your selection of odd or even.

Now this happens to be one of those programming situations where the flow chart appears to be far, far more involved than the program that implements it. All of the decisions and writing carried out by the flow chart in Fig. 11-9 is done in the few lines between the comment, OF ENTIRE CASE and the line that specifies WRITE ('ENTER TO SPIN THE WHEEL'). This particular example very clearly demonstrates the power of Pascal's CASE...OF statement. It does a whole lot of flow charting in a very few lines of program test.

Spinning Phase Flow Chart

The next step in the program is to spin the wheel. That part of the operation is flow charted for you in Fig. 11-10.

The flow chart shows the program skipping a couple of lines on the screen. The betting summary just described is to remain near the top of the screen, but the spinning effect is to be situated near the middle. Thus, you need to skip a few lines downward.

The next operation is to print an ENTER message. To be exact, the program tells the play: ENTER TO SPIN THE WHEEL.

Having worked with some roulette wheel games before in BASIC, I've found the simplest approach to "spinning the wheel" is to start that spin at some random number and then let the system cycle through a prescribed number of counts. Doing the job the more "natural" way—picking a random number and making the count advance that many places—causes some real hairy programming processes. So why do things the hard way, when a bit of creative imagination shows a much simpler alternative that works just as well?

This spinning scheme picks a random starting number between 0 and 31 and assigns it to variable NUM. That is done by letting NUM "buzz" between 0 and 31 until the operator strikes the ENTER key. Satisfying the ENTER conditional in Fig. 11-10 picks the value for NUM.

Variable TIME is then set to 1000, and the system enters a rather large and involved looping operation. This loop is responsible for doing three things. First, it causes the number on the screen to cycle between 0 and 31 (beginning at the NUM value). At the same time, it assigns colors, red or black, to the numbers as they flash on the screen. Finally, the loop is responsible for the slowing down effect of the flashing numbers and colors. All of this begins at the block labeled CLEAR DISPLAY.

CLEAR DISPLAY erases any information on the middle line of the screen. Immediately after that, however, the value of NUM variable is written there. In essence, the system displays the first in a long series of numbers that are to represent the spinning effect of the roulette wheel.

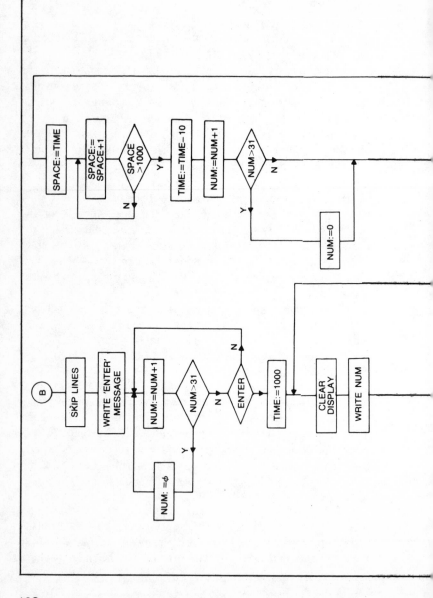

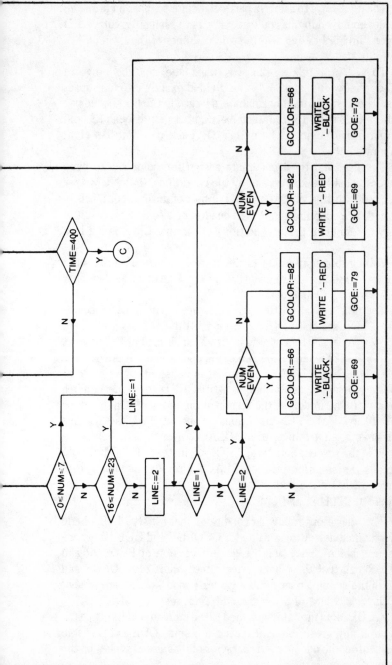

Fig. 11-10. Flow chart for the spinning phase of the ROULETTE WHEEL program.

193

The next job is to assign a particular color to that number. The scheme employed in this roulette game is to assign the color RED to even numbers falling within two quadrants of the "wheel."

Quadrants

To see how this works, you must see that the range of numbers between 0 and 31 can be divided exactly into four quadrants. The first quadrant has numbers 0 through 7, the second has numbers 8 through 15, the third has numbers 16 through 23, and the fourth has number 24 through 31. Each quadrant has eight numbers apiece.

The first and third quadrants assign the color red to even numbers. That is taken care of by the conditional $0<=NUM<=7$ combined with $16<=NUM<=23$. If either of those conditionals is satisfied, it means the count is in quadrants 1 or 3. As a result of satisfying either of those conditionals, variable LINE is set to a value of 1.

Failing to satisfy either of those two conditionals means the count must be somewhere in quadrants 2 or 4. In that case, variable LINE is set to a value of 2.

The next operations in Fig. 11-10 are a pair of LINE conditionals: LINE=1 and LINE=2. Suppose LINE=1 is satisfied. In other words, the NUM count is in either quadrant 1 or 3. The next conditional asks whether the number is odd or even. If the number is even, the NUM EVEN conditional is satisfied . The system, among a couple of other things, writes RED after the number appearing in the middle of the screen at the moment. On the other hand, if the NUM EVEN conditional is *not* satisfied, the system, again among other things, prints BLACK after the number in the middle of the screen. Satisfying LINE=2, instead of LINE=1, just reverses the situation printing BLACK after the number if it is even and RED if it's odd.

Values For GCOLOR, and GOE

The operations following conditions that satisfy LINE=1 and LINE=2 include setting a value for GCOLOR and GOE. What are those variables? They are the game's version of PCOLOR and POE. Recall that the player selects the values of PCOLOR and POE in the opening phase of the game. Those variables represent the player's choice of color and odd/even respectively.

GCOLOR is the color assigned to the number appearing on the screen at any given moment during the spin. GOE is a variable representing the odd or even character of that same number on the screen.

As the wheel "spins," the values assigned to variables GCOLOR and GOE switch around quite a bit. But in any event, GCOLOR is equal to either 66 or 82, the ASCII codes for B and R. GOE is equal to either 69 or 79, the ASCII codes for E and O. At any given moment during the spinning of the wheel, the color and odd/even character of the number appearing in the middle of the screen is carried as variables GCOLOR and GOE.

The final phase of the operation flow charted in Fig. 11-10 is to slow down the spinning action and eventually bring it to a stop. When things come to a halt, the existing values of GCOLOR and GOE represent the winning combinations. But that's getting ahead of the discussion.

Slow-Down Effect

The next series of steps on the flow chart begin with SPACE:=TIME and end with the conditional, TIME=400. These are the steps most responsible for changing the number that flashes on the screen and slowing down the spinning effect.

The heart of the slow-down effect is the block SPACE:=SPACE+1 and conditional SPACE *greater than* 1000. That is a time delay loop that runs until variable SPACE is greater than 1000. But what is the value of SPACE when the counting begins? The block preceding the timing loop tells you that SPACE is set equal to variable TIME.

What is TIME equal to? In the early part of this flow chart: TIME is set to 1000. On the first pass through this part of the program, the time delay certainly is not very long. Incrementing SPACE just one count satisfies the SPACE *greater than* 1000 conditional, and the timing is done. That isn't very exciting.

But notice that TIME is decreased by 10 in the step following the time delay loop. The next time the system gets around to SPACE:TIME, SPACE will be 990 and the time delay will run through 11 cycles instead of just one. After that, TIME is decreased by 10 again. The next time delay will be even longer.

The time delay operation thus grows longer each time the system executes the big loop in Fig. 11-10. And that continues until TIME=400. By then, the delay is getting close to ½ of a second, and it's time to think about stopping the spinning action.

That is how the slow-down effect of the "spin" takes place. In the meantime, variable NUM is being incremented and cycled between 0 and 31. NUM, you recall, is displayed as a number in the middle of the screen.

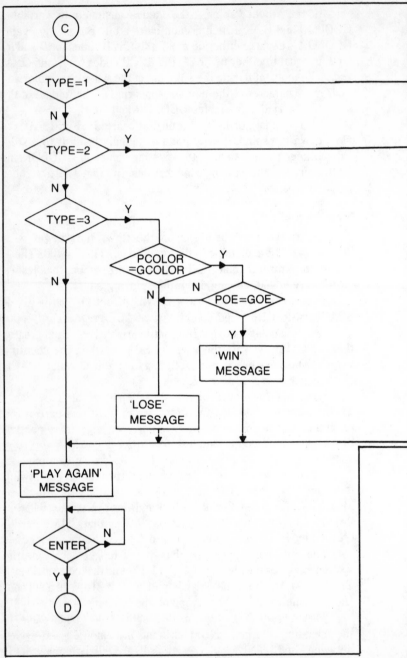

Fig. 11-11. Flow chart for the closing phase of the ROULETTE WHEEL program.

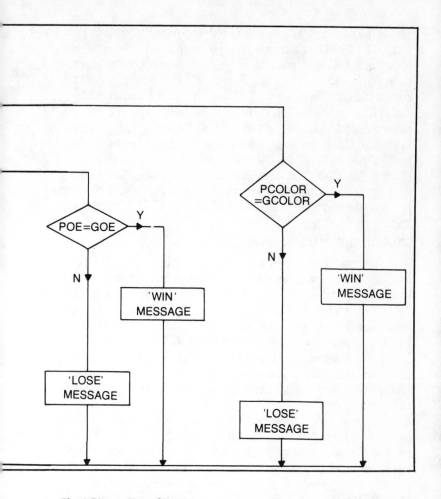

Final Phase Flow Chart

Figure 11-11 is the flow chart for the final phase of the game. It is here that the system compares the winning number and color with the player's bet.

The exact nature and extent of the comparison operations depend on the value of variable TYPE, the type of bet the player made before spinning the wheel. If TYPE=1, the system compares PCOLOR (the player's choice of color) with GCOLOR (the color of the winning number). If the two happen to be equal, as determined by conditional PCOLOR=GCOLOR, then the system prints out the appropriate WIN message. If the colors do not match, however, the system prints out the LOSE message.

If the player selected bet TYPE 2, the system compares POE and GOE, the player's choice of odd or even against the odd/even nature of the winning number. The system then prints the appropriate WIN or LOSE message. Selecting TYPE 3 merely calls for comparing both the color variables and the odd/even variables.

To wrap up the play, the system prints a PLAY AGAIN message, and waits at conditional ENTER for a reply from the keyboard. Upon getting that reply, the program cycles all the way back to the TYPE OF BET selection operations shown on the flow chart in Fig. 11-8. The whole business thus begins all over again. The actual program steps for the flow chart in Fig. 11-11 fall between the comment line, SHOW RESULTS SEQUENCE, to the end.

GRAPHIC SLOT MACHINE GAME

Slot machines are popular gadgets in the world of popular betting. Here is a program that simulates the action of a slot machine in a highly graphic fashion. This is another program that can be best appreciated after playing with it on your computer for a while. Enter the program and have some fun with it. Then you'll be in a better position to analyze its workings.

When you first run this SLOT MACHINE program, you will see a message telling you to ENTER TO START. At the same time, the screen shows three empty slots. This is the only time the slots will be empty.

When you do that first ENTER, the fun begins. You see patterns of characters flashing through the three slots. The patterns in the slot on the left begin slowing down, and come to a stop after about five cycles. Immediately after that, the patterns in the middle slot begin slowing down; they, too, eventually come to a stop. Finally the slot on the right shows the same slow-down-and-stop effect. Now you have the final result.

This particular SLOT MACHINE program has no built-in scoring, so you'll have to work that out for yourself. Usually you win nothing if all three slots show different patterns. You will run something on the order of a 10:1 payoff if two of the slots show identical patterns. And the payoff is quite large if all three slots show the same pattern. The jackpot is usually reserved for one particular pattern (cherries) appearing in all three slots.

Graphic Format

This game doesn't show cherries, apples, wavy lines or anything like that. It could be done, but only after writing a very

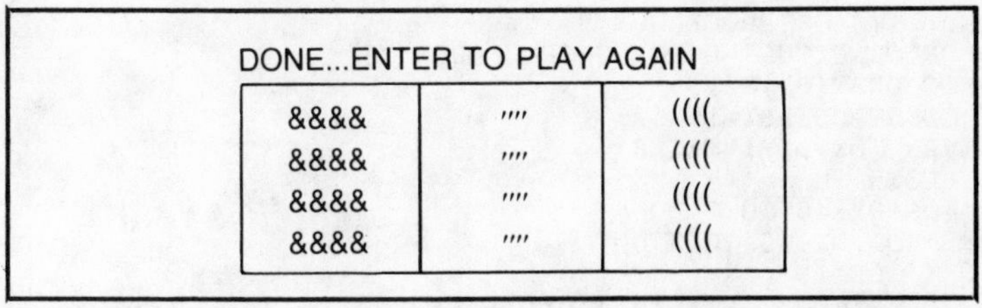

DONE...ENTER TO PLAY AGAIN		
&&&&	''''	((((
&&&&	''''	((((
&&&&	''''	((((
&&&&	''''	((((

Fig. 11-12. Graphic format for the SLOT MACHINE GAME.

complicated graphics program. It does, however, show 10 different 4×4 patterns of ASCII characters. See the example in Fig. 11-12.

Actually the slots work according to a counter that cycles between 34 and 43. If you refer to the ASCII code table in the Appendix, you will see that those numbers represent a series of punctuation marks, beginning with quotation marks and ending with the plus sign. The counters in the drawing in Fig. 11-12 happened to stop at ASCII decimal codes 38, 39 and 40—the ampersand, apostrophe and right parenthesis, respectively.

You can play the game any number of times by simply striking the ENTER key. You don't even have to feed the machine a quarter (but then the payoff is just pretend, too).

Program

Here is the program:

```
(* SLOT MACHINE *)
VAR SEED,S1,S2,S3,PHASE,M,N,P,TIMES,INTERVAL:INTEGER;
(* SLOT DRAWING PROCEDURE *)
PROC SLOTDRAW;
  VAR DX,DY:INTEGER;
  BEGIN
  WRITE(28,31);
  FOR DX:=28 TO 99 DO
    BEGIN
    PLOT(DX,13,1);
    PLOT(DX,28,1)
    END;
  FOR DY:=13 TO 28 DO
    BEGIN
    FOR DX:=28 TO 29 DO
      BEGIN
      PLOT(DX,DY,1);
      PLOT(DX+70,DY,1)
      END;
     FOR DX:=50 TO 53 DO
      BEGIN
      PLOT(DX,DY,1);
      PLOT(DX+24,DY,1)
      END
  END
```

```
END;   (* OF PROCEDURE *)
(* SLOT FIGURE DRAWING PROCEDURE *)
PROC DRAW(S1,S2,S3);
  CONST DSTART=15762;
  VAR DX,DY:INTEGER;
  BEGIN
  FOR DY:=0 TO 2 DO
    FOR DX:=0 TO 3 DO
      BEGIN
      MEM(DSTART+DX+64*DY):=S1;
      MEM(DSTART+DX+12+64*DY):=S2;
      MEM(DSTART+DX+24+64*DY):=S3
      END
  END;
(* BEGINNING OF SLOT MACHINE MAINLINE PROGRAM *)
BEGIN
SLOTDRAW;
WRITE('ENTER TO BEGIN PLAY');
(* PICK UP SEED NUMBER FOR RANDOM GENERATOR *)
WHILE INKEY<>13 DO
  BEGIN
  SEED:=SEED+1;
  IF (SEED<99) OR (SEED>999) THEN SEED:=99;
  END;
N:=SEED;
(* RESTART POINT FOR REPEATED PLAYS *)
REPEAT
(* SELECT RANDOM STARTING POINTS FOR THE THREE SLOTS *)
  FOR PHASE:=1 TO 3 DO
    BEGIN
    REPEAT
      M:=N*16807;
      IF M<0 THEN M:=ABS(M);
      N:=M;P:=M;
      P:=P MOD 61
    UNTIL (P>=34) AND (P<=43);
    CASE PHASE OF
      1:S1:=P;
      2:S2:=P;
      3:S3:=P

    UNTIL (P>=34) AND (P<=43);
    CASE PHASE OF
      1:S1:=P;
      2:S2:=P;
      3:S3:=P
    END; (* OF CASE STATEMENT *)
    END;
(* SLOW DOWN  AND STOP FIRST SLOT *)
  INTERVAL:=0;
  REPEAT
    FOR TIMES:=0 TO INTERVAL DO
      BEGIN
      DRAW(S1,S2,S3);
      S2:=S2+1;
      IF S2>43 THEN S2:=34;
      S3:=S3+1;
      IF S3>43 THEN S3:=34
      END;
```

200

```
      S1:=S1+1;
      IF S1>43 THEN S1:=34;
      INTERVAL:=INTERVAL+2
   UNTIL  INTERVAL>10;
(* SLOW DOWN  AND STOP SECOND SLOT *)
   INTERVAL:=0;
   REPEAT
     FOR TIMES:=0 TO INTERVAL DO
      BEGIN
      DRAW(S1,S2,S3);
      S3:=S3+1;
      IF S3>43 THEN S3:=34;
      END;
    S2:=S2+1;
    IF S2>43 THEN S2:=34;
    INTERVAL:=INTERVAL+2
   UNTIL INTERVAL>10;
(* SLOW DOWN AND STOP THIRD SLOT *)
   INTERVAL:=0;
   REPEAT
     FOR TIMES:=0 TO INTERVAL
       DO DRAW(S1,S2,S3);
     S3:=S3+1;
     IF S3>43 THEN S3:=34;
     INTERVAL:=INTERVAL+2
   UNTIL INTERVAL>10;
(* INVITATION TO PLAY AGAIN *)
   WRITE(28,30,'DONE ... ENTER TO  PLAY AGAIN');
   READ(TIMES);
   WRITE(28,30);
UNTIL TIMES<>13
END.
```

DRAW and SLOTDRAW Procedures

The program can be divided into three basic parts: the main-line program, procedure SLOTDRAW and procedure DRAW. The mainline program takes care of every operation except those requiring some drawing activity on the screen. The procedures take care of that task.

The SLOTDRAW procedure, the first one listed in the program, merely draws the outline of the slots. Notice the use of PLOT graphics in this case. The idea is quite similar to the one used for drawing the outline of the dice in the GRAPHIC DICE ROLL game described in an earlier section of this chapter.

The DRAW procedure appears directly after the SLOTDRAW listing. DRAW is responsible for generating the 4×4 patterns of ASCII characters within the three slot outlines. In this case, though, PLOT graphics isn't fast enough to achieve a rapid spinning effect. PLOT graphics is good enough for drawing out the slot outlines, but it is far too slow for simulating slot patterns as they spin, slow down and eventually come to a halt on the screen.

So if you look at the DRAW procedure, you will see it uses Pascal MEM graphics. The graphic charters are dumped directly into the TRS-80 video memory, and there is no time wasted going through a lot of internal conversion operations. The need for high speed graphics dictates the use of the MEM graphics procedures in this program.

You have to understand TRS-80 SET and POKE graphics in order to understand the workings of the SLOTDRAW and DRAW procedures. Indeed, if you do understand TRS-80 graphics, you won't have much trouble understanding these Pascal procedures. On the other hand, if you don't understand TRS-80 graphics, you would have trouble following any discussion that might be presented here. So it's up to you to work out the ways the DRAW and SLOTDRAW procedures work.

Win Select Phase Flow Chart

The mainline program is flow charted in Figs. 11-13 and 11-14. The operation of particular importance in this mainline program is the way in which the slot patterns slow down and stop, one at a time and from left to right. The remaining operations ought to seem somewhat familiar. They have appeared in earlier programs.

Figure 11-13 blocks out the opening phase of the game. It begins, as usual, by declaring the variables for the mainline program. Then it calls SLOTDRAW to draw the outline of the slots.

The next step is to select the seed value for the program's pseudo-random number generator. This is another of those INKEY-interrupted counting operations that ultimately ends with a number somewhere between 99 and 999. See the operations in the program that directly follow the comment, PICK UP SEED NUMBER FOR RANDOM GENERATOR.

The SLOT MACHINE program requires three random numbers between 34 and 43. Looking at the flow chart in Fig. 11-13, you can see this operation beginning and PHASE:1 and ending when the conditional, *PHASE greater than 3*, is satisfied.

The three successive PHASE conditional and PHASE counting operations simply pick the three random numbers, one at a time, and assign them to variables S1, S2 and S3, in that order. Those three S variables turn out to be the ASCII number codes for the patterns to appear on the slots.

As in the case of the ROULETTE WHEEL game described earlier in this chapter, the spinning action of the three slots *begins* at a random number, and then cycles through a prescribed number

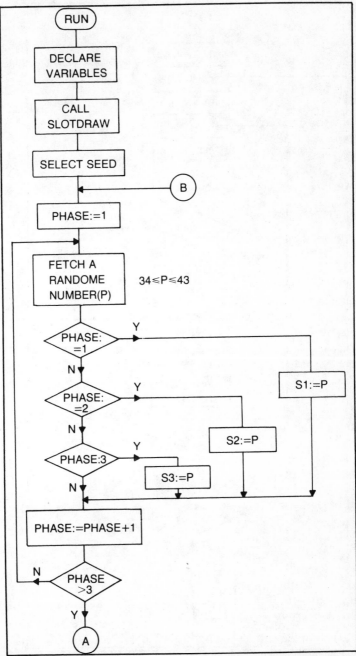

Fig. 11-13. Flow chart for the win select phase of the SLOT MACHINE GAME.

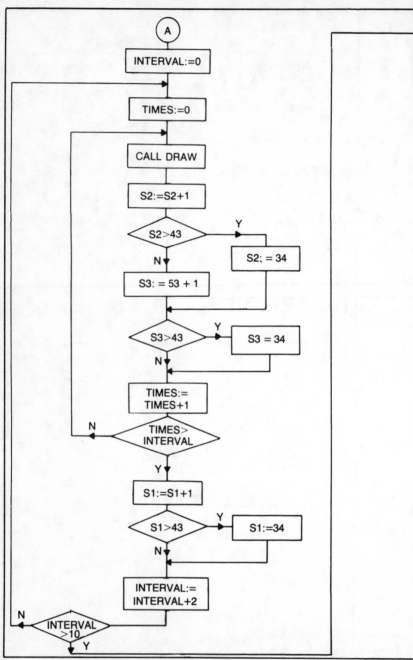

Fig. 11-14. Flow chart for the spin phase of the SLOT MACHINE GAME.

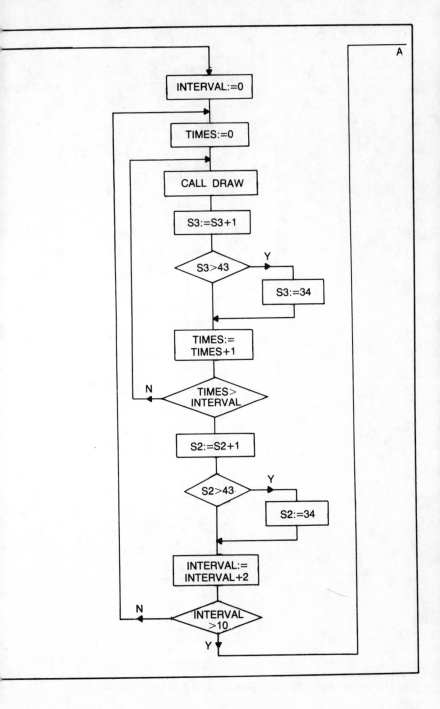

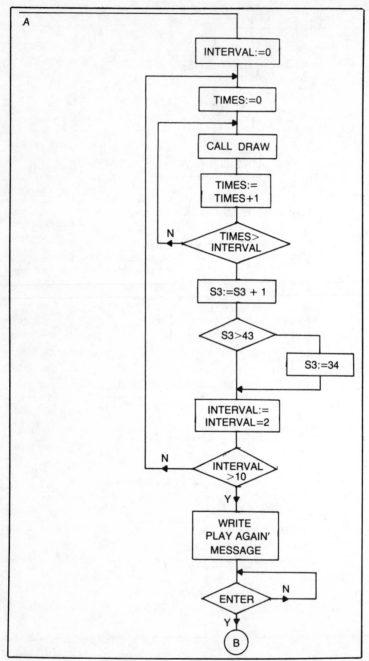

Fig. 11-14. Flow chart for the spin phase of the SLOT MACHINE GAME.

of counts. That, you recall, is a lot easier than trying to get the spinning action to stop at some random number.

By the time the operations reach the end of the flow chart in Fig. 11-13, the program has drawn the outline of the three slots on the screen and picked random starting numbers for the slot action. The latter is carried by variables S1, S2 and S3.

Spin Phase Flow Chart

Most of the operations flow charted in Fig. 11-14 represent these involved in slowing down and stopping the graphic impressions in the slot figures. The chart might appear to be very complicated at first, but it is really a set of operations that are repeated until the spinning action is done.

The slow-down-and-stop action is achieved in a fashion that is quite different from that of the ROULETTE WHEEL. Rather than injecting an increasingly long time delay into the display action of the slot that is slowing down, this scheme sets up an increasingly large ratio between the number of times the slot counters are incremented.

For example, the instant the first slot is to begin slowing down its rate of change, it is changing just as frequently as the other two. But then the second and third slots are incremented twice before the first one is. The second and third are incremented four times before the third one changes, and so on, until the two "fast" slots are changing 10 times faster than the one that is supposed to stop.

After the spinning action for the first slot is over, the counting for the middle slot begins taking place less often than that of the last slot. The first slot is supposed to be stopped now, so its count isn't changing at all.

Eventually the counting rate ratio between the second and third slot reaches such a large number that the second or middle slot stops. The first and middle figures remain stationary while the third slot slows to a stop. This is a reliable little trick that creates a rather convincing impression of a slot machine action.

Throughout the flow chart in Fig. 11-13, variable INTERVAL determines how many times the slowing-down counter will cycle before it stops. Note that there are three blocks labeled INTERVAL:=0. Each of them marks the beginning of a slow-down-and-stop operation.

Variable TIMES sets the counting ratio between the slot that is supposed to slow down and the slot(s) that are to remain running at full speed. The operation CALL DRAW is inserted into the counting loops for the three phases of the spinning action. DRAW is the procedure responsible for printing the ASCII character pattern inside the slot figures. Since the figures on the screen have to be updated with every count of the fast counters, it figures that the operation should take place with every count. A lot of the operations in Fig. 11-14 merely lock the counting range of variables S1, S2 and S3 between 34 and 43, the ASCII codes for the slot machine patterns.

Now that you know what the variables are for, you should be able to follow the flow chart fairly well. Note that all three S variables are included in the first counting loop, but that variable S1 is missing from the second and third counting loop. Why is S1 missing from those two counting loops? It isn't supposed to change its value once it comes to a stop. Likewise, variable S2 is present in the first and second counting loops, but not the third.

Finally, the third counting loop involves only the S3 variable. You can see these three counting cycles programmed as SLOW-DOWN AND STOP FIRST SLOT, SLOW DOWN AND STOP SECOND SLOT and SLOW DOWN AND STOP THIRD SLOT in the mainline program.

Returning to Fig. 11-14, the play ends with a message, DONE . . . ENTER TO PLAY AGAIN. The player can "pull the arm" again by striking the ENTER key. That action satisfies the ENTER conditional and sends control back to point B, the PHASE:=1 operation, in Fig. 11-13. There the program picks up a new set of random numbers for the S counters.

Chapter 12
Some Computer
Graphics In A Pascal Format

Judging from the title of the previous chapter, one would conclude that it dealt with a variety of games of chance. And indeed it did. But perhaps you noticed the strong emphasis on flow chart analysis of the programs. That chapter emphasized the programs' operations from a flow chart perspective, and the Pascal structure seemed to be set into the background.

Now this chapter deals with computer graphics. Here, again, it will live up to its promise. However, the emphasis will be upon Pascal structures, how they develop and how they can be modified.

A LINE SKETCHING PROGRAM

TRS-80 Tiny Pascal lends itself quite nicely to a computerized version of the popular Etch-A-Sketch™ toy. Here the drawing of straight line segments is controlled by striking the appropriate keys on the keyboard: *D* for a downward step, *U* for an upward step, *L* for a left step and *R* for a right step. The whole thing adds up to a nice pastime, especially for youngsters.

Here is the program for the first version:

```
(* SKETCH V.1 *)
VAR X,Y,ERROR,EXIT,MOVE:INTEGER;
BEGIN
WRITE(28,31);
WRITE('ENTER UP, DOWN, LEFT, RIGHT OR END');
Y:=3;X:=0;
PLOT(X,Y,1);
REPEAT
  REPEAT
    ERROR:=0;EXIT:=0;
```

```
      REPEAT
        MOVE:=INKEY
      UNTIL MOVE<>0;
      CASE MOVE OF
        'U':IF Y>3 THEN Y:=Y-1;
        'D':IF Y<47 THEN Y:=Y+1;
        'L':IF X>0 THEN X:=X-1;
        'R':IF X<127 THEN X:=X+1;
        'E':EXIT:=1
        ELSE ERROR:=1
      END; (* OF CASE STATEMENT *)
    UNTIL NOT ERROR;
    PLOT(X,Y,1)
  UNTIL EXIT
END.
```

Enter, compile and run SKETCH V.1. Play with it and make a mental note of any shortcomings you might find. You will have a chance to correct some of the program's annoying characteristics later in this section.

Structure

Take special note of the Pascal structure in this program. It begins by declaring the variables and then goes to a block that starts with BEGIN and terminates at END. With the exception of the opening remark and declaration lines, the entire program is enclosed within that one big block. This scheme can be represented this way:

> REMARK
> DECLARATION
> BLOCK.

The clock, itself, is divided into a number of first-order statements. The first-order statements within the block look like this:

> WRITE expression;
> WRITE expression;
> ASSIGNMENT; ASSIGNMENT;
> PLOT expression;
> REPEAT
>   statements
> UNTIL EXIT

In all, there are only six statements of the first order. Remember that REPEAT ... UNTIL is just one statement. The rest of the program is written within that one first-order REPEAT ... UNTIL statement.

Technically speaking, there are only two statements within the first-order REPEAT...UNTIL. They are:

```
REPEAT
    statements
UNTIL NOT ERROR;
PLOT(X,Y,1)
```

For our present purposes, these are the program's second-order statements. They are the two highest-order statements within the first-order REPEAT...UNTIL statement. Putting things together as described so far, the Pascal structure of SKETCH V.1 looks like this:

```
REMARK
VARIABLE DECLARATION
BEGIN
WRITE expression;
WRITE expression;
ASSIGNMENT; ASSIGNMENT;
PLOT expression;
REPEAT
    REPEAT
        statements
    UNTIL NOT ERROR;
    PLOT expression
UNTIL EXIT
END.
```

The indented lines represent the second-order statements of this program.

The second-order REPEAT...UNTIL statement is composed of statements of the third order:

```
ASSIGNMENT;ASSIGNMENT;
REPEAT
    statement
UNTIL MOVE Ø;
CASE MOVE OF
    case statements
END;
```

That figures out to a total of four third-order statements. Like REPEAT...UNTIL, CASE...OF...END makes up just one statement.

Now the third-order REPEAT...UNTIL statement is made up of just one fourth-order statement, MOVE:=INKEY. And there are five case statements. That accounts for the entire SKETCH V.1 program.

Indentation Scheme

While indentations are used throughout this book to separate the different orders of statements, such a procedure is not necessary as far as the computer is concerned. The indentations make it easier to pick out the different orders and see the Pascal structure more clearly.

Without using the indentation scheme, a programmer runs the risk of losing sight of which UNTIL goes with which REPEAT. Likewise, there can be some trouble matching up ENDs and BEGINs.

But the advantages of using the indentation scheme to clarify the orders of Pascal statements is perhaps no better realized than when it is time to modify a finished program. To see how this works out, let's modify the SKETCH V.1 program.

Blinking Routine

One of the shortcomings of the program is that the user cannot see where the "blip" is whenever it is laying on a previously drawn line segment. The "blip" is white, and so is any line segment it might be tracing over. The simplest and perhaps most effective way to cure this particular difficulty is by having the "blip" blink off and on.

Writing a blinking routine isn't difficult. It is just a matter of writing a PLOT(X, Y, $\emptyset$) ... PLOT(X, Y, 1) sequence somewhere in the program. PLOT(X, Y, $\emptyset$) effectively turns off the blip, while PLOT(X, Y, 1) turns it on again. The only question concerns where to insert that sequence in the program.

It turns out that most of the program's execution time is spent looping around the third-order statement, REPEAT ... UNTIL MOVE<>$\emptyset$. So why not include the two PLOT statements within that REPEAT ... UNTIL loop?

Put your system into the EDIT mode, and insert the off/on PLOT statements to make the REPEAT ... UNTIL look like this:

```
REPEAT
  PLOT(X,Y,∅);
  MOVE:=INKEY;
  PLOT(X,Y,1)
UNTIL MOVE<>∅;
```

That adds two more fourth-order statements to the program. Allowing the original MOVE:=INKEY to fall between the two new PLOT statements provides some time delay between turning the blip off and on.

Compile the program again and try it out for yourself. You will find a vast improvement in the ease of drawing lines on the screen.

There is yet another desirable sort of modification, giving the operator a chance to erase previously drawn line segments and skip over parts of the screen without leaving a white trail behind. Properly handled, the erasing and skipping modifications amount to one and the same thing. The modification, however, is far more extensive than adding the blinking effect.

The basic idea is to give the operator the option of operating the sketching program in one of two different modes: a PLOT mode and an X-OUT mode. In the PLOT mode, the thing works just as before, plotting a line wherever the blip is directed. In the new X-OUT mode, however, the blip effectively erases anything in its path. That includes previously drawn line segments as well as portions of the screen that are already blank.

The little blip still blinks off and on in either mode. You can still see where it is, even in the X-OUT mode.

SKETCH V.2 Program

The following revised version of SKETCH can be created by doing some EDIT surgery on the existing version. Here is what the new version, SKETCH V.2, should look like when the modifications are completed:

```
(* SKETCH V.2 *)
VAR X,Y,ERROR,EXIT,MOVE,BLANK:INTEGER;
BEGIN
WRITE(28,31);
WRITE('ENTER UP,DOWN,LEFT,RIGHT,X-OUT,PLOT OR END');
Y:=3;X:=0;BLANK:=0;
REPEAT
  REPEAT
    ERROR:=0;EXIT:=0;
    REPEAT
      IF BLANK THEN PLOT(X,Y,1)
        ELSE PLOT(X,Y,0);
      MOVE:=INKEY;
      IF BLANK THEN PLOT(X,Y,0)
        ELSE PLOT(X,Y,1)
    UNTIL MOVE<>0;
    CASE MOVE OF
      'U':IF Y>3 THEN Y:=Y-1;
      'D':IF Y<47 THEN Y:=Y+1;
      'L':IF X>0 THEN X:=X-1;
```

```
        'R':IF X<127 THEN X:=X+1;
        'E':EXIT:=1;
        'X':BLANK:=1;
        'P':BLANK:=0
        ELSE ERROR:=1
    END;
  UNTIL NOT ERROR;
  IF BLANK THEN PLOT(X,Y,0)
    ELSE PLOT(X,Y,1)
UNTIL EXIT
END.
```

Now the mode of operation, PLOT or X-OUT, is signaled by the value of a new variable, BLANK. The program is in the PLOT mode whenever BLANK = 0. It is in the X-OUT mode whenever BLANK=1. So the first modifications involve adding BLANK to the variable declaration line, and initializing BLANK at 0 before starting the first-order REPEAT...UNTIL loop. Initializing the BLANK in this fashion automatically puts the program into the PLOT mode when the program is first started. That's not necessary, but it's nice.

Statement Analysis

Looking at the third-order statements, the CASE statement must have provisions for accepting the PLOT and X-OUT characters from the keyboard, So the X and P cases are added. Striking the X key sets BLANK to 1, and striking the P key returns it to zero.

Another third-order statement is affected by the mode of operation. The case in point is the PLOT statement that concludes the first-order REPEAT...UNTIL statement. Instead of always plotting a point with PLOT(X,Y,1) the statement must erase the point with a PLOT(X,Y,0) when the program is in the X-OUT mode. What was originally a simple PLOT statement now becomes a conditional statement. IF BLANK (=1 is implied), THEN PLOT(X,Y,0) ELSE (BLANK=0 is implied) PLOT(X,Y,1).

Buried in the program at the fourth order is the blip blinking feature. In the original version (modified to include the blinking effect), the off-first-then-on-again sequence was appropriate. And it is still appropriate whenever the system is in the PLOT mode. But in the X-OUT mode, the blinking sequence must be reversed. Otherwise, the blip will leave behind a spot of light in both modes, thus defeating the purpose of the entire modification. So the blink PLOT statements are written as conditional statements that depend on whether the system is in the PLOT or X-OUT mode.

While these modifications have been done for you here, you can perhaps see how difficult the job would have been if the programmer had no understanding of Pascal structures. Using the indentation scheme to separate the different orders of statements helped considerably.

The modifications did not alter the general structure of the original SKETCH program. All the first-order statements remained first-order statements, second orders remained second orders, etc. Indeed the modifications for creating the second version of SKETCH introduced more statements, but there were no changes in the orders of statements. The program is fundamentally the same.

So the program, SKETCH V.2, lets you sketch all sorts of interesting figures on the screen. When it comes to designing computer games, wouldn't it be nice if you could transfer the figure created via the SKETCH V.2 to a game program? Suppose, for example, you want to write a program for some sort of space wars game. You need some complex figures to do the job in the most interesting fashion. You can create interesting figures with SKETCH V.2, but it isn't always easy to come up with the program steps for drawing such figures for other purposes.

SKETCH V.3 Program

The following program, SKETCH V.3, modifies the basic SKETCH idea so that you can determine the plotting points for every line segment in the figure. You can draw a figure as with SKETCH V.2, use the new figure to determine the coordinates of every point in the figure, and then use those coordinates for recreating the same figure within another program.

Unfortunately it takes a great deal of sophisticated programming to create a figure with the SKETCH program, and then transfer it automatically to another program that will use the figure. By way of a compromise, the scheme suggested here makes it necessary for you to write down the coordinates of the plots. Re-enter them when you are writing the new program. Maybe that sounds like too much work, but then so does trying to create a complex figure from nothing more than abstract PLOT coordinates.

The SKETCH V.3 program is essentially identical to SKETCH V.2 right down to the point where you do an END command. Using SKETCH V.2, striking the E key simply brings the program to an end. But when using the SKETCH V.3 version, striking the E key begins the copy phase of the job.

In that copy phase, the program scans the screen horizontally, from left to right. Then it drops down one and scans it from left to right. The scanning operation stops, however, whenever the point being scanned happens to be a line segment which you "drew" on the screen during the drawing phase of the program. Whenever the program stops at such a segment, it writes out the PLOT coordinates for you. Then you can copy down the coordinates and strike the ENTER key to continue the scanning operation. The program comes to an end after it has scanned the entire screen for you.

Now you have a written record of the PLOT coordinates for the figure. They can be entered into a game program at any later time.

```
(* SKETCH V.3 *)
VAR X,Y,ERROR,EXIT,MOVE,BLANK:INTEGER;
BEGIN
WRITE(28,31);
WRITE('ENTER UP,DOWN,LEFT,RIGHT,X-OUT,PLOT OR END');
Y:=3;X:=0;BLANK:=0;
REPEAT
  REPEAT
    ERROR:=0;EXIT:=0;
    REPEAT
      IF BLANK THEN PLOT(X,Y,1)
        ELSE PLOT(X,Y,0);
      MOVE:=INKEY;
      IF BLANK THEN PLOT(X,Y,0)
        ELSE PLOT(X,Y,1)
    UNTIL MOVE<>0;
    CASE MOVE OF
      'U':IF Y>3 THEN Y:=Y-1;
      'D':IF Y<47 THEN Y:=Y+1;
      'L':IF X>0 THEN X:=X-1;
      'R':IF X<127 THEN X:=X+1;
      'E':EXIT:=1;
      'X':BLANK:=1;
      'P':BLANK:=0
      ELSE ERROR:=1
    END;
  UNTIL NOT ERROR;
  IF BLANK THEN PLOT(X,Y,0)
    ELSE PLOT(X,Y,1)
UNTIL EXIT;
WRITE(28,30,'COPY PHASE -- ENTER TO START');
WHILE INKEY<>13 DO;
FOR Y:=3 TO 47 DO
  FOR X:=0 TO 127 DO
    IF POINT(X,Y) THEN
      BEGIN
      WRITE(28,30,X#,',',Y#,32,32,'ENTER TO CONTINUE');
      REPEAT
        PLOT(X,Y,0);
        MOVE:=INKEY;
```

```
        PLOT(X,Y,1)
      UNTIL  MOVE=13
      END;
WRITE(28,30,'DONE')
END.
```

COPY PHASE Operation

You can see from the listing for SKETCH V.3 that it is identical to SKETCH V.2 down to the line following UNTIL EXIT. Version 2 ends after that, but version 3 enters the COPY PHASE of the program.

As far as the COPY PHASE of SKETCH V.3 is concerned, it is a 4-statement operation. From a structural point of view, it is built around these first-order statements:

WRITE expression
WHILE expression DO;
FOR expression TO expression DO
    statements
WRITE expression

After that, the entire program comes to an END.

The first-order FOR. . . TO. . .DO statement is made up of a single second-order statement, a FOR expression TO expression DO. That one second-order statement encompasses a single, third-order IF expression THEN statement. Finally, the IF. . .THEN statement includes a BEGIN. . .END statement made up of three fourth-order statements and a set of three fifth-order statements.

Statements within statements within statements within statements is what Pascal structure is all about. Get accustomed to Pascal structure, and you're on your way to being an effective Pascal programmer.

MISSILE SHOOT GAME

Here is a program for video game buffs. A sequence of 10 enemy ballistic missiles invades your air space. It is your responsibility to shoot them down with your own antiballistic missile. Except for the scoring and instruction messages, the game is entirely one of animated graphics.

Figure 12-1 shows how the screen might look during a game of MISSILE SHOOT. The missile near the top of the screen is flying from left to right. That is the enemy missile.

The little missile figure at the bottom of the screen is your own antiballistic missile. You fire it by striking the ENTER key. If you "lead" the enemy missile properly, you will hit and destroy it, and rack up a point in the SCORE column.

The tricky part of the game is that the altitude and speed of the enemy missile are never known in advance. They simply appear at the left side of the screen. Some come in at low altitudes and some approach at high altitudes. There is no correspondence between the speed and altitude of the enemy missile.

The speed of your antiballistic missile is always the same, and that is a feature in the player's favor. Actually, that's about the only thing in the player's favor. Even the timing between the approach of new enemy missiles varies.

This is a comparatively complex game program. The compiled version, if you write it exactly as shown here, occupies something on the order of 1300 bytes of memory. It isn't the length of the program that is of primary importance at this point in the discussion. Aside from being an unusually long Pascal program it uses some rather involved Pascal structures. You are going to find a great deal of space in this section devoted to analyzing the structural peculiarities of this program. It's important, believe me.

The first thing you should do, however, is enter the program into your computer and play with it for a while. That experience will give you some advantages when it comes to analyzing how the structure works.

The structure for a program of this size has little meaning, however, until you understand all the little processes involved. So

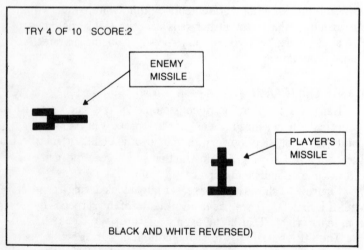

Fig. 12-1. Screen format for MISSILE SHOOT game.

the second step in our analysis project is to break the program down in a flow chart fashion.

Finally, you will have a chance to see the Pascal structuring. If that isn't enough to keep you busy for a while, you can then get involved in modifying the program to make it work even better. You migth add some features that will heighten the excitement of playing with it.

Program

Here is the program for the first version of MISSILE SHOOT:

```
(* MISSILE SHOOT V.1 *)
VAR MSTART,MSPEED,N,SCORE,TRY,GDELAY,APLACE,MPLACE:
  INTEGER;
    FFLAG,MDELAY,FIRE,MDONE,AMISS,HIT,MTRY,AGAIN,SEED:
      INTEGER;
FUNC RND(RLOW,RHIGH);
  VAR M,P:INTEGER;
  BEGIN
  REPEAT
    M:=N*3125;
    IF M<0 THEN M:=ABS(M);
    N:=M;P:=M;
    P:=P MOD RHIGH
  UNTIL (P>=RLOW) AND (P<=RHIGH);
  RND:=P
  END;   (* OF FUNCTION *)
FUNC SEED;
  VAR SEED:INTEGER;
  BEGIN
  SEED:=SEED+1;
  IF SEED>999 THEN SEED:=99
  END;   (* OF FUNCTION *)
PROC MFIG(MPLACE,PHASE);
  VAR MX:INTEGER;
  BEGIN
  IF PHASE=1 THEN
    BEGIN
    MEM(MPLACE):=162;
    MEM(MPLACE+1):=191;
    FOR MX:=2 TO 5 DO
      MEM(MPLACE+MX):=140
    END
  ELSE
    BEGIN
    FOR MX:=0 TO 1 DO
      MEM(MPLACE+MX):=32;
  FOR MX:=2 TO 5 DO
    MEM(MPLACE+MX):=32
    END
  END;   (* OF PROCEDURE *)
PROC AFIG(APLACE,PHASE);
  VAR AY:INTEGER;
  BEGIN
```

```
  IF PHASE=1 THEN
    BEGIN
    MEM(APLACE):=136;
    MEM(APLACE+1):=191;
    MEM(APLACE+2):=132;
    MEM(APLACE+64):=188;
    MEM(APLACE+65):=191;
    MEM(APLACE+66):=188
    END
  ELSE
    BEGIN
    FOR AY:=0 TO 2 DO
      MEM(APLACE+AY):=32;
    FOR AY:=64 TO 66 DO
      MEM(APLACE+AY):=32
    END
END; (* OF PROCEDURE *)
PROC SPEED(DELAY);
  VAR TIME:INTEGER;
  BEGIN
  FOR TIME:=0 TO DELAY DO;
  END;  (* OF  PROCEDURE *)
PROC UPDATE(TRY,SCORE);
  BEGIN
  WRITE(28,30);
  WRITE('TRY ',TRY#,' OF 10          SCORE:' ,SCORE#)
  END;
(* BEGINNING OF MAINLINE PROGRAM *)
BEGIN
N:=SEED;
AGAIN:=0;
WHILE AGAIN<>32 DO
  BEGIN
  WRITE(28,31,215,'** MISSILLE SHOOTING GAME **',13
    ,13);
  WRITE('TEN MISSILES WILL INVADE YOUR AIR SPACE.'
    ,13);
  WRITE('STRIKE THE ENTER KEY TO FIRE YOUR
    ANTIBALLISTIC',13);
  WRITE('MISSILE.',13,13,'DO ENTER TO START THE
    GAME ...');
  WHILE INKEY<>13 DO;
  WRITE(28,31);
  SCORE:=0;
  FOR TRY:=1 TO 10 DO
    BEGIN
    UPDATE(TRY,SCORE);
    MSTART:=15488+64*RND(0,5);
    MPLACE:=MSTART;
    MSPEED:=10*RND(1,5);
    GDELAY:=RND(100,1000);
    APLACE:=16224;
    AFIG(APLACE,1);
    SPEED(GDELAY);
    FFLAG:=0;MDONE:=0;AMISS:=0;HIT:=0;
    REPEAT
      MDELAY:=0;
      REPEAT
        IF NOT FFLAG THEN
```

220

```
            BEGIN
            FIRE:=INKEY;
            IF FIRE=13 THEN
               FFLAG:=1
            END;
         MDELAY:=MDELAY+1
      UNTIL MDELAY>=MSPEED;
      MFIG(MPLACE,0);
      MPLACE:=MPLACE+1;
      IF NOT (MPLACE>=MSTART+57) THEN
         BEGIN
         MFIG(MPLACE,1);
         IF FFLAG THEN
            BEGIN
            AFIG(APLACE,0);
            APLACE:=APLACE-64;
            IF NOT (APLACE<15487) THEN
               BEGIN
               AFIG(APLACE,1);
               FOR MTRY:=1 TO 5 DO
                  IF (MTRY+MPLACE)=APLACE THEN
                     BEGIN
                     HIT:=1;
                     SCORE:=SCORE+1;
                     MFIG(MPLACE,0);
                     AFIG(APLACE,0)
                     END;
               END
            ELSE
               BEGIN
               AMISS:=1;
               MFIG(MPLACE,0);
               END;
         END
      ELSE
         FFLAG:=0;
      END
   ELSE
      BEGIN
      MDONE:=1;
      AFIG(APLACE,0)
      END;
   UNTIL((MDONE=1) OR (AMISS=1) OR (HIT=1));
   UPDATE(TRY,SCORE);
   END;
   WRITE(13,'GAME DONE -- DO ENTER TO PLAY AGAIN');
   WRITE(13,205,'STRIKE THE SPACE BAR TO END THE
      PROGRAM');
   REPEAT
      AGAIN:=INKEY;
      N:=SEED
   UNTIL (AGAIN=13) OR (AGAIN=32);
   END
END.
```

Declaring Mainline Program Values

The first stages of the flow chart and structure analysis of
MISSILE SHOOT V.1 are straightforward. There are a lot of lines

of program information in that opening part of the task. But it doesn't add up to anything significantly different from what has been done before.

The first operation on the flow chart in Fig. 12-2, for instance, is to declare all the variables for the mainline program. Sure, there are quite a few variables. They take up two declaration lines. But variables shouldn't frighten you by now. They are just semi-descriptive names of values that will change from time to time during the execution of the main part of the program.

After declaring the mainline variables, the flow chart indicates some definitions of functions and procedures. As usual, Pascal functions and procedures follow the declaration of mainline variables.

This particular program happens to have two functions and four procedures. Look at the program listing and count them. These functions and procedures take up about one-third of the entire program.

RND Function

The first function defined in the program listing is called RND, and it works from two variables from the mainline program, RLOW and RHIGH. This function should look rather familiar to you. It has been used a number of times earlier in this book, and its job is to generate a quasi-random set of integers between values RLOW and RHIGH. In this MISSILE SHOOT program, the RND function is called a number of times for different purposes. RND, for example, sets the altitude of the enemy attack missile (variable MSTART), the attack missile's speed (variable MSPEED), and the delay interval between successive attacks (variable GDELAY).

SEED Function

You should realize from earlier discussions that the random number generator will tend to duplicate the same sequence of quasi-random numbers unless it is seeded with a number that is generated in a random fashion. That is the purpose of the second function in the program known as SEED.

Function SEED is called from a couple of different places in the mainline program. Each time it is called, it ensures a non-repeating sequence of missile attacks. That scheme keeps the game fair for players who haven't played the game in the past and have no feeling for what is going to happen next.

So there are the two functions for the program. Now look at the first procedure.

MFIG Procedure

Procedure MFIG is responsible for drawing and erasing the attack missile figure on the screen. Its variable from the mainline program are MPLACE and PHASE. MPLACE is a number that sets the position of the enemy missile on the screen, while PHASE is equal to either 1 or 0, depending upon whether the procedure is supposed to draw or erase the figure.

If procedure MFIG(16550, 1) is called from the mainline program, it will draw the enemy missile figure, beginning at graphics point 16550. The viewer gets the impression that the figure is moving from left to right across the screen when the missile figure is first erased from its present position and then redrawn one graphics position to the right. The following sequence of calls illustrates how this works:

```
PLACE:=16550;
MFIG(PLACE, 1);
MFIG(PLACE, 0);
MFIG(PLACE+1, 1);
MFIG(PLACE+1, 0);
MFIG(PLACE+2, 1);
```

That particular sequence of operations first initializes the position of the enemy missile at graphics point 16550, and then it calls the MFIG procedure to draw the figure. Immediately after that, MFIG(PLACE, 0) erases the figure. The sequence then calls for redrawing the figure one place to the left of where it was originally drawn. The same figure is erased after that, and a new version is drawn two places to the left of the original point. The overall effect is a smooth movement of the enemy missile from left to right across the screen. Of course, the sequence continues as long as the figure is to remain moving in that direction.

Notice that procedure MFIG uses MEM graphics as opposed to the slower PLOT graphics. You will have to refer to the table of TRS-80 ASCII graphics in the Appendix if you want to see how the procedure assembles the enemy missile figure.

AFIG, SPEED and UPDATE Procedures

Procedure AFIG draws or erases the image of the player's missile. The basic operation of this procedure is identical to that of

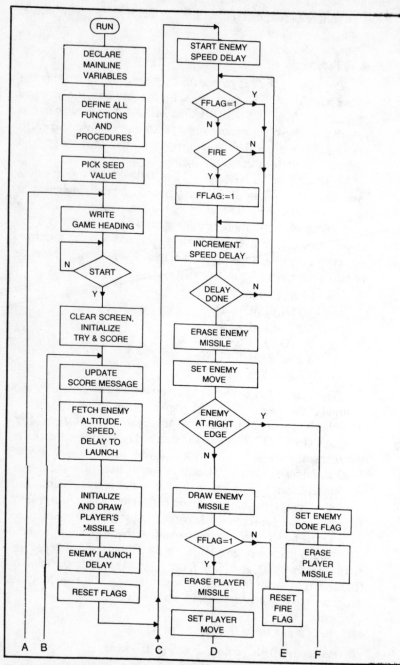

Fig. 12-2. Flow chart for MISSILE SHOOT game.

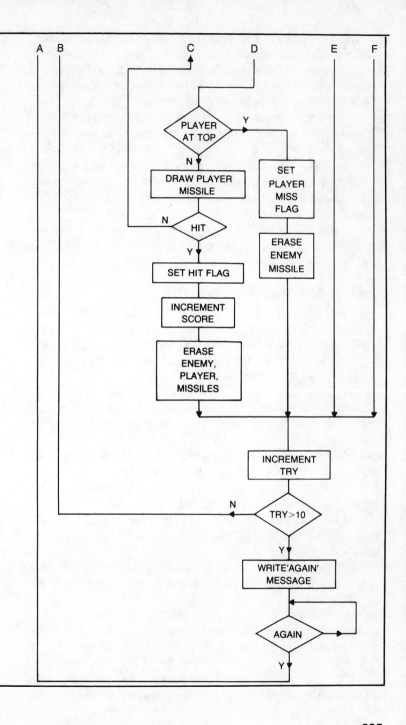

A B C D E F

PLAYER AT TOP

N

DRAW PLAYER MISSILE

N

HIT

Y

SET HIT FLAG

INCREMENT SCORE

ERASE ENEMY, PLAYER, MISSILES

Y

SET PLAYER MISS FLAG

ERASE ENEMY MISSILE

INCREMENT TRY

N

TRY>10

Y

WRITE 'AGAIN' MESSAGE

AGAIN

Y

the MFIG procedure. The figure is drawn a bit differently, however, and the missile moves from bottom to top, rather than from left to right across the screen. Variables APLACE and PHASE for procedure AFIG indicate the current position of the player's missile and whether it should be drawn or erased.

The third procedure in the program listing is called SPEED. This is nothing more than a time delay subroutine that occupies the time necessary for counting variable TIME from 0 to DELAY. Variable DELAY is carried to the SPEED procedure from the mainline program. Variable TIME, however, is used only within this particular procedure, and is not declared in the list of variables for the mainline program.

Procedure UPDATE simply updates the scoring on the screen, generating the figures for writing out the TRY value and SCORE. Now that wasn't too bad, was it?

Beginning Operations

Returning to the flow chart in Fig. 12-2, the next step following the definition of all the functions and procedures is picking the SEED value for the random number generator. That step determines the sequence of enemy missile altitudes, speeds and delays for the entire game program.

The flow chart then calls for writing out the heading messages and waiting for the player to strike the ENTER key to get the game started. Once the game is started, the system clears the screen and initializes the TRY and SCORE variables. TRY is a mainline variable that keeps track of the number of attacks in a game. The game, as shown here, runs for 10 successive attacks, so you will find TRY incrementing from 1 to 10 as the game progresses. The game comes to an end after the tenth TRY.

SCORE, as you might imagine, is the player's score counter. It increments each time the player manages to lob his missile into the attack missile.

All of that gets a particular game started. The remainder of the program controls events for a given attack sequence within the 10-TRY game.

According to the flow chart, the next operation is that of updating the score on the screen. You can find this point in the program listing as the line, UPDATE(TRY, SCORE), two lines below the statement, FOR TRY:=1 TO 10 DO.

The system picks random numbers for the enemy missile's attack altitude, speed and delay. These operations appear in the program listing as a sequence of assignment statements involving MSTART, MPLACE, MSPEED and GDELAY.

The enemy missile is ready for a TRY at this point in the process. First, the system has to draw the player's missile at its initial position at the bottom of the screen. That is done by the assignment sequence, APLACE:=16224 and AFIG(APLACE, 1), in the program listing. The operations appear on the flow chart in Fig. 12-2 as INITIALIZE AND DRAW PLAYER'S MISSILE.

Flag Variables

The next step is to delay the launch of the enemy missile, and that is done by SPEED(GDELAY) in the program. Just before the enemy missile is actually launched, however, it is necessary to reset a group of flags.

The flags in this game are just variables taking on values of 1 or 0, depending upon the events that have transpired during the game. FFLAG, for example, has a value of 0 if the enemy missile has been launched, but the player's missile has not. Once the player's missile is launched, FFLAG is set to a value of 1.

MDONE is another flag variable. This one indicates whether or not the enemy missile has reached the right-hand extreme of its travel across the screen. That variable is at 0 until that criterion is reached. At that time, MDONE is set to 1.

AMISS is a flag variable that indicates whether or not the player's missile has reached the top of the screen. HIT is the last flag in the group, and it signals whether or not a contact has occurred between the two missiles. In both of these instances, a 0 indicates "no" and a 1 indicates "yes."

Everything is ready for an attack at this point. But the sequence of events that follows depends upon whether or not the player's missile has been launched. See the FFLAG=1 conditional in the flow chart.

If the player's missile has not been fired, conditional FFLAG=1 is *not* satisfied, and the player is given a chance to do so by means of the FIRE conditional. If, during that time, the player strikes the ENTER key to fire the missile, the FIRE conditional is satisfied and FFLAG is set to 1. FFLAG then remains at a value of 1 throughout the attack sequence, indicating that the player has indeed launched his missile. Notice that the FIRE conditional is bypassed once FFLAG is set to 1.

Looping Operation

After checking out the status of the player's missile firing opportunity, the system increments the speed delay. If the speed delay is not done, the DELAY DONE conditional is not satisfied, and the flag checking sequence is repeated. The system thus loops around this sequence until the speed delay is done.

The purpose of this particular looping operation is to give the player an opportunity to launch his missile *and* provide a time delay necessary for making the enemy missile move at a reasonably slow pace across the screen. The loop, in other words, actually performs two functions at one time. The animation effect could be seriously degraded if these two operations were performed separately. The INKEY operation for triggering the player's missile requires frequent repetition to be reliable. There is no point in building a separate loop for that INKEY operation when the missile speed control requires the same sort of operation.

So the loop between conditionals FFLAG=1 and DELAY DONE in Fig. 12-2 does double duty. These operations can be found in the program listing as a REPEAT . . . UNTIL loop that begins with the statement, MDELAY:=∅.

Animation Sequence

The next group of operations are responsible for the actual animation effects and picking up the end points of the attack sequence. The animation effects involve moving the enemy missile across the screen by using the MFIG procedure and incrementing its MPLACE value. The player's missile is likewise moved up the screen, provided it has been launched.

The three end points for the repeating animation sequence have been described already: the enemy missile reaching the right-hand extreme of its travel (indicating either a missed shot or none at all), the player's missile reaching the top of the screen (indicating a missed shot), or the two figures colliding (indicating a successful shot on the player's part).

No matter how the sequence turns out, the TRY counter is incremented by the INCREMENT TRY block in Fig. 12-2. If TRY is less than 10, the game loops back to the point where it updates the score and sets up another launching sequence.

But if it happens that TRY is greater than 10, it is time to conclude the game. The system prints out an appropriate message and waits for the player to satisfy the AGAIN conditional by striking the ENTER key. Then the system loops back to the point where it writes the new game heading and waits for another ENTER operation to initialize the TRY and SCORE counters.

If you have made a conscientious effort to understand the Pascal language as you have progressed through this book, you should have little trouble following the first half of the structure in the Pascal program listing for this game. But things might begin looking a bit peculiar at the point where the animation sequence begins.

On the flow chart in Fig. 12-2, the sequence in question begins with the conditional ENEMY AT RIGHT EDGE and ends at INCREMENT TRY. The flow chart looks rather ordinary and, hopefully, you have little trouble following it.

The Pascal listing for this sequence begins with IF NOT (MPLACE>=MSTART+57) THEN and runs down through the statement, UNTIL ((MDONE=1) OR (AMISS=1) OR (HIT=1)). Structurally speaking, the whole animation procedure is one big, fat IF . . . THEN . . . ELSE statement. Translated into terms more consistent with the flow chart, that sequence—the Pascal structure—reads something like this:

```
IF the enemy missile is NOT at the right edge of the screen
THEN   BEGIN
    draw the enemy missile;
    IF the player missile has been launched THEN
        BEGIN
        erase the player missile;
        move the player missile up one line;
        IF the player missile is NOT at the top of the screen THEN
            BEGIN
            draw the player missile figure;
            check to see if there is contact
            IF there is contact THEN
                BEGIN
                set HIT flag to 1;
                increment the SCORE;
                erase the enemy missile figure;
                erase the player missile figure
                END; sequence begun 5 lines above
            END   the sequence begun 10 lines above
        ELSE    alternative to player missile NOT at top
            BEGIN
            set AMISS flag to 1;
            erase enemy missile figure
            END;   the sequence begun 3 lines above
    ELSE    alternative to player missile having been launched
            set FIRE flag to zero
    END   the sequence begun 26 lines above
```

ELSE   alternative to enemy missile NOT at right edge
  BEGIN
  set MDONE flag to 1;
  erase the player missile figure
  END; the sequence begun 3 lines above

You were promised in an earlier chapter that Pascal IF . . .
THEN . . . ELSE statements would prove quite valuable. And here
they are, nested four deep to handle an impressive set of program
operations. To be sure, it is possible to do the same sort of thing
using the IF . . . THEN . . . ELSE statements in BASIC, but BASIC
programmers rarely think in terms of highly structured formats.
Instead, we get off the hook with a lot of GOTO statements that eat
up big doses of time and memory. Tiny Pascal does not include
GOTO statements, so Pascal programmers are forced into the
highly structured and quite efficient form of thinking.

Incidentally, Standard Pascal does include a GOTO statement
that many programmers tend to abuse. In a manner of speaking, it's
fortunate that Chung and Yuen—the originators of Tiny Pascal—
saw fit to leave the GOTO statement out of their version of Pascal.
To catch the essence and elegance of the nested IF . . . THEN
structure demonstrated in this game program, try looking at a more
general example.

FLOW CHART FOR IF . . . THEN . . . ELSE PROGRAMMING

Figure 12-3 is the flow chart for a general sequence of conditionals and operations. It really makes no difference what the
conditionals are testing or what the DO statements are doing. The
important thing here is the structure of the thing. Example 12-1
shows the Pascal structure for such a scheme:

Example 12-1

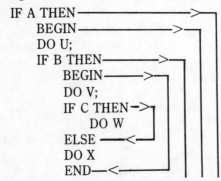

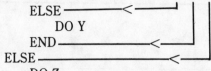

```
ELSE ———————<———┘
    DO Y
END————————<—┐
ELSE ————————————<—┘
    DO Z;
```

The arrows and lines drawn onto the program point out the corresponding elements of the nested statements. Structurally speaking, the program is of the form:

```
IF A THEN
    statement
ELSE
DO Z;
```

That statement, however, takes this form:

```
BEGIN
statement
END
```

So considering just the first- and second-order statements, the program in Example 12-1 looks like:

```
IF A THEN
    BEGIN
    statement
    END
    ELSE
    DO Z;
```

Now the statement in that version takes the general form:

```
DO U;
IF BE THEN
    statement
ELSE
    DO Y
```

Merging that with what has been done thus far:

```
IF A THEN
    BEGIN
    DO U;
    IF B THEN
    statement
    ELSE
    DO Y
    END
ELSE
    DO Z;
```

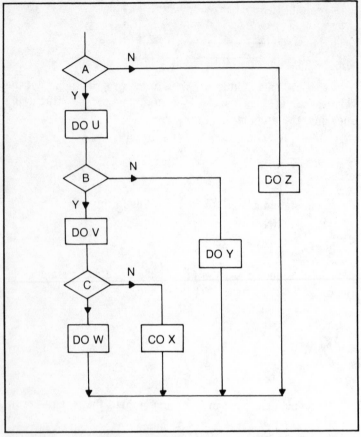

Fig. 12-3. Flow chart for a general nested, IF...THEN...ELSE programming situation.

If you are following the evolution of this pattern, you might suspect that the statement in this instance takes the form:

```
BEGIN
DO V;
    IF C THEN
        DO W
    ELSE
        DO X
```

Fit that segment into the evolutionary scheme, and you end up with the program as it appears in Example 12-1.

The nested IF . . . THEN . . . ELSE statements in the MISSILE SHOOT game follow the same general pattern. Some of the operations within the statements are a bit more involved, but that does not alter the fact that Pascal programs are, indeed, built around nested statements.

THE ULTIMATE IN GRAPHICS: REAL-TIME ANIMATION

It is one thing to draw a picture of some sort on the CRT screen. But it is quite something else to make that picture behave in a complex, animated fashion.

Computer animation works on the same principle as animated films. The basic idea is to show a series of still pictures in a sequence that is rapid enough to fool the eye into thinking the pictures are moving.

The real problem with computer animation is not the nature of the programs, themselves, but the magnitude of the programming task. This section offers a simple 4-frame animation sequence as an example. In principle, there is nothing at all tricky about the process. At the risk of being overly repetitive, I must say there is a lot of work involved in getting the sequence running on the screen.

There can be little room for argument about the fact that real-time animation must be carried out using MEM graphics. PLOT graphics is far too slow on the TRS-80 to allow the rapid sequencing of complicated pictures. The pictures must be drawn directly into the system's video memory.

Where do the "pictures" come from? The pictures must be built up, one element at a time, according to the TRS-80 graphics code listed in the Appendix. These elements have to be carefully selected and then worked into a program as part of a MEM statement.

Recall that a Tiny Pascal MEM statement takes the general form, MEM(expression):=expression. In the context of MEM graphics, this statement takes the special form, MEM(address):=graphic code, where *address* is the position of the element on the screen and *graphic code* is the ASCII code number for the element.

The allowable range of addresses for MEM graphics is between decimal 15360 and 16383. Do any MEM operations outside that range, and you run the risk of destroying your own program, the Tiny Pascal program, or both.

If you want to try some graphics to get a feeling for the idea, try Example 12-2.

Example 12-2

```
(* SEE GRAPHICS *)
VAR N: INTEGER;
```

```
BEGIN
WRITE (28, 31);
FOR N:=15360 TO 15422 DO
    MEM(N) :=N-15231
END;
```

That will print out the TRS-80 graphics. The screen addresses run between 15360 (upper left-hand corner) and 15422 (almost to the end of the second line). If you work through the math in that example, you will find that the graphics codes run between 129 and 191, the entire family of graphic elements listed in the Appendix.

Planning the Frames

The first step in preparing a real-time animation sequence is to plan the frames. A helpful tool in this case is Radio Shack's TRS-80 Video Display Worksheet. Pads of these worksheets are available through any Radio Shack store that handles TRS-80 equipment and supplies.

The handy feature of these worksheets is the way they draw out the six segments for each character space. You will have to work out the MEM addressing on those sheets for yourself, however. At the time of this writing, Radio Shack isn't including video address coordinates on the worksheets. The TAB, PRINT and PLOT coordinates are there, but the POKE/PEEK coordinates — (BASIC's counterpart of Pascal's MEM) are not.

Sketch the figure for the first frame on the worksheet, being careful to follow the character-segment lines. You will have to compromise on the resolution at times, showing some jagged lines where you would rather have smooth ones, but the overall resolution isn't bad. At least the resolution is good enough for doing some fantastic graphics.

Translation Into TRS-80 Graphic Code Numbers

So sketch out the figure, and fill in the dark areas of the screen. When you're done with this part of the job, you will have a good idea of what graphic elements you will need to produce the desired image. Now here comes a time-consuming part that calls for your full attention, translating the drawn graphic elements into TRS-80 graphic code numbers.

You can write the program so that it draws the picture elements in any order you want. There is no reason why one drawing pattern would be better than any other. As long as you have a choice, you might as well be systematic about it. The more sys-

234

tematic you are at this point, the less chance you have of making errors.

So list the graphics code numbers as they would appear as the picture is scanned from left to right, and from top to bottom. List the first horizontal line of codes from left to right, proceeded to the next line down, and list the codes for that line.

Scanning the picture in that particular fashion won't make it any easier for the system to draw it. The computer can build MEM images with the elements presented in any order. The advantage is that the systematic scanning lets you double check or troubleshoot your listing much easier. It makes it easier to locate an element you might want to change.

Starting Address

Once you have the orderly listing of graphics codes, pick a starting address and assign it to the first element to be drawn. If you decided to follow the scanning scheme I have just suggested, that first address will represent the position of the picture element in the upper left-hand corner of the image.

The next picture element to the right will then have the starting address, plus 1. The next element ought to take the starting address plus 2, and so on, to the end of the first line.

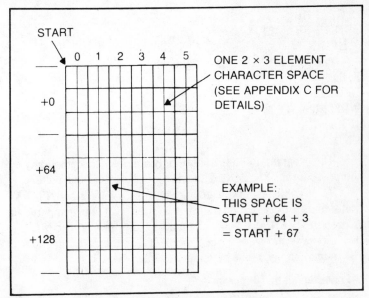

Fig. 12-4. Example of field drawing an animation figure.

Begin the second line by adding 64 to the starting address. There are 64 graphics elements in each line on the screen. So adding 64 to any of the addresses sets up the system for drawing a new element directly below the old one.

The second element in the second line thus has an address equal to the starting address plus 65. The third element's address is the starting address plus 66, and so on through the end of the second line.

The third line begins at the starting address plus 128, and the left-to-right scanning is achieved by incrementing that number. See the drawing in Fig. 12-4.

Once you have the listing of addresses and element codes, you can assign them to a series of MEM statements, perhaps a rather long series. In the worst case, there will be a MEM statement for every element in the picture.

MEM Statements Program

At any rate, you can assign a procedure name to the picture, and enter it into your computer. Suppose, for instance, you name the procedure 1FRAME. You can then check it on the computer by writing procedure 1FRAME and all your MEM statements into a program. This sort of program will do the job:

Example 12-3

```
(* GRAPHICS *)
PROC 1 FRAME;
   BEGIN
      (all your MEM statements here)
END;
BEGIN
WRITE(28,31);
1FRAME
END.
```

The program, itself is exceedingly simple. The complexity of the procedure, 1FRAME, depends on the size of your picture.

Then go through the same process to develop a set of MEM statements for the second frame, and enter it into the computer as procedure 1FRAME. You can then test the new procedure as a separate program, or you can combine it with the first frame to see the animation sequence beginning to take shape.

2-Frame Animation Program

Here is a little 2-frame animation program:

Example 12-4

```
(* GRAPHICS *)
VAR DELAY;INTEGER;
PROC 1FRAME;
  BEGIN
      (MEM statements for frame 1 here)
END;
PROC 2FRAME;
  BEGIN
      (MEM statement for frame 2 here)

END;
BEGIN   REPEAT
WRITE(28,31);
1FRAME
FOR DELAY:=0 TO 100 DO;
WRITE(28,31);
2FRAME;
FOR DELAY:=0 TO 100 DO
UNTIL DELAY<>DELAY
END.
```

The program displays the two frames, one at a time and in an unending sequence. A delay interval inserted after drawing each frame slows down the action to a reasonable rate. You can slow the rate even more by increasing the delay interval.

Now suppose the idea is to build a 2-frame sequence of a figure running across the screen. The two frames, themselves, show the figure in two basic running positions. As the program is shown in Example 12-4, the figure won't make any progress across the screen. The animation will take place in just one spot.

To give the figure some motion across the screen—in addition to the animation—simply increment the value of the starting address. Run a frame, clear the screen, increment the starting address, and draw the second frame. That would make the figure move from left to right across the screen.

Decrementing the starting address for the frames makes the figure move to the left. Incrementing in steps of 64 makes the figure move downward. Decrementing the starting address by 64 makes it move upward.

Be careful when planning these address changing programs. You certainly don't want the figure (or any part of it) to wander outside the video memory space.

Before taking a look at a specific example of some real-time animation, consider this important point. There will be times when you don't want to clear the entire screen between successive animation frames. Perhaps you are running two animated figures at the same time, and you don't want to erase both images at the same time.

The way around that little problem is to write an erasing procedure for each figure. The erasing procedure would do a MEM(addresses):=32 through the area covered by the image. Write a FOR...TO...DO loop to cycle the *addresses* through the frame area, and let the code 32 erase the character spaces as it goes along.

In a sense, this is pinpoint erasing. It saves any other images that might be on the screen at the same time.

Figures 12-5 through 12-8 show four frames for an animation sequence. The sequence in this case represents the figure of a little girl who can both run and jump. Ultimately, the program will show the girl running across the screen, occasionally hopping up into the air. You will see variable GPLACE as the starting address and all of the graphics codes written in a systematic manner below each of the frames.

Frame 1 Program

Here is a program for displaying Frame 1 Fig. 12-5 on the screen. The reason for running this program is to test the accuracy of the drawing code numbers. You will note that statements from Fig. 12-5 that call for placing a blank space on the screen are omitted from the program. There is no need to specify them, because the screen is always cleared before the figure is drawn. A blank space will thus be a blank space, whether you specify it in the graphics program or not.

Example 12-5

```
(* GIRL AT PLAY V.1 *)
VAR DELAY,GPLACE:INTEGER;
(* FRAME 1 PROCEDURE *)
PROC FR1(GPLACE,PHASE);
  VAR DX,DY:INTEGER;
  BEGIN
  IF NOT PHASE THEN
    FOR DY:=0 TO 2 DO
      FOR DX:=0 TO 4 DO
        MEM(GPLACE+DX+64*DY):=32
  ELSE
    BEGIN
    MEM(GPLACE):=136;
```

```
      MEM(GPLACE+1):=175;
      MEM(GPLACE+2):=159;
      MEM(GPLACE+65):=187;
      MEM(GPLACE+66):=191;
      MEM(GPLACE+67):=157;
      MEM(GPLACE+128):=178;
      MEM(GPLACE+129):=159;
      MEM(GPLACE+130):=135;
      MEM(GPLACE+131):=175;
      MEM(GPLACE+132):=180
      END
  END;
(* BEGINNING OF MAINLINE *)
BEGIN
WRITE(28,31);
GPLACE:=15770;
REPEAT
  FR1(GPLACE,1);
  FOR DELAY:=0 TO 1000  DO;
  FR1(GPLACE,0);
  FOR DELAY:=0 TO 500 DO;
  FR1(GPLACE,0)
UNTIL DELAY<>DELAY
END.
```

Two variables, GPLACE and PHASE, are carried to the FR1 frame-drawing feature. GPLACE designates the starting address of the figure-drawing operation, and PHASE indicates whether the figure should be drawn (PHASE=1) or erased (PHASE=0).

The mainline program thus calls for alternately drawing and erasing the figure, inserting time delays between each operation. The program cycles indefinitely, or until you strike the BREAK key twice in succession.

Enter and compile the program in Example 12-5. Run it to check the accuracy of the drawing and erasing feature.

Program With MEM Statements For Frame 2

Example 12-6 is extended to include the MEM drawing statements for Frame 2 in Fig. 12-6. The mainline program animates the figure to some extent by drawing Frame 1, erasing it, drawing Frame 2, erasing it, and going back to Frame 1 again.

Note that the erasing operations for both frames is now specified as a separate procedure, ER12. That saves some unnecessary duplication of erasing steps in the two figure-drawing procedures.

Example 12-6

```
(* GIRL AT PLAY V.2 *)
VAR DELAY,GPLACE:INTEGER;
(* ERASE PROCEDURE -- 1,2 *)
```

```
PROC ER12(GPLACE);
  VAR DX,DY:INTEGER;
  BEGIN
  FOR DY:=0 TO 2 DO
    FOR DX:=0 TO 4 DO
      MEM(GPLACE+DX+64*DY):=32
  END;
(* FRAME 1 PROCEDURE *)
PROC FR1(GPLACE,PHASE);
  BEGIN
  IF NOT PHASE THEN ER12(GPLACE)
  ELSE
    BEGIN
    MEM(GPLACE):=136;
    MEM(GPLACE+1):=175;
    MEM(GPLACE+2):=159;
    MEM(GPLACE+65):=187;
    MEM(GPLACE+66):=191;
    MEM(GPLACE+67):=157;
    MEM(GPLACE+128):=178;
    MEM(GPLACE+129):=159;
    MEM(GPLACE+130):=135;
    MEM(GPLACE+131):=175;
    MEM(GPLACE+132):=180
    END
  END;
(* FRAME 2 PROCEDURE *)
PROC FR2(GPLACE,PHASE);
  BEGIN
  IF NOT PHASE THEN ER12(GPLACE)
  ELSE
    BEGIN
    MEM(GPLACE):=136;
    MEM(GPLACE+1):=175;
    MEM(GPLACE+2):=159;
    MEM(GPLACE+65):=187;
    MEM(GPLACE+66):=191;
    MEM(GPLACE+67):=157;
    MEM(GPLACE+128):=130;
    MEM(GPLACE+129):=131;
    MEM(GPLACE+130):=191;
    MEM(GPLACE+131):=179
    END
END;
(* BEGINNING OF MAINLINE *)
BEGIN
WRITE(28,31);
GPLACE:=15770;
REPEAT
  FR1(GPLACE,1);
  FOR DELAY:=0 TO 10 DO;
  FR1(GPLACE,0);
  FR2(GPLACE,1);
  FOR DELAY:=0 TO 10 DO;
  FR2(GPLACE,0)
UNTIL DELAY<>DELAY
END.
```

240

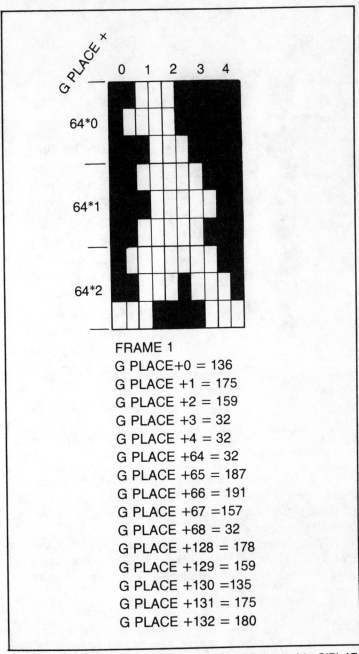

FRAME 1
G PLACE+0 = 136
G PLACE +1 = 175
G PLACE +2 = 159
G PLACE +3 = 32
G PLACE +4 = 32
G PLACE +64 = 32
G PLACE +65 = 187
G PLACE +66 = 191
G PLACE +67 =157
G PLACE +68 = 32
G PLACE +128 = 178
G PLACE +129 = 159
G PLACE +130 =135
G PLACE +131 = 175
G PLACE +132 = 180

Fig. 12-5. Preliminary drawing and graphics codes for Frame 1 of the GIRL AT PLAY animation sequence.

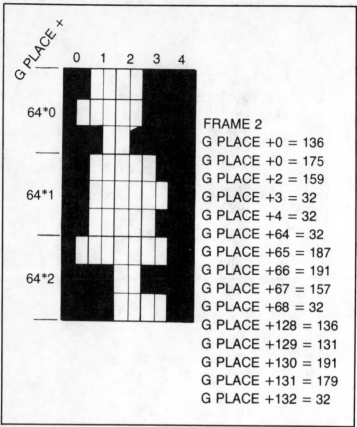

Fig. 12-6. Preliminary drawing and graphics codes for Frame 2 of the GIRL AT PLAY animation sequence.

With the program in Example 12-6, the figure of the girl should appear to run at one place on the screen. If you want to slow her down a little bit, just extend the DELAY range in the mainline portion of the program.

If the program is in good working order, you are ready to add some translation effect to the figure. The idea is to make the girl move from left to right across the screen as her legs show the running effect.

Revised Version Of The Mainline Program

There is no need to change any of the procedures as they appear in Example 12-6, but you do have to rework the mainline program. Use the Tiny Pascal editing feature to do this, and you

will save the trouble of having to enter all the procedures again.
Here is the revised version of the mainline program:

Example 12-7

```
(* BEGINNING OF MAINLINE *)
BEGIN
WRITE(28,31);
REPEAT
  GPLACE:=15810;
  REPEAT
    FR1(GPLACE,1);
    FOR DELAY:=0 TO 100 DO;
    FR1(GPLACE,0);
    GPLACE:=GPLACE+1;
    FR2(GPLACE,1);
    FOR DELAY:=0  TO 100 DO;
    FR2(GPLACE,0)
  UNTIL GPLACE=15873
UNTIL DELAY<>DELAY
END.
```

Compile and run this version, and you'll see the little girl
stroll across the screen. The next task is to enter procedures for
drawing Frames 3 and 4, based on the codes generated from Figs.
12-7 and 12-8. Use the system's edit mode to insert the ER34
erasing procedure just after ER12, and FR3 and FR4 procedures
just after the FR2 procedure already stored in your system.

Procedures For Frames 3 and 4

Here are the new procedures for the GIRL AT PLAY program:

Example 12-8

```
(* ERASE PROCEDURE -- 3,4 *)
PROC ER34(GPLACE);
  VAR DX,DY:INTEGER;
  BEGIN
  FOR DY:=0 TO 3 DO
    FOR DX:=0 TO 7 DO
      MEM(GPLACE+DX+64*DY):=32
  END;
(* FRAME 3 PROCEDURE *)
PROC FR3(GPLACE,PHASE);
  BEGIN
  IF NOT PHASE THEN ER34(GPLACE)
  ELSE
BEGIN
MEM(GPLACE+5):=176;
MEM(GPLACE+64):=139;
MEM(GPLACE+65):=180;
MEM(GPLACE+67):=175;
MEM(GPLACE+68):=159;
```

```
    MEM(GPLACE+70):=184;
    MEM(GPLACE+71):=135;
    MEM(GPLACE+129):=131;
    MEM(GPLACE+130):=179;
    MEM(GPLACE+131):=191;
    MEM(GPLACE+132):=191;
    MEM(GPLACE+133):=179;
    MEM(GPLACE+134):=131;
    MEM(GPLACE+192):=140;
    MEM(GPLACE+193):=143;
    MEM(GPLACE+194):=129;
    MEM(GPLACE+198):=143;
    MEM(GPLACE+199):=140
    END
END;
(* FRAME 4 PROCEDURE *)
PROC FR4(GPLACE,PHASE);
  BEGIN
  IF NOT PHASE THEN ER34(GPLACE)
  ELSE
    BEGIN
    MEM(GPLACE+5):=176;
    MEM(GPLACE+67):=175;
    MEM(GPLACE+68):=159;
    MEM(GPLACE+128):=176;
    MEM(GPLACE+129):=158;
    MEM(GPLACE+130):=135;
    MEM(GPLACE+131):=175;
    MEM(GPLACE+132):=159;
    MEM(GPLACE+133):=139;
    MEM(GPLACE+134):=173;
    MEM(GPLACE+135):=176;
    MEM(GPLACE+193):=176;
    MEM(GPLACE+194):=190;
    MEM(GPLACE+195):=135;
    MEM(GPLACE+196):=139;
    MEM(GPLACE+197):=189;
    MEM(GPLACE+198):=176
    END
END;
```

Editing The Mainline Program

Now edit the mainline program to test the operation of procedures ER34, FR3 and FR4:

Example 12-9

```
(* MAINLINE *)
BEGIN
WRITE(28,31);
GPLACE:=15810;
REPEAT
    FR3(GPLACE,1);
    FOR DELAY:=0 TO 100 DO;
```

244

```
        FR3(GPLACE,Ø);
        FR4(GPLACE,1);
        FOR DELAY:=Ø TO 1ØØ DO;
        FR4(GPLACE,Ø)
UNTIL DELAY<*DELAY
END.
```

What you should have now is the mainline program in Example 12-9 coming after procedures FR3 and FR4 in Example 12-8. The program's variable declaration line should appear as it does in Example 12-6, followed by ER12 from that same example. The ER34 listing from Example 12-8 should follow ER12, and then you should find listings for procedures FR1 and FR2 as they are presented in Example 12-6.

If you are confused by the placement of all this, here is a more brief description:

Variable declaration line

```
PROC ER12(GPLACE);
PROC ER34(GPLACE);
PROC FR1(GPLACE ,PHASE);
PROC FR2(GPLACE,PHASE);
PROC FR3(GPLACE,PHASE);
PROC FR4(GPLACE,PHASE);
MAINLINE PROGRAM FROM EXAMPLE 12-9
```

Compile and run the program as it stands at this time. You should see the figure jumping up and down, near the left hand side of the screen. Debug any parts of the figure that might seem defective. Now you are ready to put together a complete mainline program, one that combines the running and jumping motions.

To be on the safe side, you ought to save the program on cassette tape before putting together the final mainline program. Just in case you make a mistake in setting the values for GPLACE, you will have a copy of all the procedures on that tape. Remember, running the figure outside the video memory will most likely destroy the entire program, and you've invested a considerable amount of time getting it into the machine.

Reworking The Mainline Program

With the program saved on tape, rework the mainline program to look like this one:

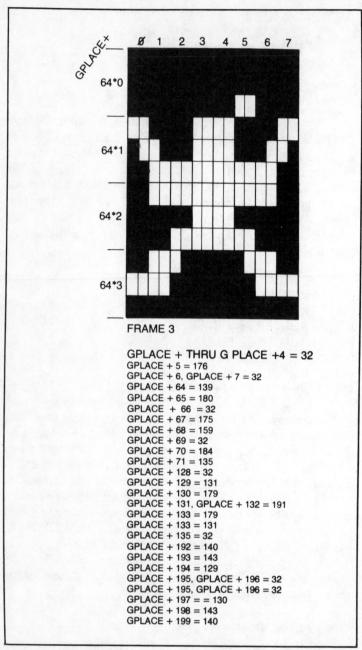

FRAME 3

GPLACE + THRU G PLACE +4 = 32
GPLACE + 5 = 176
GPLACE + 6, GPLACE + 7 = 32
GPLACE + 64 = 139
GPLACE + 65 = 180
GPLACE + 66 = 32
GPLACE + 67 = 175
GPLACE + 68 = 159
GPLACE + 69 = 32
GPLACE + 70 = 184
GPLACE + 71 = 135
GPLACE + 128 = 32
GPLACE + 129 = 131
GPLACE + 130 = 179
GPLACE + 131, GPLACE + 132 = 191
GPLACE + 133 = 179
GPLACE + 133 = 131
GPLACE + 135 = 32
GPLACE + 192 = 140
GPLACE + 193 = 143
GPLACE + 194 = 129
GPLACE + 195, GPLACE + 196 = 32
GPLACE + 195, GPLACE + 196 = 32
GPLACE + 197 = = 130
GPLACE + 198 = 143
GPLACE + 199 = 140

Fig. 12-7. Preliminary drawing and graphics codes for Frame 3 of the GIRL AT PLAY animation sequence.

246

Example 12-10

```
(* BEGINNING OF MAINLINE *)
BEGIN
WRITE(28,31);
REPEAT
  GPLACE:=15810;
  REPEAT
    FR1(GPLACE,1);
    FOR DELAY:=0 TO 10 DO;
    FR1(GPLACE,0);
    GPLACE:=GPLACE+1;
    IF (GPLACE=15825) OR (GPLACE=15835) THEN
      BEGIN
      FOR UD:=0 TO 4 DO
        BEGIN
        FR4(GPLACE-64*UD,1);
        FOR DELAY:=0 TO 5 DO;
        FR4(GPLACE-64*UD,0);
        FR3(GPLACE-64*UD,1);
        FOR DELAY:=0 TO 5 DO;
        FR3(GPLACE-64*UD,0)
        END;
      FOR UD:=4 DOWNTO 0 DO
        BEGIN
        FR3(GPLACE-64*UD,1);
        FOR DELAY:=0 TO 5 DO;
        FR3(GPLACE-64*UD,0);
        FR4(GPLACE-64*UD,1);
        FOR DELAY:=0 TO 5 DO;
        FR4(GPLACE-64*UD,0)
        END;
      GPLACE:=GPLACE+1
      END;
    FR2(GPLACE,1);
    FOR DELAY:=0 TO 10 DO;
    FR2(GPLACE,0);
  UNTIL GPLACE=15873
UNTIL DELAY<>DELAY
END·
```

This mainline adds a new variable, UD. So you must edit the original variable declaration line to include it. The new line should look like this:

VAR DELAY, GPLACE,UD:INTEGER;

After making that little chance, the program is ready to compile and run. You should see the girl running across the screen, jumping up and down at two different places along the way.

The way she flaps her arms and legs around when jumping makes one think she might be trying to fly. Certainly you are free to tinker with the mainline program to get just about any animation effect you want.

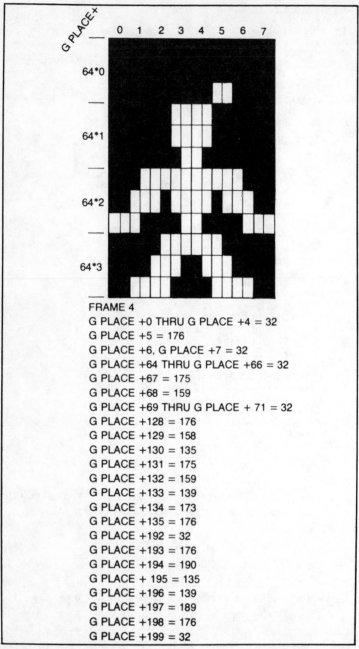

FRAME 4
G PLACE +0 THRU G PLACE +4 = 32
G PLACE +5 = 176
G PLACE +6, G PLACE +7 = 32
G PLACE +64 THRU G PLACE +66 = 32
G PLACE +67 = 175
G PLACE +68 = 159
G PLACE +69 THRU G PLACE + 71 = 32
G PLACE +128 = 176
G PLACE +129 = 158
G PLACE +130 = 135
G PLACE +131 = 175
G PLACE +132 = 159
G PLACE +133 = 139
G PLACE +134 = 173
G PLACE +135 = 176
G PLACE +192 = 32
G PLACE +193 = 176
G PLACE +194 = 190
G PLACE + 195 = 135
G PLACE +196 = 139
G PLACE +197 = 189
G PLACE +198 = 176
G PLACE +199 = 32

Fig. 12-8. Preliminary drawing and graphics codes for Frame 4 of the GIRL AT PLAY animation sequence.

Complete GIRL AT PLAY Program

This chapter closes with a complete listing for GIRL AT PLAY. If you have been having any difficulties with the animation examples, try checking your listing—line by line—against this one.

```
  (* GIRL AT PLAY V.3 *)
VAR DELAY,GPLACE:INTEGER;
(* ERASE PROCEDURE -- 1,2 *)
PROC ER12(GPLACE);
  VAR DX,DY:INTEGER;
  BEGIN
  FOR DY:=0 TO 2 DO
    FOR DX:=0 TO 4 DO
      MEM(GPLACE+DX+64*DY):=32
  END;
(* ERASE PROCEDURE -- 3,4 *)
PROC ER34(GPLACE);
  VAR DX,DY:INTEGER;
  BEGIN
  FOR DY:=0 TO 3 DO
    FOR DX:=0 TO 7 DO
      MEM(GPLACE+DX+64*DY):=32
  END;
(* FRAME 1 PROCEDURE *)
PROC FR1(GPLACE,PHASE);
  BEGIN
  IF NOT PHASE THEN ER12(GPLACE)
  ELSE
    BEGIN
    MEM(GPLACE):=136;
    MEM(GPLACE+1):=175;
    MEM(GPLACE+2):=159;
    MEM(GPLACE+65):=187;
    MEM(GPLACE+66):=191;
    MEM(GPLACE+67):=157;
    MEM(GPLACE+128):=178;
    MEM(GPLACE+129):=159;
    MEM(GPLACE+130):=135;
    MEM(GPLACE+131):=175;
    MEM(GPLACE+132):=180
    END
  END;
(* FRAME 2 PROCEDURE *)
PROC FR2(GPLACE,PHASE);
  BEGIN
  IF NOT PHASE THEN ER12(GPLACE)
  ELSE
    BEGIN
    MEM(GPLACE):=136;
    MEM(GPLACE+1):=175;
    MEM(GPLACE+2):=159;
    MEM(GPLACE+65):=187;
    MEM(GPLACE+66):=191;
    MEM(GPLACE+67):=157;
    MEM(GPLACE+128):=130;
```

```
    MEM(GPLACE+129):=131;
    MEM(GPLACE+130):=191;
    MEM(GPLACE+131):=179
    END
END;
(* FRAME 3 PROCEDURE *)
PROC FR3(GPLACE,PHASE);
  BEGIN
  IF NOT PHASE THEN ER34(GPLACE)
  ELSE
-   BEGIN
    MEM(GPLACE+5):=176;
    MEM(GPLACE+64):=139;
    MEM(GPLACE+65):=180;
    MEM(GPLACE+67):=175;
    MEM(GPLACE+68):=159;
    MEM(GPLACE+70):=184;
    MEM(GPLACE+71):=135;
    MEM(GPLACE+129):=131;
    MEM(GPLACE+130):=179;
    MEM(GPLACE+131):=191;
    MEM(GPLACE+132):=191;
    MEM(GPLACE+133):=179;
    MEM(GPLACE+134):=131;
    MEM(GPLACE+192):=140;
    MEM(GPLACE+193):=143;
    MEM(GPLACE+194):=129;
    MEM(GPLACE+198):=143;
    MEM(GPLACE+199):=140
    END
END;
(* FRAME 4 PROCEDURE *)
PROC FR4(GPLACE,PHASE);
  BEGIN
  IF NOT PHASE THEN ER34(GPLACE)
  ELSE
    BEGIN
    MEM(GPLACE+5):=176;
    MEM(GPLACE+67):=175;
    MEM(GPLACE+68):=159;
    MEM(GPLACE+128):=176;
    MEM(GPLACE+129):=158;
    MEM(GPLACE+130):=135;
    MEM(GPLACE+131):=175;
    MEM(GPLACE+132):=159;
    MEM(GPLACE+133):=139;
    MEM(GPLACE+134):=173;
    MEM(GPLACE+135):=176;
    MEM(GPLACE+193):=176;
    MEM(GPLACE+194):=190;
    MEM(GPLACE+195):=135;
    MEM(GPLACE+196):=139;
    MEM(GPLACE+197):=189;
    MEM(GPLACE+198):=176
    END
END;
(* BEGINNING OF MAINLINE *)
BEGIN
```

```
WRITE(28,31);
REPEAT
  GPLACE:=15810;
  REPEAT
    FR1(GPLACE,1);
    FOR DELAY:=0 TO 10 DO;
    FR1(GPLACE,0);
    GPLACE:=GPLACE+1;
    IF (GPLACE=15825) OR (GPLACE=15835) THEN
      BEGIN
      FOR UD:=0 TO 4 DO
        BEGIN
        FR4(GPLACE-64*UD,1);
        FOR DELAY:=0 TO 5 DO;
        FR4(GPLACE-64*UD,0);
        FR3(GPLACE-64*UD,1);
        FOR DELAY:=0 TO 5 DO;
        FR3(GPLACE-64*UD,0)
        END;
      FOR UD:=4 DOWNTO 0 DO
        BEGIN
        FR3(GPLACE-64*UD,1);
        FOR DELAY:=0 TO 5 DO;
        FR3(GPLACE-64*UD,0);
        FR4(GPLACE-64*UD,1);
        FOR DELAY:=0 TO 5 DO;
        FR4(GPLACE-64*UD,0)
        END;
      GPLACE:=GPLACE+1
      END;
    FR2(GPLACE,1);
    FOR DELAY:=0 TO 10 DO;
    FR2(GPLACE,0);
  UNTIL GPLACE=15873
UNTIL DELAY<>DELAY
END
```

Chapter 13
Some Just For Fun Pastimes

The three Tiny Pascal programs offered in this chapter are of rather modest proportions, but they can be fun for one or two players. The text accompanying these programs simply describes their operating features and points out a couple of special programming steps.

ONE PLAYER HIGH/LOW GAME

A "high/low" game presented earlier in this book required two players, one to enter the mystery number and another to discover it. This version is intended for one player. The program selects the mystery number.

Format

Upon running the program, you will first see the heading, ** ONE PLAYER HIGH/LOW GAME**, followed by the request, ENTER TO START. Between the time you start the program and do the ENTER, variable SEED counts like crazy between 0 and 1000. There is no telling where that counter will be when you strike the ENTER key to start the game, so the SEED value makes a fine "mystery" number for the game.

After striking the ENTER key to get things started, you see OK, THE MYSTERY NUMBER IS IN PLACE, AND IT IS A NUMBER BETWEEN 0 and 1000. ENTER YOUR FIRST GUESS.

You respond by entering any number you want. The program will tell you whether the number is TOO LARGE, TOO SMALL or YOU GOT IT!!!.

If the number you entered is less than or greater than the mystery number, you are asked to enter your next guess. But if (and when) you enter the number that matches the mystery number, YOU GOT IT!!! flashes on and off 10 times, followed by a listing of the mystery number and the number of tries you used to find the right number.

Program

Here is the program:

```
(* ONE-PLAYER HIGH/LOW *)
VAR SEED,PNUM,SCORE,TIME,AGAIN,PHASE:INTEGER;
BEGIN
WRITE(28,31,215,'** ONE-PLAYER HIGH/LOW **',13,13);
WRITE('ENTER TO START...');
WHILE INKEY<>13 DO
  BEGIN
  IF (SEED<0) OR (SEED>1000) THEN
    SEED:=500;
  SEED:=SEED+1
  END;
REPEAT
  WRITE(28,31,'OK, THE MYSTERY NUMBER IS IN PLACE,',13);
  WRITE('AND IT IS A NUMBER BETWEEN 0 AND 1000.',13,13);
  WRITE('ENTER YOUR FIRST GUESS...',13);
  SCORE:=0;
  REPEAT
    READ (PNUM#);
    WRITE(28,31);
    IF PNUM>SEED THEN
      WRITE(PNUM#,32,'IS TOO LARGE',13,'TRY AGAIN ... )
    ELSE IF PNUM<SEED THEN
      WRITE(PNUM#,32,'IS TOO SMALL',13,'TRY AGAIN...');
    SCORE:=SCORE+1
  UNTIL PNUM=SEED;
FOR PHASE:=0 TO 10 DO
  BEGIN
  WRITE(28,31,220,'YOU GOT IT!!!');
  FOR TIME:=0 TO 100 DO;
  WRITE(28,31);
  FOR TIME:=0 TO 100 DO;
  END;
```

```
WRITE( 13,'THE MYSTERY NUMBER WAS ',SEED#,13,13);
WRITE('YOU GOT IT IN ',SCORE#,' TRIES.',13,13);
WRITE('ENTER TO PLAY AGAIN...');
WRITE( 13,'OR STRIKE THE SPACE BAR TO END THE PROGRAM.');
AGAIN:=0;
WHILE NOT((AGAIN=32)  OR (AGAIN=13)) DO
BEGIN
AGAIN:=INKEY;
IF SEED>1000 THEN SEED:=0;
SEED:=SEED+1
END
UNTIL AGAIN=32;
WRITE( 28,31 )
END.
```

A TWO PLAYER HANGMAN GAME

The game of HANGMAN illustrated here adds some special excitement to the old pencil-and-paper version. It is a two player game. One player is responsible for entering a "secret" word into the program, and the other player's job is to figure out what that word is. The guesser is allowed 10 wrong guesses before he or she is effectively hanged.

Format

Running the program, you first see HANGMAN: ENTER YOUR SECRET WORD. USE NO MORE THAN 10 LETTERS, AND MAKE SURE YOUR VICTIM IS NOT LOOKING OVER YOUR SHOULDER!

The player acting as the hangman can then enter up to 10 letters—no punctuation, spaces or numerals allowed. In fact, the program locks out the keyboard for everything but the 26 letters of the alphabet.

The hangman strikes the ENTER key when the spelling is done. Then the program reprints the word and asks whether or not it is OK. The hangman responds with a Y or N. If the response is N (for "no"), the hangman has a chance to enter the secret word again. This little feature makes it possible to correct errors in spelling, change your mind about the secret word and so on.

After responding to the OK? with a Y, the system clears the screen and prints VICTIM: DO YOUR THING TO SAVE YOUR NECK. . . At that time some dashes appear near the center of the screen. Each dash represents a letter in the secret word.

The victim, or guesser, types a letter on the keyboard. If it is a letter included in the secret word, it appears among the dashes and at the places it should appear in the finished word.

But if the letter is not part of the secret word, it is printed at the bottom of the screen. The "hang" counter is moved one step closer to the deadly count of 10.

The guesser continues entering letters until one of two things happen. Either the secret word is completely filled in or the tenth wrong guess occurs. In the former case, the victim's neck is saved. If the victim doesn't match the letters after 10 wrong guesses, it's all over. ARRGH—YOU ARE DEAD . . .

The program makes use of three arrays. One of these arrays, STR, keeps track of the letters in the secret word. Array PSTR keeps track of the victim's correct guesses, and WSTR saves the list of wrong guesses.

Program

If you are a bit weak when it comes to working with arrays, you might find a thorough study of this program quite helpful.

```
(* HANGMAN *)
VAR N,C,OK,X,LINE,DONE,WN,PN,PC,PW:INTEGER;
STR:ARRAY(10) OF INTEGER;
PSTR:ARRAY(10) OF INTEGER;
WSTR:ARRAY(10) OF INTEGER;
BEGIN
(* HANGMAN ENTERS THE SECRET WORD *)
REPEAT
  WRITE(28,31,'HANGMAN: ENTER YOUR SECRET WORD',13);
  WRITE('(UP TO 10 LETTERS)...',13,13);
  N:=1;C:=0;OK:=0;
  REPEAT
    REPEAT
      C:=INKEY
    UNTIL (C=13) OR ((C>=65) AND (C<=90));
    IF C<>13 THEN
      BEGIN
      STR(N):=C;
      WRITE(STR(N));
      N:=N+1
      END
  UNTIL (C=13) OR (N>10);
  N:=N-1;
  WRITE(28,31,'THE SECRET WORD IS:',32);
  FOR X:=1 TO N DO WRITE(STR(X));
  WRITE(13,'IS THE WORD OK? YES OR NO ...');
  READ(OK)
UNTIL OK='Y';
(* BEGINNING OF THE "VICTIM" PHASE *)
FOR X:=0 TO 100 DO
  BEGIN
  PSTR(X):=0;
```

```
      WSTR(X):=0
    END;
WN:=1;PN:=0;
WHILE (PN<N) AND (WN<=10) DO
    BEGIN
    WRITE(28,31,'VICTIM: DO YOUR THING TO SAVE YOUR
      NECK ...');
    FOR LINE:=1 TO 8 DO WRITE(13);
    PN:=0;
    WRITE(215);
    FOR X:=1 TO N DO
      BEGIN
      IF PSTR(X)=STR(X) THEN
        BEGIN
        WRITE(STR(X),32);
        PN:=PN+1
        END
      ELSE WRITE(45,32);
      END;
    IF PN<N THEN
      BEGIN
      REPEAT
        WRITE(13,'PICK A LETTER ...',13);
        WRITE('WRONG LETTERS ALREADY USED ARE:',13);
        FOR X:=1 TO WN DO WRITE(WSTR(X),32);
        READ(PC)
      UNTIL (PC>=65) AND (PC<=90);
      PW:=0;
      FOR X:=1 TO N DO
        IF PC=STR(X) THEN
          BEGIN
          PW:=PW+1;
          PSTR(X):=PC
          END;
        IF PW=0 THEN
          BEGIN
          WSTR(WN):=PC;
          WN:=WN+1
          END;
      END;
    END;
WRITE(13);
IF PN>=N THEN
    FOR X:=1 TO 10 DO
      BEGIN
      WRITE('YOU JUST SAVED YOURSELF!!!');
      FOR DONE:=0 TO 250 DO;
      WRITE(29,30);
      FOR DONE:=0 TO 50 DO;
      END
ELSE WRITE('ARRGH -- YOU ARE DEAD')
END.
```

MAKING HEADLINES

Editors of small town newspapers are sometimes hard pressed to come up with some good headlines. Here is little program intended to make up any number of headlines on demand.

Actually it is a goofy little thing that is at least good for a few chuckles. The program prints out a noun, verb and another noun to simulate the effect of a complete sentence. The silly part of the whole thing is that the nouns and verb are selected at random from a prepared list.

Indeed, MOUSE GIVES BIRTH TO ELEPHANT is headline material. If you don't happen to agree with that point, you can certainly make up some nouns and verbs of your own choosing. Just don't tell anyone you got the idea for X-rated computer programs from this book!

There is one point of technical interest in this program. You have seen that Tiny Pascal doesn't handle string information very well, at least not as easily as Level II, TRS-80 BASIC. Well, here is a way to assemble strings, using the CASE statement.

```
(* HEADLINES *)
VAR AGAIN,N,LINE,SEED:INTEGER;
FUNC RND(RLOW,RHIGH);
  VAR M,P:INTEGER;
  BEGIN
  REPEAT
    M:=N*3125;
    IF M<0 THEN M:=ABS(M);
    N:=M;P:=M;
    P:=P MOD RHIGH
  UNTIL (P>=RLOW) AND (P<=RHIGH);
  RND:=P
  END;
PROC SETUP(NOUN,VERB);
  BEGIN
  CASE NOUN OF
    1:WRITE('BOY');
    2:WRITE('CAT');
    3:WRITE('DOG');
    4:WRITE('ELEPHANT');
    5:WRITE('GOOSE');
    6:WRITE('SNAKE');
    7:WRITE('SNAIL');
    8:WRITE('MOUSE');
    9:WRITE('FLEA');
   10:WRITE('TURTLE')
    END;
  CASE VERB OF
    1:WRITE('EATS');
    2:WRITE('JUMPS OVER');
    3:WRITE('BEATS UP');
    4:WRITE('HASSLES');
    5:WRITE('GIVES BIRTH TO');
    6:WRITE('CRAWLS UNDER');
    7:WRITE('REARRANGES FACE OF');
    8:WRITE('FALLS IN LOVE WITH');
    9:WRITE('SHOOTS');
```

```
    10:WRITE('ROBS')
      END;
   WRITE(32)
END;
(* BEGIN MAINLINE PROGRAM *)
BEGIN
WRITE(28,31);
FOR LINE:=1 TO 8 DO WRITE(13);
WRITE(210,'"TODAY',39,'S HEADLINES, TOMORROW',39,'S
   NEWS"',13);
WRITE(13,'SEE IT ALL HERE BY STRIKING THE ENTER
   KEY...',13);
WHILE INKEY<>13 DO
   BEGIN
   IF (SEED<99) OR (SEED>999) THEN SEED:=99;
   SEED:=SEED+1
   END;
N:=SEED;
WRITE(28,31);
WRITE(215,'**** HEADLINE ****');
FOR LINE:=1 TO 8 DO WRITE(13);
  WHILE AGAIN=AGAIN DO
     BEGIN
     SETUP(RND(1,10),0);
     SETUP(0,RND(1,10));
     SETUP(RND(1,10),0);
     FOR AGAIN:=0 TO 5000 DO;
     WRITE(29,30)
     END
END.
```

Chapter 14
Writing Your Own Pascal Programs

Most sources of information about Pascal programming, including this book, praise the language's highly structured form. Pascal lends itself to structured programming methods and, indeed, rises out of a need for encouraging all programmers to use structured programming.

STRUCTURED PROGRAMMING

What is structured programming? It is a logical process for writing and organizing computer programs that fits virtually any computer language. Any programmer taking the trouble to master at least the basic elements of structured programming can save a great deal of programming time, especially when it comes to debugging and cleaning up a new program. Using commonly accepted methods of structured programming also makes it easier for others to follow the operations in a program and get a feeling for the intent of the original programmer.

While the topic of structured programming is appropriate to any book about writing programs, it is especially relevant to Pascal. In fact, learning to use Pascal properly automatically leads one to use some of the basic ideas of structured programming. If I were ever to write a book about structured programming, I would use Pascal as the model and then eventually show how the same ideas can be applied to other programming languages.

Even though it is unlikely that anyone could completely describe structured programming in a single chapter of one book, it is quite possible to outline the basic ideas, especially if they're framed in the context of Pascal, even Tiny Pascal. This is such a chapter.

By the time you complete your study of this chapter, you ought to be able to set up some pretty sophisticated Pascal programs of your own. Even if you don't do a whole lot of Pascal programming in the future, you will at least be convinced that structured programming is a powerful tool.

TOP-DOWN VERSUS BOTTOM-UP PROGRAMMING

In an academic sense, there are two distinctly different ways to approach the problem of writing a new computer program: from the top and down, or from the bottom and up.

When using the top-down approach, the program gradually evolves around a master program. On paper, the programmer starts out by listing the major operations in the order they are to occur. Maybe the list really begins as a general flow chart—one showing blocks for the basic operations and just the more critical conditional steps.

After the programmer is satisfied that the main sequence of operations is taking the project in the right direction, it is time to begin sketching in some details. We won't deal with too much detail at first, just enough to point out the sorts of things that should happen within each of the major operations.

With the secondary steps thus outlined, the programmer begins elaborating in even greater detail. And the process of filling in more and more detail continues until the program is finally done.

Top-down programming is an evolutionary process that begins with a few major points, and then grows to have subpoints within points and then points within the subpoints. In a sense, the matter of writing programs from the "top-down" is like making a formal outline for a term paper. It begins with a select group of major points and gradually breaks down into any number of levels of subpoints.

The essential character of top-down programming is that the overall program gradually develops. This is done instead of first building a lot of complete program "modules," and assembling all the modules with a mainline program. The contrasting idea, incidentally, is the essence of bottom-up structuring.

When writing a program from the bottom and upward, the main idea is to divide the programming operation into a lot of separate modules of operations. One module does one of the jobs, another does a different sort of task and so on. Each module is complete within itself. Of course, the programmer doesn't have a full program until the little modules are strung together.

The modules, for example, could be described as subroutines or procedures. Each can be run and tested on the computer before they are "cast into concrete." When the programmer has all the modules designed and debugged, it is time to call them in the appropriate sequence from a master program.

If the modules have been designed properly, the master program should turn out to be relatively simple. At least it shouldn't take long to get the master program written and running.

Top-down and bottom-up programming both have their merits and drawbacks. While some programmers suggest that one is always better than the other, the practical reality of the matter is that competent programmers end up using both approaches.

The next section in this chapter goes through an example of a Tiny Pascal program that is written in a top-down fashion. The section after that illustrates a purely bottom-up programming procedure, and the final section demonstrates the advisability of using both approaches at the same time.

WRITING A TINY PASCAL PROGRAM FROM THE TOP AND DOWN

Suppose you want to write a program for testing your reflexes. The general idea is to write a GET READY . . . message on the screen. At some undetermined time later, turn on a square of light. The experimenter is supposed to strike the ENTER key as soon as the light appears, as soon as possible. The reaction time then appears, in milliseconds, after the experimenter makes the response.

Preliminary Flow Chart for Reflexes Program

Figure 14-1 shows a preliminary flow chart for this particular program. The first five blocks spell out the initial operations: CLEAR THE SCREEN, WRITE THE HEADING, PICK A RANDOM DELAY NUMBER and INITIALIZE THE DELAY COUNTER. After doing those things, the program halts until the user strikes the ENTER key to signal he or she is ready to begin the experiment.

After the experimenter signals the time to start a trial, the flow chart shows CLEAR THE SCREEN, WRITE "GET READY"

MESSAGE and BEGIN DELAY. These operations mark the beginning of the part of the experiment where the user is anxiously waiting for the signal light to go on.

Since it is possible to "cheat" the experiment by continuously tapping on the ENTER key during the waiting interval, it is necessary to work the program so that this sort of cheating immediately prints out a TOO SOON message and ends the program.

If the DELAY DONE conditional is *not* satisfied—the timing interval isn't over and the signal light hasn't yet appeared—the flow chart shows an ENTER conditional. That ENTER is looking for an illegal tap of the ENTER key. If that ENTER conditional is satisfied, the program does a WRITE "TOO SOON" MESSAGE and bypasses all the other steps to bring things to an end.

If the user doesn't tap the ENTER key before the right signal appears, the ENTER conditional is *not* satisfied. The "get ready" timing procedes without interruption. Once the delay is done (conditional DELAY DONE is satisfied), the system turns on a square of light (SHOW SQUARE) and starts the millisecond timer (START TIMER).

The timer continues running until its ENTER conditional is satisfied. In other words, the timer runs until the experimenter strikes the ENTER key. The moment that ENTER conditional is satisfied, the flow chart calls for STOP TIMER, SHOW TIME COUNT and END.

The flow chart in Fig. 14-1 simply shows the general sequence of operations and, in a general way, defines the nature of each of the operations. There are a lot of details that must be filled in, but at this point in the top-down process the programmer shouldn't be overly concerned. He should not become confused and carried away with a lot of little details. This is simply an overall sketch of what is to be done.

Outline of the Reflex Program

There are no references to specific programming languages. The flow chart, as it stands, can apply to any kind of computer system that has a keyboard input and a CRT input. It is actually possible to begin writing something of a program without regard to the language to be used. Such a procedure is beyond the scope of this book. For our purposes, the next step is to sketch out the main operations in a Tiny Pascal, TRS-80 format. Example 14-1 is a preliminary pencil-and-paper outline of the program.

Example 14-1

```
(* REACTION TIME *)
VAR LINE, START, TIME, DELAY, ENTER, STOP:
    INTEGER;
BEGIN
WRITE(28, 31, '** REACTION TIME TEST **');
FOR LINE:=1 TO 8 DO WRITE(13);
WRITE ('STRIKE ENTER KEY TO START . . .');
pick random number for delay TIME variable;
zero the reaction time counter;
READ(START);
WRITE (28, 31, 'GET READY . . .');
DELAY:=Ø;
WHILE (DELAY<TIME) AND (ENTER=Ø) DO
    BEGIN
    ENTER:=INKEY;
    DELAY:=DELAY+1
    END;
IF ENTER=Ø THEN
    BEGIN
show the square of light;
REPEAT
        increment reaction time counter;
        STOP:=INKEY
    UNTIL STOP=13;
    WRITE (13, status of the reaction time counter#)
ELSE WRITE (13, 'TOO SOON . . . RUN AGAIN')
END.
```

Stubs

The program, as it appears in Example 14-1, is not ready to enter and run. There are too many operations still described in general terms. See the lines written in lower case letters. The ideas that aren't specified in formal Pascal are sometimes called *stubs*.

Even though Example 14-1 still contains some stubs, it is complete from a structural viewpoint. All the basic elements are indicated as either formal Pascal syntax or stubs; and that is the hallmark of top-down programming. In this first pass through the program, you have a BEGIN and an END. All that remains to be done, as far as writing the program is concerned, is to replace the stubs with formal Pascal operations.

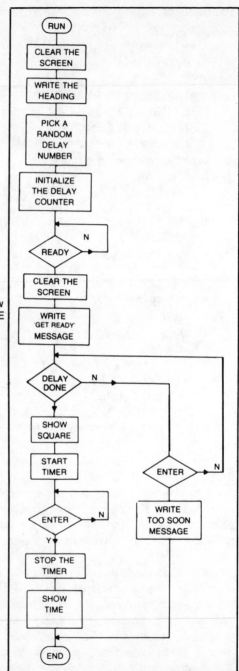

Fig. 14-1. Preliminary flow chart for REACTION TIME program. See Examples 14-1 through 14-4.

264

Some top-down programmers would like to take the semi-program in Example 14-1 and work it so that it can be entered and run. The program wouldn't do everything, but it would execute the operations that have been formalized to this point. Getting that partial program into the computer has at least two advantages.

Executable Version of Example 14-1

First, it gives you a chance to work out any little details such as the spacing of the lines and messages on the screen. Second, running this much of the program makes it easier to enter the remaining parts as you develop them. Here is a workable version of the listing in Example 14-1.

Example 14-2

```
(* REACTION TIME*)
VAR LINE, START, TIME, DELAY, ENTER, STOP:
    INTEGER;
BEGIN
WRITE (28, 31, '** REACTION TIME TEST **');
FOR LINE:=1 TO 8 DO WRITE (13);
WRITE ('STRIKE THE ENTER KEY TO START . . .');
READ (START);
WRITE (28, 31, 'GET READY . . .');
DELAY:=0; ENTER:=0;
TIME:=1000;
WHILE (DELAY<TIME) AND (ENTER=0) DO
    BEGIN
    ENTER:=INKEY;
    DELAY:=DELAY+1
    END;
IF ENTER=0 THEN
    BEGIN
    REPEAT
        STOP:=INKEY
    UNTIL STOP=13
    END
ELSE WRITE (13, 'TOO SOON . . . RUN AGAIN')
END.
```

The program in Example 14-2 does not do everything specified on the original flow chart. Rather, it is an executable version of the preliminary program in Example 14-1. The stubs are left out, but in some cases they have to be replaced with a reasonable substitute.

265

For example, it is possible to skip the operation, "zero the reaction time counter," and run without incrementing that counter and showing its status near the end of the program. Thus, any references to the reaction time counter can be skipped for the time being.

You cannot test the workings of the DELAY operation, however, without having some value for variable TIME. In the final version of the program, TIME will be selected by a random number generator. Since the preliminary version doesn't include a formal representation of that number generator, variable TIME must be set by some other means, temporarily, that is. So the program in Example 14-2 shows a TIME:=1000 statement. That statement will be deleted later on.

Like the stubs for working with the reaction time counter, the process of showing the square of light is simply omitted. You can thus enter the program as it is shown in Example 14-2. Given the fact that some operations are missing, it still runs in a meaningful fashion.

Actually, I must confess that my first version of Example 14-2 did not run properly. It wouldn't compile completely because I accidentally omitted the END that belongs after the statement, UNTIL STOP=13. Look at Example 14-1, and you'll find it is missing there, too. I mention this little accident on my part to emphasize the fact that running a partial program which is being evolved in a top-down fashion is a good way to uncover problems while everything is still of manageable proportions.

Running the Program

Running the program as it stands in Example 14-2, you should first see the heading messages. The message, ** REACTION TIME TEST **, ought to be centered at the top of the screen. Make a note to include a 215 tab operation in the WRITE statement the next time.

Upon striking the ENTER key to start the test, the GET READY message appears at the upper left-hand corner of the screen. That's okay. To test the TOO SOON feature, strike the ENTER key within about 5 seconds. You should get the TOO SOON message.

Run the program again, and wait about 10 seconds before striking the ENTER key. If the DELAY counting is working, the program will come to an end without showing the TOO MUCH message.

That completes the first series of tests on this top-down preparation. It is now time to fill in some of the stubs.

Square of Light Stub

Maybe the most meaningful stub to work into the program is the one for lighting the square of light at the end of the delay interval. While you're at it, you might as well write in the random number generator and set TIME equal to that number.

Example 14-3
```
(* REACTION TIME *)
VAR LINE, START, TIME, DELAY, ENTER, STOP:
    INTEGER;
      N, M, P, DY, DX:INTEGER;
BEGIN
WRITE(28, 31, 215, '** REACTION TIME TEST **');
FOR LINE:=1 TO 8 DO WRITE(13);
WRITE('STRIKE ENTER KEY TO START. . .');
REPEAT
    M:=N*3125;
    IF M Ø THEN M:=ABS(M);
    N:=M;P:=M;
    P:=P MOD 5ØØØ
UNTIL (P>=1ØØØ) AND (P<=5ØØØ);
READ(START);
WRITE(28, 31, 'GET READY . . .');
DELAY:=Ø; ENTER:=Ø;
TIME:=P;
WHILE(DELAY TIME) AND (ENTER=Ø) DO
    BEGIN
    ENTER:=INKEY;
    DELAY:=DELAY+1
    END;
IF ENTER=Ø THEN
    BEGIN
    FOR DY:=1 TO 4 DO
        FOR DX:=1 TO 8 DO PLOT(DX+32, DY+5, 1);
    REPEAT
        STOP:=INKEY
    UNTIL STOP =13
    END
ELSE WRITE(13, 'TOO SOON . . . RUN AGAIN')
END.
```

Enter and run this version, and you should see the square of light blinking on at the end of some randomly selected interval. The response time counter isn't in the program, at least not yet. But the program can run. Of course, it is possible to work out any syntax errors and change any little operating feature that isn't working quite as expected.

As an example of the latter (not being completely satisfied with a feature), I wasn't especially pleased with the way the system draws the square of light. It's drawn too slowly, and a user who is really fast on the draw might strike the enter key before the square is completely drawn. So I made a note to replace the PLOT graphic in that case with a MEM graphic which will, of course, draw that square a whole lot faster.

Reaction Time Counter

The next and final major step is to work in the reaction time counter.

Example 14-4

```
(* REACTION TIME *)
VAR LINE, START, TIME, DELAY, ENTER, STOP:
    INTEGER;
    N, M, P, DY, DX, COUNTER:INTEGER;
BEGIN
WRITE(28, 31, 215, '** REACTION TIME TEST **');
FOR LINE:=1 TO 8 DO WRITE(13);
WRITE('STRIKE THE ENTER KEY TO START. . .');
REPEAT
    M:=N*3125;
    IF M<Ø THEN M:= ABS(M);
    N:=M;P:=M;
    P:=P MOD 5ØØØ
UNTIL (P>=1ØØØ) AND (P<=5ØØØ);
COUNTER:=Ø;
READ(START);
WRITE(28, 31, 'GET READY. . .');
DELAY:=Ø; ENTER:=Ø;
TIME:=P;
WHILE (DELAY<TIME) AND (ENTER= Ø) DO
    BEGIN
    ENTER:=INKEY;
```

```
        DELAY:=DELAY+1
        END;
    IF ENTER=0 THEN
        BEGIN
        FOR DY:=1 TO 4 DO
            FOR DX:=1 TO 8 DO PLOT(DX+32,  DY+5, 1);
        REPEAT
            COUNTER:=COUNTER+1;
            STOP:=INKEY
        UNTIL STOP=13;
        WRITE(13, 13, 'REACTION TIME IS',
            (COUNTER*2)#, 'THOUSANDTHS OF A SECOND');
            END
    ELSE WRITE(13, 'TOO SOON . . . RUN AGAIN')
    END.
```

Example 14-4 represents the complete REACTION TIME TEST program, at least as far as it was defined in the original flow chart and program in Example 14-1. It turns out that my concern about being able to hit the ENTER key before the square was completely drawn was a needless concern. Upon trying to beat the square, I found it couldn't be done. That's the sort of thing that the top-down approach to programming can resolve for you.

Perhaps you would like to work on the program a bit more, doing things such as adding a more complete set of instructions at the beginning and tinkering with the COUNTER to make it a bit more accurate. That is up to you, the programmer.

At any rate, the program was developed here in a top-down fashion. In a matter of speaking, the program was "complete" from the start. All the additional work involved adding in the stubs and debugging the routine. The next section of this chapter deals with the matter of writing a program in a bottom-up fashion.

WRITING A TINY PASCAL PROGRAM FROM THE BOTTOM AND UP

The basic idea behind writing a program from the bottom-up is to work out a set of complete program *modules* —major sections of the program that are, in themselves, completely workable and free of bugs. The final step is to string all those modules together with a main program.

Preliminary Flow Chart for an Arrow Shooting Game

Figure 14-2 shows the preliminary flow chart for an arrow shooting game. The idea is to launch an arrow figure at a large white square that is bouncing up and down on the right-hand side of the screen. If you hit the square with the arrow, the score shows an additional point. If you miss, there is no added score.

The game runs for 10 arrow shots. The trick is that you never know exactly where the arrow will be positioned along the left-hand side of the screen. So there is some skill involved.

For the sake of writing the program in a bottom-up fashion, the operations can be divided into a number of basic steps. First, there are the operations involved in doing the heading: writing the heading messages, clearing the screen and picking a seed number for the random number generator.

The second set of operations concern fixing the random position of the arrow at the left-hand side of the screen. At about the same time, the target square ought to begin bouncing up and down on the right-hand side of the screen.

The next major block of operations are responsible for launching the arrow at the target figure. Then the program calls for a set of conditional steps that determine whether the arrow reaches the right-hand side fo the screen without touching the target figure (that amounts to a missed shot), or whether the arrow strikes the target figure (that's a hit).

Finally, the program updates the score and tests for the tenth shot. If the tenth shot has just occurred, the program concludes. Otherwise, it loops back up to the point where the arrow figure is drawn again in a new, randomly selected point on the left side of the screen.

That amounts to a complete flow chart representation of the program's main events. There are some details that have to be resolved, but that can wait until later in the bottom-up process.

Heading Information Module

Getting the programming process underway, you are free to start with any of the major operations, structural modules, to be specific. For the sake of getting started, begin with the easiest module, the one that prints out the heading information.

That part of the program might look something like this:

Example 14-5

```
(*ARROW SHOOT *)
(*HEADING*)
WRITE(28, 31, 220, '** ARROW SHOOT GAME **', 13,
    13);
WRITE('STRIKE THE ENTER KEY TO START');
```

```
WHILE INKEY<>13 DO
    BEGIN
    IF (SEED<99) OR (SEED>999) THEN SEED:=99;
    SEED:=SEED+1
    END;
```

That looks pretty good for a program module. It clears the screen, prints the name of the game across the middle of the top line, and then counts SEED numbers rather rapidly until the player strikes the ENTER key to get the game started. The problem is that it isn't a complete Pascal program as it stands. In order to check it out, you must fill in some details. Declare the SEED variable, begin the block with BEGIN and end it with END.

Even if you do round out the module in Example 14-5 so that it can be run on the computer, you have no way of knowing whether or not the SEED counter is actually picking up a number between 99 and 999 when the user strikes the ENTER key. So you also have to write in a testing line. A good test line in this case is WRITE(SEED#). That will write out the selected SEED number for you.

Here is a suggested on-line program for the heading module:

Example 14-6

```
(* ARROW SHOOT *)
VAR SEED:INTEGER;
BEGIN
(* HEADING *)
WRITE(28, 31, 220, '** ARROW SHOOT GAME **', 13,
    13);
WRITE('STRIKE ENTER KEY TO START');
WHILE INKEY<>13 DO
    BEGIN
    IF (SEED<99) OR (SEED>999) THEN SEED:=99;
    SEED:=SEED+1
    END;
WRITE (SEED#)
END.
```

Enter Example 14-6 into your computer, and you will find it runs just fine. I ran it 10 times in succession and never came up with the same seed number twice. Of course, all of the SEED values were between 99 and 999.

That completes the work on one module. Now you can either keep it in program memory, using it every time you test another

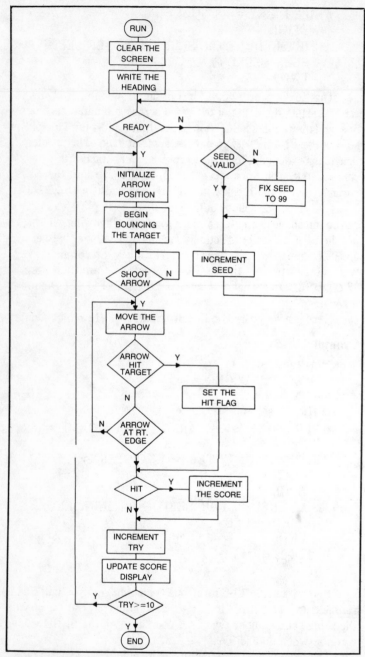

Fig. 14-2. Preliminary flow chart for ARROW SHOOT program. See Examples 14-5 through 14-16.

module, or write it down so that it can be cleared from memory. It is generally better in the long run to record the module (without the test lines) on paper; then wipe out the whole thing to make room for the next module. Getting modules interacting at this point in the process can cause more trouble than it's worth.

Incidentally, I thought the 220 tabulation code moved the ** ARROW SHOOT GAME ** heading too far to the right. So when I copied the program onto paper, I changed that number to 215.

Target-Moving Module

It really doesn't make much difference which major operation you choose for the second module in this particular bottom-up process. I was quite interested in the technique of making the white square move up and down along the right-hand side of the screen, so I picked that as the next module.

Example 14-7

```
(* START MOVING THE TARGET *)
TARGET:=16310; PHASE:=-1;
REPEAT
    REPEAT
        TARGET:=TARGET+64*PHASE;
        FOR DX:=1 TO 3 DO
            MEM(TARGET+DX):=191;
        FOR DELAY:=0 TO 100 DO;
        FOR DX:= 1 TO 3 DO
            MEM(TARGET+DX):=32
    UNTIL(TARGET<15424) OR (TARGET>16315);
    PHASE:=PHASE*(-1)
UNTIL(arrow hits the target) OR (arrow hits the right
    side);
```

Example 14-7 indicates the general flow of operations for making a lighted square move up and down on the left side of the screen. It cannot be compiled and tested, however, until you write in some other statements. For example:

Example 14-8

```
(* ARROW SHOOT *)
VAR TARGET, PHASE, DX, DELAY: INTEGER;
BEGIN
( * START MOVING THE TARGET *)
TARGET: = 16310; PHASE: = -1;
    REPEAT
```

```
        REPEAT
            TARGET:=TARGET+64*PHASE;
            FOR DX:=1 TO 3 DO
                MEM(TARGET+DX) :=191;
            FOR DELAY:=Ø TO 1ØØ DO;
            FOR DX:=1 TO 3 DO
                MEM(TARGET+DX) :=32
        UNTIL (TARGET 15424) OR (TARGET 16315);
        PHASE:=PHASE*(-1)
    UNTIL TARGET TARGET
END.
```

This target-moving module can be run and tested in the form shown in Example 14-8. The statement, UNTIL TARGET TARGET, is included for testing purposes. It makes certain the program continues running until you strike the BREAK key to get out of it.

You might want to experiment with the time delay line that actually sets the speed of the bouncing target. That is the line, FOR DELAY:=Ø TO 1ØØ DO. Just change around the value of 1ØØ to something larger to slow down the bouncing effect. Making that same number smaller increases the bouncing speed.

When you are satisfied with the target bouncing module, record your figures on paper for future reference. Remember that many of the statements in Example 14-8 are included just for testing purposes. The extra statements won't appear in the version that will be inserted into the final program at a later time.

Arrow-Moving Module

The next module ought to be the one that fires the arrow figure from left to right across the screen. Here is a working draft of that arrow-moving module.

Example 14-9

```
( * FIRE THE ARROW *)
SARROW:=15424+ random number between Ø and 15;
ARROW:=SARROW;
REPEAT
    ARROW:=ARROW+1;
    MEM(ARROW):=94;
    FOR DELAY:=Ø TO 1Ø DO;
    MEM(ARROW) :=32
UNTIL (ARROW>=SARROW+63) OR (ARROW=target
    position);
```

That is just the general approach and how it will look in the finished program. To run and test it, you have to fit in some other statements.

Example 14-10

```
( * ARROW SHOOT *)
VAR SARROW, ARROW, DELAY:INTEGER;
BEGIN
( * FIRE THE ARROW *)
SARROW:=15424;
ARROW:=SARROW;
REPEAT
    ARROW:=ARROW+1;
    MEM(ARROW):=94;
    FOR DELAY:=0 TO 10 DO;
    MEM(ARROW):=32
UNTIL (ARROW=SARROW+63)
END.
```

Every time you run the module in Example 14-10, you see a little arrow flying across the top of the screen, from left to right. You might want to insert a WRITE (28,31) statement after the BEGIN. That will clear the program statements from the screen before the arrow is launched. It really doesn't make any difference at this point.

Maybe you have noticed that there is no reason to work with these module in any particular order. That is generally the case when doing bottom-up programming. Sometimes, though, a bit of common sense dictates working with a couple of modules in a particular order. So far, it hasn't made any real difference which modules you tackle next.

Random Number Generator Module

The only remaining module of any significant complexity is the one that generates the random number for setting the initial vertical position of the arrow figure. You have already seen the random number generator a number of times through this book, so there is no need to present it here in a general form. Instead, go directly to the testing form that can be run on the computer:

Example 14-11

```
( * ARROW SHOOT * )
VAR N,M,P, SEED: INTEGER;
BEGIN
(* INITIALIZE ARROW POSITION *)
N:=SEED;
REPEAT
    REPEAT
    M:=N*3125;
    IF M<∅ THEN M:=ABS(M);
    N:=M;P:=M;
    P:=P MOD 15;
    UNTIL (P>=∅) AND (P<=15);
    WRITE(P#,32)
UNTIL P<>P
END.
```

This testing routine fills the screen with random numbers between ∅ and 15. Let it run for a while; then strike the BREAK key to stop it. Check to make certain all numbers between ∅ and 15 are indeed generated by the program. Oops, that isn't right! There are no 15s in the list.

That is easy to fix, though. Just change P:=P MOD 15 to read P:=P MOD 17. Try the program again, and you will see the 15s are there. Checking these little modules certainly pays off.

To this point, everything has been written and tested in a piecemeal fashion. There are a couple of minor steps yet to be prepared such as the scorekeeping, counting the number of arrows shot and making the decisions about when to end the overall program. Those details, however, can be included as you assemble the modules into a finished program.

Entering Heading Operations

Clear out the program memory, and start stringing things together from the beginning. First enter the heading operations from Example 14-12. Don't worry about declaring all the variables for the program. Just work with the ones required for the module you're entering at the moment.

When the HEADING module is in place, your programming should look something like this:

Example 14-12

```
(* ARROW SHOOT *)
VAR SEED:INTEGER;
BEGIN
(* HEADING *)
WRITE(28,31,215, '** ARROW SHOOT GAME **',13,13);
WRITE('YOU HAVE 10 CHANCES TO HIT A
    MOVING TARGET WITH AN ARROW',13);
WRITE('WHEN YOU WANT TO SHOOT THAT
    ARROW, JUST STRIKE THE ENTER');
WRITE(13,32, 'KEY.',13,13,13, 'STRIKE THE ENTER
    KEY TO START...');
WHILE INKEY 13 DO
    BEGIN
    IF(SEED<99) OR (SEED>999) THEN SEED:=99;
    SEED:=SEED+1
    END;
END.
```

That is a bit different from the original version outlined in Example 14-5 and tested by Example 14-6. But the changes do not affect the actual operation of the program. They merely help clarify what the player is supposed to do. Nothing is cast in concrete when it comes to embellishing a program as you work it into its final form.

N: = SEED Statement

Run this part of the program to make sure everything is working as expected. Then, since the SEED number is now available, add on the random number generating algorithm from Example 14-11, leaving out the REPEAT...UNTIL loop that forced it to run continuously for testing purposes. After making a few more minor adjustments the program should look much like this:

Example 14-13

```
(* ARROW SHOOT *)
VAR SEED,N,M,P:INTEGER;
BEGIN
(* HEADING *)
WRITE(28,31,215, '** ARROW SHOOT GAME **',13,13);
WRITE ('YOU HAVE 10 CHANCES TO HIT A
```

```
      MOVING TARGET WITH AN ARROW; 13);
WRITE('WHEN YOU WANT TO SHOOT THAT
      ARROW, JUST STRIKE THE ENTER');
WRITE(13,'KEY.',13,13,13,'STRIKE THE ENTER
      KEY TO START...');
WHILE INKEY<>13 DO
      BEGIN
      IF (SEED<99) OR (SEED>999) THEN SEED:=99;
      SEED:=SEED+1
      END;
(* INITIALIZE ARROW POSITION *)
N:=SEED;
REPEAT
      M:=N*3125;
      IF M<Ø THEN M:=ABS(M);
      N:=M;P:=M;
      PL=P MOD 17
UNTIL (P>=Ø) AND (P<=15);
END.
```

The statement, N:=SEED is the one that ties the two modules together.

Adding The Arrow-Firing Module

Now add on the module that positions and fires the arrow across the screen. That comes from Example 14-9.

Example 14-14

```
(* ARROW SHOOT *)
VAR SEED,N,M,P,SARROW, ARROW, DELAY:
      INTEGER;
BEGIN
(* HEADING *)
WRITE(28,31,215,'** ARROW SHOOT GAME **',13,13);
WRITE('YOU HAVE 1Ø CHANCES TO HIT A
      MOVING TARGET WITH AN ARROW. ',13);
WRITE('WHEN YOU WANT TO SHOOT THAT
      ARROW, JUST STRIKE THE ENTER ');
WRITE(13,'KEY.',13,13,13,'STRIKE THE ENTER
      KEY TO START...');
WHILE INKEY<>13 DO
      BEGIN
```

```
                IF (SEED<99) OR (SEED>999) THEN SEED:=99;
                SEED:=SEED+1
                END;
            (* INITIALIZE ARROW POSITION *)
            N:=SEED;
            REPEAT
                M:=N*3125;
                IF M<Ø THEN M:=ABS(M):
                N:=M;P:=M;
                P:=P MOD 17
            UNTIL (P>=Ø) AND (P<=13);
            (* FIRE THE ARROW *)
            WRITE(28,31);
            SARROW=15424+64*P;
            ARROW:=SARROW;
            MEM(SARROW):=94;
            WHILE INKEY<>13 DO;
            MEM(SARROW):=32;
            REPEAT
                ARROW:=ARROW+1;
                MEM(ARROW):=94;
                FOR DELAY:=Ø TO 1Ø DO;
                MEM(ARROW):=32
            UNTIL (ARROW=SARROW+63);
            END.
```

Several new statements are required to merge FIRE THE
ARROW module with INITIALIZE ARROW POSITION. The new
ones are a WRITE(28,31) which clears the heading messages from
the screen; WHILE INKEY 13 to stop the progress of the program
until the player strike the ENTER key to fire the arrow, and an
extra set of statements that first draw the arrow figure and then
erase it. Both are required for showing the arrow in its initial
position.

Working In The Target-Moving Module

Before attempting to test the program to the point illustrated
by Example 14-15, note a slight change in the range of random
numbers. In the INITIALIZE ARROW POSITION module, a
statement that read UNTIL (P>=Ø) AND (P<=15) now reads
UNTIL (P>=Ø) AND (P<=13). The range of random numbers had
to be reduced from 15 to 13 at the upper end. The modified
initialization statement, SARROW:=15424+64*4, made it possi-

ble to run the arrow out of the video memory and into places where it can totally mess up the program, Tiny Pascal's programming and just about everything else in the system.

Running the program as it stands thus far, you can see the headings, strike the ENTER key to start the game, see the arrow figure in a randomly selected position, and then fire the arrow across the screen. The program simply ends when the arrow reaches the extreme right-hand side of the screen.

By this time, you should be able to appreciate some clear distinctions between top-down and bottom-up program design methods. Both methods work, but their similarity seems to end at that.

The next step is a trickier one. Working in the START MOVING THE TARGET module (from Example 14-7) is not simply a matter of sticking it onto the end of the existing program and perhaps adding a few transition statements. Rather, this new module has to be closely meshed with the FIRE THE ARROW MODULE. The two have to mesh in such a way that the target can be bouncing while the arrow figure is being initialized and fired across the screen.

Example 14-15 is the result of merging the START MOVING THE TARGET with FIRE THE ARROW. Frankly, this was quite a tough job. The listing represents the result of a lot of cut-and-try modifications as well as thoughtful programming.

Example 14-15

```
(* ARROW SHOOT *)
VAR SEED, N, M, P,SARROW, ARROW, DELAY:
    INTEGER;
DX,TARGET,FARROW,PHASE,DARROW:INTEGER;
BEGIN
(* HEADING *)
WRITE(28,31,215,'**ARROW SHOOT GAME **)',13,13);
WRITE('YOU HAVE 1Ø CHANCES TO HIT A MOVING
    TARGET WITH AN ARROW. ',13);
WRITE('WHEN YOU WANT TO SHOOT THAT ARROW,
    JUST STRIKE THE ENTER ');
WRITE(13,'KEY. ',13,13,13,'STRIKE THE ENTER
    KEY TO START... ');
WHILE INKEY<>13 DO
    BEGIN
        IF (SEED<99) OR (SEED>999) THEN SEED:=99;
```

```
                    SEED:=SEED+1
                    END;
        (* INITIALIZE ARROW POSITION *)
        N:=SEED;
        REPEAT
            M:=N*3125;
            IF M<0 THEN M:=ABS(M);
            N:=M;P:=M;
            P:=P MOD 17
        UNTIL (P>=0) AND (P<=13);
        (* INITIALIZE FIGURES *)
        WRITE(28,31);
        SARROW:=15424+64*P;ARROW:=SARROW;
        MEM(SARROW):=94;
        FARROW:=0;PHASE:=-1;
        TARGET:=16310;
        (* START MOVING THE TARGET *)
        REPEAT
            TARGET:=TARGET+64*PHASE;
            FOR DX:=1 TO 3 DO
                MEM(TARGET+DX):=191;
            DELAY:=0;
            WHILE DELAY<10 DO
                BEGIN
                IF NOT FARROW THEN
                    BEGIN
                    FARROW:=INKEY;
                    IF FARROW=13 THEN
                        FARROW:=1
                    ELSE
                        FARROW:=0;
                    END
                ELSE IF (FARROW=1) AND (ARROW<
                    (SARROW+63)) THEN
                    BEGIN
                    MEM(ARROW):=32;
                    ARROW:=ARROW+1;
                    MEM(ARROW):=94
                    END;
                DELAY:=DELAY+1
                END;
            IF (TARGET<15424) OR (TARGET>16315)THEN
```

281

```
        PHASE:=PHASE*(-1);
    FOR DX:=1 TO 3 DO
        MEM(TARGET+DX):=32
    UNTIL (ARROW=TARGET) OR (ARROW>=(SARROW
    +63))
    END.
```

Now all of the modules developed at earlier points in this bottom-up programming process are incorporated into a master program. All that remains to be done is fit in the scoring feature and, perhaps, touch up a few minor points.

Final Version Of The Arrow Shooting Game

Here is the final version:

Example 14-16

```
  (* ARROW SHOOT *)
VAR SEED,N,M,P,SARROW,ARROW,DELAY:INTEGER;
  DX,TARGET,FARROW,PHASE,SCORE,TRY:INTEGER;
  RATE,HIT:INTEGER;
BEGIN
(* HEADING *)
WRITE(28,31,215,'** ARROW SHOOT GAME **)',13,13);
WRITE('YOU HAVE 10 CHANCES TO HIT A MOVING TARGET
  WITH AN ARROW.',13);
WRITE('WHEN YOU WANT TO SHOOT THAT ARROW, JUST
  STRIKE THE ENTER');
WRITE(13,'KEY.',13,13,13,'ENTER DESIRED LEVEL OF
  DIFFICULTY:');
REPEAT
WRITE(13,13,200,'1 - BEGINNER',13,200,'2 - PRETTY
  GOOD',13,200,'3 - EXPERT',13);
  READ(RATE#)
UNTIL (RATE>=1) AND (RATE<=3);
WRITE(28,31,'OK, STRIKE THE ENTER KEY TO START...');
WHILE INKEY<>13 DO
  BEGIN
  IF (SEED<99) OR (SEED>999)  THEN SEED:=99;
  SEED:=SEED+1
  END;
(* INITIALIZE ARROW POSITION *)
N:=SEED;
WRITE(28,31);
SCORE:=0;TRY:=0;
REPEAT
  TRY:=TRY+1;HIT:=0;
  WRITE(29,30,'TRY:',TRY#,200,'SCORE:',SCORE#);
  REPEAT
    M:=N*3125;
    IF M<0 THEN M:=ABS(M);
    N:=M;P:=M;
    P:=P MOD 17
  UNTIL (P>=0) AND (P<=13);
```

282

```
(* INITIALIZE ARROW AND TARGET *)
  SARROW:=15424+64*P;ARROW:=SARROW;
  MEM(SARROW):=94;
  FARROW:=0;PHASE:=-1;
  TARGET:=16310;
(* START MOVING THE TARGET *)
  REPEAT
  TARGET:=TARGET+64*PHASE;
    FOR DX:=1 TO 3 DO
      MEM(TARGET+DX):=191;
    DELAY:=0;
    WHILE DELAY<(40-10*RATE) DO
      BEGIN
      IF NOT FARROW THEN
        BEGIN
        FARROW:=INKEY;
        IF FARROW=13 THEN
          FARROW:=1
        ELSE
          FARROW:=0;
        END
      ELSE IF (FARROW=1) AND (ARROW<(SARROW+63)) THEN
        BEGIN
        MEM(ARROW):=32;
        ARROW:=ARROW+1;
        MEM(ARROW):=94;
        IF ARROW=TARGET THEN
          HIT:=1
        END;
      DELAY:=DELAY+1
      END;
    IF (TARGET<15424) OR (TARGET>16315) THEN
    PHASE:=PHASE*(-1);
    FOR DX:=1 TO 3 DO
      MEM(TARGET+DX):=32;
  UNTIL (HIT=1) OR (ARROW>=(SARROW+63));
  IF HIT THEN
    SCORE:=SCORE+1;
UNTIL TRY=10;
WRITE(29,30,'GAME DONE',13,'FINAL SCORE IS ',SCORE#,'
OUT OF 10',13,13,'ENTER R TO PLAY AGAIN...');
END.
```

That was a lot of work. The important thing, however, is that the program works, and it is fun to play.

The fact that the bottom-up procedures for writing this program seemed rather involved is no accident. Indeed, it is often more work to assemble a program via the bottom-up route than by the top-down method. But the bottom-up procedure yielded a fine program here; one can only wonder if it would have been any easier and faster to do it by the top-down method.

COMBINING TOP-DOWN AND BOTTOM-UP PROGRAMMING

Perhaps you suspect by now that the most effective way to prepare structured programs is by applying both the top-down and bottom-up methods. It is quite likely the ARROW SHOOT program would have gone together a bit easier if some top-down methods had been used in at least a couple of places.

The game used in this illustration might be called SCREW-BALL GOLF. The game consists of nine different "hole" frames. The idea is to get to the hole in the present frame with a little ball figure. The player works through 10 different hole frames, and a scoring feature keeps track of the total number of strokes required for hitting all 10 holes. The idea is to play 9 holes with the lowest possible stroke score.

The catch is that the ball is a screwball. It moves in a spiral path rather than a straight line. Before making each stroke, the player must specify the amount of horizontal, vertical and total distance motion.

It isn't an easy game. The tricky ball motion isn't the end of the challenge. The holes rarely show up in the same position each time.

Preliminary Flow Chart For SCREWBALL GOLF

Figure 14-3 shows the preliminary flow chart for SCREW-BALL GOLF. The first phase of the game merely spells out some heading information and gives the system a chance to pick a random seed number for the random number generator.

The second phase sets the positions of the current hole and initial position of the ball. The player specifies the motion parameters for the stroke.

After the player makes the swing, the ball begins to move in its screwy way, hopefully toward the hole. This phase of the operation is terminated by one of three conditionals: BALL AT HOLE, BALL IN ROUGH or MOVE DONE.

Satisfying the BALL AT HOLE conditional is a matter of getting the ball to the hole. That's the goal of every swing. The ball must not be allowed to roam off the screen, however, and the BALL IN ROUGH conditional is responsible for detecting that undesirable state.

As mentioned earlier, the player specifies the total distance the ball is to travel. So there is a need for a MOVE DONE conditional.

Any one of these three conditionals end up having the ball stop moving. If the ball happens to be at the hole, as detected by the HOLE FLAG conditional, the system increments the hole number, checks to see if all 10 holes have been played, and then either starts a new hole frame or ends the game.

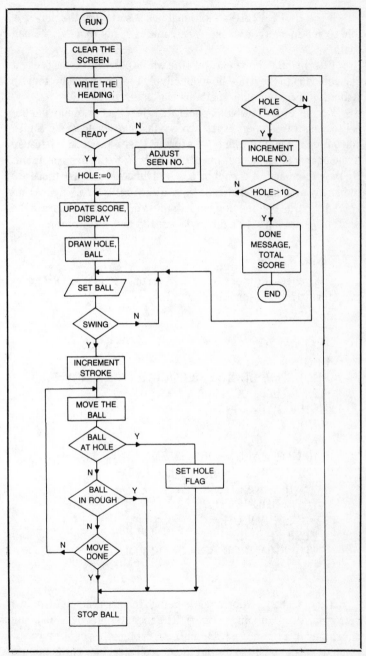

Fig. 14-3. Preliminary flow chart for SCREWBALL GOLF. See Examples 14-17 through 14-21.

If the HOLE FLAG conditional is *not* satisfied, the player is told to set up another stroke. The game is ready to move the ball again.

Bear in mind, however, that the whole purpose of this present discussion is to illustrate how effectively top-down and bottom-up structured programming methods can be used together.

For instance, it would appear that the process of moving the ball across the screen in its screwy fashion would make a nice bottom-up module. It cannot be a formal Pascal procedure because it must carry the final position of the ball back to the main program. On the other hand, it cannot be a Pascal function because there are too many non-mathematical steps (drawing the ball figure) involved. So this ball moving module must be an integral part of the main program, and it ought to be written and tested first.

MOVE BALL Module

The general flow of events, in a partial Tiny Pascal Programming format, looks something like this:

Example 14-17

```
(* MOVE BALL *)
BEGIN
FHOLE:=∅; BDONE:=∅;ROUGH:=∅; SWING:=∅;
player sets up ball motion
WHILE SWING 13 DO;
REPEAT
  move the ball
  IF NOT BALL=HOLE THEN
    IF NOT ball in the rough THEN
      IF move is done THEN
          BDONE:=1
      ELSE ROUGH:=1
    ELSE FHOLE:=1;
UNTIL FHOLE OR BDONE OR ROUGH
END.
```

That is a ball motion module being treated as an element in a bottom-up programming process. The module, however, is being developed in a top-down fashion. It isn't complete yet as there are some details to be filled in. But the overall structure of the thing is set.

Example 14-18

```
(* SCREWBALL GOLF *)
VAR DY, DX, XBALL, YBALL, DE-
    LAY, FHOLE, DMOVE, BDONE, ROUGH:INTEGER;
    MOVE:INTEGER;
BEGIN
(*MOVE BALL *)
WRITE(28,31);
FOR DY:=0 TO 2 DO
    FOR DX:=0 TO 4 DO
        PLOT(120+DX,10+DY,1);
FHOLE:=0;BDONE:=0;ROUGH:=0;
XBALL:=0;YBALL:=12;DMOVE:=200;
PLOT(XBALL,YBALL,1);
WHILE INKEY<>13 DO;
MOVE:=0;
REPEAT
    PLOT(XBALL,YBALL,0);
    XBALL:=XBALL+1;
    IF NOT POINT(XBALL,YBALL) THEN
        IF NOT ((XBAL>127) OR (XBALL<0) OR
            (YBALL>47) OR
            (YBALL<0)) THEN
        BEGIN
        PLOT(XBALL,YBALL,1);
        MOVE:=MOVE+1;
        IF MOVE>=DMOVE THEN
            BDONE:=1;
        FOR DELAY:=0 TO 20 DO;
        END
        ELSE ROUGH:=1
    ELSE
        BEGIN
        FHOLE:=1;
        PLOT(XBALL,YBALL,0)
        END;
UNTIL FHOLE OR BDONE OR ROUGH
END.
```

Checking FHOLE, BDONE and ROUGH

The MOVE BALL module in Example 14-18 can be run on the computer for testing purposes. The ball can be fired across the

287

screen to the hole, doing an automatic hole-in-one shot. The idea is to see whether or not the FHOLE scheme really works.

Check out the BDONE scheme (the one that allows only a certain distance of motion). Modify the program so that variable DMOVE is initialized to 5Ø instead of 2ØØ. That way the ball should stop short of the hole.

To check the ROUGH detector, return the DMOVE initializing point back to 2ØØ. Raise the initial position of the ball so that it cannot hit the hole. That will run the ball off the screen and into the rough. To make that modification, initialize YBALL at 8 instead of 12.

Those tests for FHOLE, BDONE and ROUGH are a little awkward because they call for modifying the actual program listing. An alternative would be to write in some READ statements that allow you to set the values of ball motion and DMOVE from the keyboard. That way it is possible to test the different operations each time the program is run.

With the major flags thus checked out, it is time to work in some more programming. Making the ball move through its screwy motions seems to be the appropriate part to handle next.

Screwball Motions

Figure 14-4 shows the four different screwball motions for this SCREWBALL GOLF game. The basic pattern of motion is made up of six horizontal increments, four vertical increments, two horizontals and then two more vertical increments. This 6, 4, 2, 2 pattern makes up a 14-increment cycle of motion.

Motion 1 is basically a movement to the upper right, motion 2 works the ball in an upward and to the left direction, motion 3 moves the ball downward and to the right, while motion 4 carries it downward and to the left. Of course, it is possible to come up with a lot of other combinations of screwball motions. But these suffice for an interesting and challenging round of golf.

Example 14-19 shows the motion controls fit into the program in a top-down fashion. It is a matter of taking the program in Example 14-18, adding in some motion control functions and rounding out the process with a few more mainline statements. The new version, incidentally, also contains the READ statements for letting the user specify the distance and direction of the ball's motion.

Example 14-19

```
(* SCREWBALL GOLF *)
VAR DY, DX, XBALL, YBALL, DELAY, FHOLE,
```

```
        DMOVE, BDONE, ROUGH:INTEGER;
            MOVE, UD, RL, CYC:INTEGER;
FUNC MOT (UD, RL);
        BEGIN
        IF (UD='U') AND (RL='R') THEN MOT:=1
        ELSE IF (UD='U') AND (RL='L') THEN MOT:=2
        ELSE IF (UD='D') AND (RL='R') THEN MOT:=3
        ELSE IF (UD='D') AND (RL='L') THEN MOT:=4
        ELSE MOT:=0
        END;
FUNC PHASE (MOT, CYC);
        BEGIN
        IF MOT=0 THEN PHASE:=0
            ELSE CASE CYC OF
                1, 2, 3, 4, 5, 6: CASE MOT OF
                                1, 3: PHASE:=1;
                                2, 4: PHASE:=2
                                END;
                7, 8, 9, 10: CASE MOT OF
                                1, 2: PHASE:=4;
                                3, 4: PHASE:=3
                                END;
                11, 12: CASE MOT OF
                                2, 4: PHASE:=1;
                                1, 3: PHASE:=2
                                END;
                13, 14: CASE MOT OF
                                1, 2: PHASE:=3;
                                3, 4:PHASE:=4
                                END
            END
        END;
    BEGIN
    (* INITIALIZE *)
    WRITE (28, 31);
    FOR DY:=0 TO 2 DO
        FOR DX:=0 TO 4 DO
                PLOT(120+DX,10+DY,1);
    FHOLE:=0;BDONE:=0;ROUGH:=0;
    XBALL:=0;YBALL:=12;
    PLOT(XBALL, YBALL, 1);
    WRITE (28, 30);
```

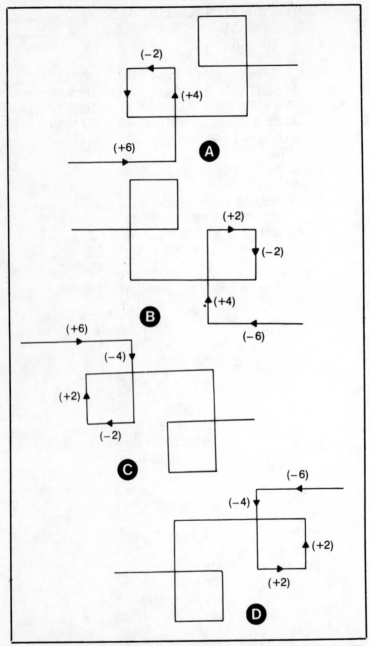

Fig. 14-4. Patterns of ball motion for SCREWBALL GOLF. (A) Up and right. (B) Up and left. (C) Down and right. (D) Down and left.

```
(* SET UP THE STROKE *)
WRITE (13, 30, 'UP OR DOWN?');
READ (UD);
WRITE (29, 30, 'LEFT OR RIGHT?');
READ(RL);
WRITE(29, 30, 'DISTANCE ');
READ(DMOVE#);
(* DO THE STROKE *)
MOVE:=0;CYC:=1;
REPEAT
    PLOT(XBALL, YBALL, 0);
    CASE PHASE (MOT(UD, RL), CYC) OF
        1: XBALL:=XBALL+1;
        2: XBALL:=XBALL-1;
        3: YBALL:=YBALL+1;
        4: YBALL:=YBALL-1;
        END;
    IF NOT POINT(XBALL, YBALL) THEN
        IF NOT ((XBALL>127)  OR (XBALL<0)
          OR  (YBALL>47) OR
                (YBALL<0)) THEN
        BEGIN
        PLOT(XBALL, YBALL,1);
        MOVE:=MOVE+1;
        CYC:=CYC+1;
        IF CYC>=14 THEN CYC:=1;
        IF MOVE>=DMOVE THEN BDONE:=1;
        FOR DELAY:=0 TO 10 DO;
        END
        ELSE ROUGH:=1;
    ELSE
        BEGIN
        FHOLE:=1;
        PLOT(XBALL, YBALL, 0)
        END;
    UNTIL FHOLE OR BDONE OR ROUGH
    END.
```

The program isn't complete, so you cannot expect a full range of tests at this time. The only motion specification that does anything significant is a DOWN, RIGHT at a distance of maybe a 100 or more. You cannot hit the hole, not yet, anyway.

Multiple Stroke Feature

The next draft of the SCREWBALL GOLF program extends the listing to let the player make any number of strokes required for getting to the hole. Adding a STROKE counter and display seemed to work in at the same time.

In the process of fitting the multiple stroke feature, I uncovered a major bug in the game. The ball could not be hit out of the rough. It wasn't possible to pick up that problem while running Example 14-19, but it certainly showed up this time around.

The cure amounts to pulling the ball one increment out of the rough. To penalize an overzealous player, the STROKE counter is automatically incremented by two whenever the ball is hit out of the rough condition. That was a little wrinkle that occurred to me only after dealing with the ROUGH problem. Working with both bottom-up and top-down programming methods often suggest new wrinkles to make programs work more efficiently or effectively.

One-Hole Golf Game Program

I then played with the program for a while, and decided to fit in a random number generator to set the intitial positions of the ball and hole. You will find that feature, along with the STROKE and ROUGH ideas, fits into Example 14-20. The program listing, as it stands in Example 14-20, is a nice one-hole of SCREWBALL GOLF. Maybe you'll want to conclude the programming at this point.

Example 14-20

```
(* SCREWBALL GOLF *)
VAR DY, DX, XBALL, YBALL, DELAY, FHOLE, DMOVE,
    BDONE, ROUGH:INTEGER;
    MOVE, UD, RL, CYC, STROKE, SEED, N,
    XHOLE, YHOLE:INTEGER;
FUNC MOT(UD, RL);
    BEGIN
    IF (UD='U') AND (RL='R') THEN MOT:=1
    ELSE IF (UD='U') AND (RL='L') THEN MOT:=2
    ELSE IF (UD='D') AND (RL='R') THEN MOT:=3
    ELSE IF (UD='D') AND (RL='L') THEN MOT:=4
    ELSE MOT:=∅
    END;
FUNC PHASE (MOT, CYC);
    BEGIN
    IF MOT:=∅ THEN PHASE:=∅
```

```
            ELSE CASE CYC OF
                1, 2, 3, 4, 5, 6: CASE MOT OF
                            1, 3: PHASE:=1;
                            2, 4: PHASE:=2
                            END;
                7, 8, 9, 10: CASE MOT OF
                            1, 2: PHASE:=4;
                            3, 4: PHASE:=3
                            END;
                11, 12: CASE MOT OF
                            2, 4: PHASE:=1;
                            1, 3: PHASE:=2
                            END;
                13, 14: CASE MOT OF
                            1, 2: PHASE:=3;
                            3, 4: PHASE:=4
                            END
            END
        END;
    FUNC RND (RLOW, RPIGH);
        VAR M,P:INTEGER;
        BEGIN
        REPEAT
            M:=N+3125;
            IF M<0 THEN M:=ABS(M);
            N:=M;P:=M;
            P:=P MOD RHIGH
        UNTIL (P>=RLOW) AND (P<=RHIGH);
        RND:=P
        END;
    (* BEGINNING OF MAINLINE PROGRAM *)
    BEGIN
    WRITE(28, 31, 215, '** SCREWBALL GOLF GAME **');
    WRITE(13, 13, 'YOUR ARE ABOUT TO PLAY 10
        HOLES OF GOLF');
    WRITE (13, 'WITH A SCREWBALL—THAT IS A
        KIND OF BALL,');
    WRITE (13, 'AND NOT SOME KIND OF PARTNER!');
    WRITE(13, 13, 'STRIKE ENTER KEY TO START . . .');
    WHILE INKEY <>13 DO
        BEGIN
        IF (SEED<99) OR (SEED>999) THEN SEED:=99;
```

293

```
        SEED:=SEED+1
        END;
    N:=SEED;
    (* INITIALIZE *)
    WRITE (28, 31);
    XHOLE:=RND(100, 120); YHOLE:=RND(10, 40);
    FOR DY:=0 TO 2 DO
        FOR DX:=0 TO 4 DO
            PLOT(XHOLE+DX, YHOLD+DY,1);
    XBALL:=0;YBALL:=RND(10, 30);
    FHOLE:=0;STROKE:=0;
    REPEAT
        BDONE:=0; ROUGH:=0;
        PLOT(XBALL, YBALL,1);
        WRITE(28, 30);
    (* SET UP THE STROKE *)
    WRITE (13, 30, 'UP OR DOWN?');
    READ(UD);
    WRITE (29, 30, 'LEFT OR RIGHT?');
    READ(RL);
    WRITE (29, 30, 'DISTANCE ');
    READ(DMOVE#);
    STROKE:=STROKE+1;
    WRITE(27, 30, 'STROKE ', STROKE#);
    (* DO THE STROKE *)
    MOVE:=0; CYC:=1;
    REPEAT
        PLOT(XBALL, YBALL,0);
        CASE PHASE (MOT(UD,RL), CYC) OR
            1:XBALL:=XBALL+ 1;
            2:XBALL:=XBALL- 1;
            3:YBALL:=YBALL+1;
            4:YBALL:=YBALL-1
            END;
        IF NOT POINT (XBALL, YBALL) THEN
            IF NOT(XBALL>=127) OR (XBALL<=0) OR
                (BALL>=47) OR (YBALL<=6)) THEN
                BEGIN
                PLOT (XBALL, YBALL, 1);
                MOVE:=MOVE+1;
                CYC:=CYC+1;
                IF CYC>=14 THEN CYC:=1;
```

294

```
                        IF MOVE>=DMOVE THEN BDONE:=1;
                        FOR DELAY:=0 TO 10 DO;
                        END
                    ELSE
                        BEGIN
                        ROUGH:=1;
                        STROKE:=STROKE+2;
                        WRITE (220, 'IN THE ROUGH—LOSE
                            2 STROKES');
                        FOR DELAY:=0 TO 2500 DO;
                        IF XBALL<=0 THEN XBALL:=XBALL+1
                        ELSE IF  XBALL>=127   THEN
                            XBALL:=XBALL−1
                        ELSE IF YBALL<=6 THEN YBALL:=
                            YBALL+1
                        ELSE IF  YBALL>=47 THEN YBALL:
                            =YBALL−1
                        END
                ELSE
                    BEGIN
                    FHOLE:=1;
                    PLOT(XBALL, YBALL, 0)
                    END;
                UNTIL FHOLE OR BDONE OR ROUGH;
            UNTIL FHOLE
            END.
```

Nine-Hole Version

All that remains is to polish off the top-down procedure by
fitting in a HOLE counter, something to keep track of the strokes
for nine different holes. Here is the finished version of the
SCREWBALL GOLF game:

```
(* SCREWBALL GOLF *)
VAR DY,DX,XBALL,YBALL,DELAY,FHOLE,DMOVE,BDONE,ROUGH:
    INTEGER;
  MOVE,UD,RL,CYC,STROKE,SEED,N,XHOLE,YHOLE,HOLE
    INTEGER;
FUNC MOT(UD,RL);
  BEGIN
  IF (UD='U') AND (RL='R') THEN MOT:=1
  ELSE IF (UD='U') AND (RL='L') THEN MOT:=2
  ELSE IFJ (UD='D') AND (RL='R') THEN MOT:=3
  ELSE IF (UD='D') AND (RL='L') THEN MOT:=4
  ELSE MOT:=0
  END;
```

```
FUNC PHASE(MOT,CYC);
  BEGIN
  IF MOT=∅ THEN PHASE:=∅
  ELSE CASE CYC OF
    1,2,3,4,5,6: CASE MOT OF
                      1,3:PHASE:=1;
                      2,4:PHASE:=2
                     END;
    7,8,9,1∅: CASE MOT OF
                  1,2: PHASE:=4;
                  3,4: PHASE:=3
                  END;
    11,12: CASE MOT OF
                2,4: PHASE:=1;
                3,4: PHASE:=2
                END;
    13,14: CASE MOT OF
                1,2: PHASE:=3;
                3,4: PHASE:=4
                END
    END
  END;
FUNC RND(RLOW,RHIGH);
  VAR M,P:INTEGER;
  BEGIN
  REPEAT
    M:=N*3125;
    IF M,∅ THEN M:=ABS(M);
    N:=M;P:=M;
    P:=P MOD RHIMGH
  UNTIL (P.=RLOW) AND (P,=RHIGH);
  RND:=P
  END;
(* BEGINNING OF MAINLINE PROGRAM *)
BEGIN
WRITE(13,13,'STRIKE THE ENTER KEY TO START');
WHILE INKEY,.13 DO
  BEGIN
  IF (SEED,99) OR (SEED.999) THEN SEED:=99;
  SEED:=SEED+1
  END;
N:=SEED;
HOLE:=∅;STROKNE:=∅;
(* MOVE BALL *)
REPEAT
  HOLE:=HOLE+1;
  WRITE(28,31);
  XHOLE:=RND(1∅∅,12∅);YHOLE:=RND(1∅,4∅);
  FOR DY:=∅ TO 2 DO
    FOR DX:=∅ TO 4 DO
      PLOT(XHOLE+DX,YHOLE+DY,1);
  XBALL:=∅;YBALL:=RND(1∅,3∅);
  FHOLE:=∅;
  REPEAT
    BDONE:=∅;ROUGH:=∅;
    POLOT(XBALL,YBALL,1);
(* SET UP THE STROKE *)
```

```
    WRITE(28,3Ø,'HOLE ',HOLE#,215,
      'STROKES:',STROKE#,13);
    WRITE(29,3Ø,'UP OR DOWN?');
    READ(UD);
    WRITE(29,3Ø,'LEFT OR RIGHT?');
    READ(RL);
    WRITE(29,3Ø,'DISTANCE ');
    READ(DMOVE#);
    WRITE(2P7,3Ø);
    STROKE:=STROKE+1;
(* DO   THE STROKE *)
    MOVE:=Ø;CYC:=1;
    REPEAT
      PLOT(XBALL,YBALL,Ø);
      CASE PHASE(MOT(UD,RL),CYC) OF
        1:XBALL:=XBALL+1;
         2:XBALL:=XBALL-1;
        3:YBALL:=YBALL+1;
        4:YBALL:=YBALL-1
          END;
      IF NOT POINT(XBALL,YBALL) THEN
        IF NOT ((XBALL.127) OR (XBALL,=Ø) OR (YBALL.=47)

         OR (YBALL,=6)) THEN
         BEGIN
         PLOT(XBALL,YBALL,1);
         MOVE:=MOVE+1;
         CYC:=CYC+1;
         IF CYC.=14 THEN CYC:=1;
         RIF MOVE.=DMOVE THEN
           BDONE:=1;
         FOR DELAY:=Ø TO 1Ø  DO;
         END
      ELSE
        BEGIN
        ROUGH:=1;
        STROKE:=STROKE+2;
        WRITE(22Ø,'ROUGH  -- LOSE 2 STROKES');
        FOR DELAY:=Ø TO 25ØØ DO;
          IF XBALSL,=Ø THEN XBALL:=XBALL+1
          ELSE IF XBALL.=127 THEN   XBALL:=XBALL-1
          ELSE IF YBALL,=6  THEN YBALL:=YBALL+1
          ELSE IF YBALL.=47 THEN YBALL:=YBALL-1
        END
        ELSE
          BEGIN
          FHOLE:=1;
          PLOT(XBALL,YBAYTLL,Ø)
          END;
       UNTIL FHOLE OR BDONE OR ROUGH;
      UNTIL FHOLE;
    UNTIL HOLE.=9;
    WRITE(28,31,'NINE HOLES OF GOLF COMPLETED WITH ',
      STROKE#,' STROKES');
    WRITE(13,13,'ENTER R TO PLAY ANOTHER
      NINE HOLES...')
    END.
```

C/-P Command

There it is, the SCREWBALL GOLF program. It is debugged, polished and tested. But if you've been using the indentations in a conscientious fashion, you are finding you cannot compile it in the usual way. You get ERROR 1001 because there is not enough memory in a 16K computer for both the source and P-code versions of this program.

To deal with this situation, get the system into the MONITOR mode and enter C/-P. That command checks the syntax of the program for you, compiling without actually generating code. Debug the syntax as necessary to get the C/-P command to run through the entire program. Then, to be on the safe side, put the source program onto cassette tape, entering it as something like WS GOLF.

Once you have saved that valuable source program on tape, compile the source program in the computer by entering C/-S. That command compiles the P-code right over the source code program. The source code is thus destroyed, but there is then sufficient memory space for the P-code version.

After the system compiles the P-code, the program is ready to run. It has been a lot of work, but it is certainly worth it. Personally, I find SCREWBALL GOLF one of the most fascinating and challenging games around. If you ever want to modify the program, just load the source version from the cassette tape, make your modifications, and then check the syntax with the C/-P command again.

The really important point, as far as the work in this chapter is concerned, is that using both top-down and bottom-up programming methods make it possible to develop some pretty complicated programs. Without using a highly structured approach to this GOLF game, I seriously doubt many hobby computer people could do the job.

Chapter 15
Space Ranger Mission Game

Space war and pursuit games have been closely associated with computer games for a long time now. As long as programmers continue coming up with fresh ideas, these kinds of games promise to be around for a long time to come.

The game featured in this chapter is a space war/pursuit game that pushes Tiny Pascal very close to its limits. Actually there is no limit to the sophistication of a Tiny Pascal game, but here it is the 4.5k of RAM available for source programs that runs very short. Using the source program format suggested later in this chapter, SPACE RANGER MISSION takes up a bit over program space allowed by a 16k, Tiny Pascal system. Of the 4.5k-bytes of RAM space allowed for source and/or P-codes, the source version of this game, alone, takes up a bit over 4.2k-bytes. The shorter compiled version uses a bit over 2k-bytes.

So SPACE RANGER MISSION is a big game—a big program—in the context of Supersoft's Tiny Pascal format for 16k computer systems. But it isn't the size of the program that is important. The only practical consequence of its large size is the time and effort required for entering the source program, debugging it and generating the P-code version.

The program uses a good many of the Pascal principles described up to this point in the book. You will find only one really new concept introduced here, and even that ought to make good sense if you've followed everything carefully before.

The material in this chapter approaches the program from a number of different angles. You can study as much as you like, learning as much as you care to learn. For instance, you can simply load the source code from the master listing in the next section of this chapter, check it for syntax errors, load the source onto cassette tape for future use, compile the program and start playing the game. You really don't have to study the features of the Pascal programming at all.

But even if you decide to ignore the finer workings of the program, you will find there is a lot to learn about playing the game. It is a game of strategy and skill that can be made about as simple or as complex as you like.

In short, you can get about as much from the material in this chapter, the program and the game as you want to get from it. No matter how you decide to handle things, you are going to have a lot of fun playing SPACE RANGER MISSION.

GETTING SPACE RANGER MISSION IN AND UP

Set up your computer for Tiny Pascal. Clear out any old programming, put on a fresh pot of coffee and get ready to start loading the source program listed here.

Unless you peek ahead in this chapter and do some study of the Pascal functions and procedures used in the program, much of the source program listing won't make much sense. I have had to do away with much of the indentation of lines operations required for formal structured programming. For the sake of conserving program space, first, second and third-order statements are often run together on the same line. Multiple-statement lines are used through most of the listings for functions and procedures. And that's confusing.

So type in the source program in a literal fashion, following the listing as closely as you can. If you happen to make any serious typing errors, you will find them when you attempt to compile the source program.

I have compromised some program space, however, in order to write the mainline portion of the program in the standard structure-indentation format. That part of the job will most likely seem easier to enter.

So load the source program as listed here—the whole thing. Don't bother trying to compile it at any point along the way.

When the entire source program is into your computer, check for errors by doing a compile without generating the P-code. In other words, get into the monitor mode and do a C/−P. Any errors will show up that way.

Edit out the errors as they arise, and continue doing the C/−P until the entire listing is checked without errors. Next, load the source listing onto cassette tape, using a command and file name such as WS RNGE.

Now you are in a position to check out the program in its P-code format. Do a C/−S (compile P-code without the source). That operation writes the P-code version right over the source listing in your system memory, but that's the price we have to pay for using such long programs. Of course, that's why it was important to save the source listing on cassette tape.

Now it's time to run the program. What happens at that point is the subject of the section following the source listing.

```
(* SPACE RANGE MISSION *)
VAR OBJ,N,SEED,CHANGE,CFLAG,PHASE,ENGO,DELAY:INTEGER;
XCOORD:ARRAY(10)OF INTEGER;YCOORD:ARRAY(10)OF INTEGER;
XVEC:ARRAY(10) OF INTEGER;YVEC:ARRAY(10) OF INTEGER;
TYPE:ARRAY(10) OF INTEGER;LIVE:ARRAY(10) OF INTEGER;
(* RANDOM NO. *)
FUNC RND(RLOW,RHIGH);VAR M,P:INTEGER;
BEGIN REPEAT
M:=N*3125;IF M<0 THEN M:=ABS(M);N:=M;P:=M;
P:=P MOD RHIGH UNTIL (P>=RLOW) AND (P<=RHIGH);
RND:=P END;
(* RELATIVE COORDS *)
FUNC RCOORD(ELESHIP,ELETARG);BEGIN
RCOORD:=ELETARG-ELESHIP END;
(* RANGE *)
FUNC RANGE(XSHIP,YSHIP,XTARG,YTARG);VAR XDIST,YDIST,
   SCALE,RAD,ROOT:INTEGER;BEGIN
XDIST:=ABS(RCOORD(XSHIP,XTARG));YDIST:=ABS(RCOORD
   (YSHIP,YTARG));IF XDIST>=10*YDIST THEN RANGE:=XDIST;
IF YDIST>=10*XDIST THEN RANGE:=YDIST;
IF NOT((XDIST>=10*YDIST) OR (YDIST>=10*XDIST))
   THEN BEGIN
IF (XDIST<=100) AND (YDISST<=100) THEN SCALE:=1 ELSE
   BEGIN
SCALE:=10;XDIST:=XDIST DIV 10;YDIST:=YDIST DIV 10 END;
RAD:=SQR(XDIST)+SQR(YDIST);ROOT:=0;
REPEAT ROOT:=ROOT+1 UNTIL SQR(ROOT)>=RAD;
IF (SQR(ROOT)-RAD)>(ABS(SQR(ROOT-1)-RAD)) THEN ROOT:
   =ROOT-1;
RANGE:=ROOT*SCALE END END;
(* OBJECT STATUS *)
PROC ENESTAT(XSHIP,YSHIP,XENE,YENE,LIVE,TYPE);VAR
ENEDIST:INTEGER; BEGIN
ENEDIST:=RANGE(XSHIP,YSHIP,XENE,YENE); CASE TYPE OF
0:IF ENEDIST>100 THEN WRITE('OUT OF RANGE')
   ELSE WRITE('RANGE:',ENEDIST#,'X=',RCOORD(XSHIP,0)#,'
   Y=',RCOORD(YSHIP,0)#);
```

```
1:IF NOT LIVE THEN WRITE('DESTROYED')ELSE BEGIN
IF ENEDIST>100 THEN WRITE('NOT IN RANGE')
ELSE WRITE('RANGE:',ENEDIST#,' X=',RCOORD(XSHIP,
    XENE)#,'    Y=',RCOORD(YSHIP,YENE)#) END;
2:IF NOT LIVE THEN WRITE('RANGE:',ENEDIST#,' NAV
    INOPERATIVE')
ELSE WRITE('RANGE:',ENEDIST#,'X=',RCOORD(XSHIP,
    XENE)#,'    Y=',RCOORD(YSHIP,YENE)#) END;
WRITE(13) END;
(* MOVE SHIP *)
FUNC SHIPMOVE(ELESHIP,DIRSHIP);VAR NEWDIR:INTEGER;
    BEGIN
IF(ELESHIP+DIRSHIP<0) OR (ELESHIP+DIRSHIP>1000)
THEN SHIPMOVE:=ELESHIP ELSE SHIPMOVE:=ELESHIP+DIRSHIP
    END;
(* MAINLINE PROGRAM *)
BEGIN
(* SEED *)
WRITE(28,31,'ENTER TO START THE GAME...');
WHILE INKEY<>13 DO BEGIN
    IF(SEED<99) OR (SEED>999) THEN SEED:=99;SEED:=SEED+1
    END;
(* INITIALIZE GAME *)
N:=SEED;CFLAG:=0;PHASE:=1;WRITE(28,31);
FOR OBJ:=0 TO 1 DO BEGIN
    XCOORD(OBJ):=0;YCOORD(OBJ):=0;TYPE(OBJ):=0;LIVE(OBJ)
    :=1 END;
FOR OBJ:=2 TO 10 DO BEGIN
    XCOORD(OBJ):=RND(100,900);YCOORD(OBJ):=RND(100,900)
    END;
FOR OBJ:=2 TO 6 DO BEGIN
LIVE(OBJ):=1;TYPE(OBJ):=1;
REPEAT XVEC(OBJ):=(RND(1,3)-2);YVEC(OBJ):=(RND(1,3)-2)
UNTIL NOT((XVEC(OBJ)=0) AND (YVEC(OBJ)=0)) END;
FOR OBJ:=7 TO 10 DO BEGIN
LIVE(OBJ):=0;TYPE(OBJ):=2;XVEC(OBJ):=0;YVEC(OBJ):=0
    END;
(* START GAME *)
REPEAT
WRITE(28,31,210,'CURRENT NAVIGATION STATUS',13,13);
    REPEAT
    WRITE(28,13);CHANGE:=0;
    FOR OBJ:=1 TO 10 DO
        BEGIN
        IF NOT CFLAG THEN
            BEGIN
            DELAY:=0;
            WHILE (DELAY<10) AND (CHANGE=0) DO
                BEGIN
                CHANGE:=INKEY;
                DELAY:=DELAY+1
                END;
            IF CHANGE<>0 THEN CFLAG:=1
            END;
        CASE OBJ OF
            1:WRITE('HOME--');
            2:WRITE('ADVERSARY--');
```

302

```
      3:WRITE('HULK #1--');
      4:WRITE('HULK #2--');
      5:WRITE('HULK #3--');
      6:WRITE('HULK #4--');
      7:WRITE('NAV BEACON #1--');
      8:WRITE('NAV BEACON #2--');
      9:WRITE('NAV BEACON #3--');
     10:WRITE('NAV BEACON #4--')
     END;
  ENESTAT(XCOORD(0),YCOORD(0),XCOORD(OBJ),YCOORD(OBJ),
    LIVE(OBJ),TYPE(OBJ))
  END;
(* MOVE THINGS *)
  XCOORD(0):=SHIPMOVE(XCOORD(0),XVEC(0));
  YCOORD(0):=SHIPMOVE(YCOORD(0),YVEC(0));
  IF PHASE>0 THEN
    FOR ENGO:=2 TO 6 DO
      IF LIVE(ENGO)=1 THEN
        BEGIN
        XCOORD(ENGO):=XCOORD(ENGO)+XVEC(ENGO);
        IF (XCOORD(ENGO)<0) OR (XCOORD(ENGO)>1000)
        THEN
      XVEC(ENGO):=XVEC(ENGO)*(-1);
      YCOORD(ENGO):=YCOORD(ENGO)+YVEC(ENGO);
      IF (YCOORD(ENGO)<0) OR (YCOORD(ENGO)>1000) THEN
        YVEC(ENGO):=YVEC(ENGO)*(-1);
      END;
PHASE:=PHASE*(-1)
UNTIL CFLAG=1;
CFLAG:=0;
CASE CHANGE OF
  'U':YVEC(0):=1;
  'D':YVEC(0):=-1;
  'L':XVEC(0):=-1;
  'R':XVEC(0):=1;
  'S':BEGIN XVEC(0):=0;YVEC(0):=0 END;
  'N':FOR OBJ:=7 TO 10 DO
      IF RANGE(XCOORD(0),YCOORD(0),XCOORD(OBJ),YCOORD
      (OBJ))<=2 THEN LIVE(OBJ):=1; F':FOR OBJ:=2 TO 6 DO
        IF RANGE(XCOORD(0),YCOORD(0),XCOORD(OBJ),
          YCOORD(OBJ))<=10 THEN LIVE(OBJ):=0
  END;
UNTIL CHANGE='X'
END.
```

RUNNING SPACE RANGER MISSION

With the program compiled and the P-code version residing in memory, do a run. You should be greeted with the message ENTER TO START THE GAME . . .

Technically, the point of this simple heading is to generate a seed number for the program's quasi-random number generator. It's a trick used many different times in programs already described in this book.

Starting the Game

Strike the ENTER key to get the game started. This sort of display should then appear on the screen:

```
CURRENT NAVIGATION STATUS
HOME—RANGE:0   X=0   Y=0
ADVERSARY—NOT IN RANGE
HULK #1—NOT IN RANGE
HULK #2—NOT IN RANGE
HULK #3—NOT IN RANGE
HULK #4—NOT IN RANGE
NAV BEACON #1—RANGE:520 NAV INOPERATIVE
NAV BEACON #2—RANGE:860 NAV INOPERATIVE
NAV BEACON #3—RANGE:470 NAV INOPERATIVE
NAVBEACON #4—RANGE:1100 NAV INOPERATIVE
```

You will notice these lines appearing to blink in sequence. What you are seeing is the space navigation data being updated.

The three zeros on the HOME line should read as zeros whenever you first start the game. That is an indication you are starting the mission from home base. The range is 0 space units, and the coordinates of home base are likewise 0 and 0.

It is possible, but highly unlikely, that the lines for ADVERSARY and HULKS 1 through 4 will show anything but NOT IN RANGE at the very beginning of a game. The RANGE figures for NAV BEACON 1 through 4, however, will be different for each game. Your figures for NAV BEACON ranges will be quite different from those cited in this example.

The objective at this point is merely to check out the operation of the program, and not to start playing a game. So don't worry about the meaning of the figures on the screen at this point. Just follow the discussion for a bit.

As a first test, strike the U key several times in succession. This amounts to a "blast off," and you should see the Y figure in the HOME line beginning to increment in a negative direction. With each updating scan, that number will change in a sequence such as −4, −5, −6 and so on. At the same time, you should see the RANGE figure increasing in a positive direction.

Now strike the R key several times until you see the X figure for the HOME line beginning to increment in a negative direction. That amounts to a course change at right angles to the direction of blast-off. The RANGE figure for HOME should now show the length of the hypotenuse of a right triangle having the X and Y figures as the lengths of sides.

In the context of this space game, you have left home and set a course in space having certain X and Y components of motion. the program is continuously updating the RANGE from home as you move along.

Losing Contact With HOME

The HOME figures will continue showing the coordinates of your position in space and the distance to HOME until the distance exceeds 100 space units. At that time, your ship loses contact with home, and you are left rather alone in space.

Here is an example of what the display might look like, shortly after losing contact with HOME:

```
            CURRENT NAVIGATION STATUS
       HOME—OUT OF RANGE
       ADVERSARY—NOT IN RANGE
       HULK #1—NOT IN RANGE
       HULK #2—NOT IN RANGE
       HULK #3—NOT IN RANGE
       HULK #4—NOT IN RANGE
       NAV BEACON #1—RANGE:360 NAV INOPERATIVE
       NAV BEACON #2—RANGE:710 NAV INOPERATIVE
       NAV BEACON #3—RANGE:320 NAV INOPERATIVE
       NAV BEACON #4—RANGE:930 NAV INOPERATIVE
```

You can see that HOME is OUT OF RANGE, more than 100 space units behind. Note, however, that you are a lot closer to all four NAV BEACON stations. Compare these NAV BEACON ranges with those appearing in the previous example.

So you have left HOME, but moved closer to all four navigation beacons. That's good, because one of the objectives of your mission is to visit each of the inoperative navigation beacons (reduce the range to 0) and repair them. Once they are repaired, the display will show your ship's relative position in space.

Let me repeat, however, that the objective at this point is merely to test the working of the game program. Strike the S key about six times in rapid succession. That should stop your motion in space. The range figures for the NAV BEACON lines have been decrementing rather slowly all along, but now they should come to a complete stop.

ADVERSARY and HULK Lines

Sit back and watch the display for a while. This might seem to be a rather dull task, but keep an eye on the ADVERSARY and HULK lines. Although you are now stationary in space, these objects are not. The ADVERSARY and HULKS are moving about at random. Sooner or later, one of them is going to move into your navigation radar range.

While writing this paragraph, it so happened that HULK #4 moved within 100 space units. By the time I was ready to write down the figures, it had moved to a range of 89 space units, with X and Y coordinates of −10 and 88 respectively. Here is what the display looked like:

```
            CURRENT NAVIGATION STATUS
        HOME—OUT OF RANGE
        ADVERSARY—NOT IN RANGE
        HULK #1—NOT IN RANGE
        HULK #2—NOT IN RANGE
        HULK #3—NOT IN RANGE
        HULK #4—RANGE:89  X=−10  Y=88
        NAV BEACON#1—RANGE:360 NAV INOPERATIVE
        NAV BEACON #2—RANGE:710 NAV INOPERATIVE
        NAV BEACON #3—RANGE:320 NAV INOPERATIVE
        NAV BEACON #4—RANGE:930 NAV INOPERATIVE
```

If you think of yourself as a spaceship pilot resting motionless in deep space, it's sort of spooky watching these ADVERSARY and HULK objects move into, through and out of radar range. Once you learn how to fly your spaceship, you will want to chase down some of them. Maybe a crash course in operating the ship is in order now.

A FIRST LESSON IN SPACESHIP PILOTING

Getting a feeling for the peculiarities of piloting this spaceship is best done near HOME where you can watch the HOME navigation figures. If the program is already running, you can abort it by either striking the BREAK key or the X key. You might have to strike them several times in succession before you pick up the Tiny Pascal monitor cursor. If you have just loaded and compiled the program, simply do a run.

In any event, you should be back to the point where the HOME line reads HOME—RANGE:0 X=0 Y=0. That means you're at home and resting on the launching pad.

For navigation purposes, the universe is an X—Y coordinate system having HOME at coordinates 0, 0. All positions in space

306

relative to HOME are to the right and upward. And that means you can blast off from HOME in only two directions, to the right or upward. That is accomplished by striking the R or U keys, respectively.

You will notice that you sometimes have to strike a key several times in succession before seeing a response on the navigation readout. The control mechanisms on your ship aren't very precise, mainly because you are living in a day when the earth's space program has been suffering from all sorts of problems for the better part of a century. That also accounts for why the NAV BEACON objects are inoperative.

Your first piloting lesson will amount to leaving home and flying around within the 100 space-unit range of your radar. The five control keys you will need for the lesson are: U, upward motion, an increasing and upward motion from HOME; D, downward motion, a decreasing and downward motion toward HOME; R, right-direction motion, an increasing and right motion from HOME; L, left-direction, a decreasing and left motion toward HOME; and S, dead stop relative to HOME.

The only way you know you are moving at all relative to home is by noting changes in the RANGE figure and one or both of the X-Y direction figures. Of course, you know you are moving away from home when the RANGE figure is steadily increasing. You are moving toward home when the RANGE figure shows a steady decrease.

The actual direction you are moving relative to home can be deduced from the X and Y coordinate figures. If, for example, the X figure is increasing, your motion has a right-motion component. If that same figure is decreasing, your motion must have a left-direction component instead.

Using the same line of thinking, an increasing value of Y indicates you are moving up and away from home. A decreasing value shows your motion has a downward component.

You can fly combinations of X and Y directions at the same time. But it is obviously impossible to fly to the right and to the left at the same time.

If things ever get out of hand and you lose track of which direction you are flying, just strike the S key to stop things. That will give you time to plan your next navigation step.

One further important point is that your ship cannot fly ouside the 1000 by 1000 space-unit coordinates of the universe. If you happen to run into the "edge of the universe," the component of motion in the direction of the edge will simply fail to work. For example, suppose you are flying to the left and upward. You hit the left-hand edge of the universe, but there is plenty of space above. All you will notice is that the left-hand component of motion (the X figure) will stop changing suddenly. The Y figure will continue increasing, but the X figure stops. It is up to you to spot these things and take the appropriate action.

So blast off with an upward (U key), right-hand (R key) motion or a combination of the two. Fly some short distance from home, stop (S key) and make a change in course. Fly around, staying within the 100 space-unit range for the time being. Get accustomed to the fussy controls, having to strike the control keys several times in rapid succession before seeing the desired results.

When you think you are getting the hang of it, fly a bit beyond the 100 space-unit range of your navigation radar. Don't go too far out because you want to find your way back.

How do you know which way to go when you've lost navigation contact? That little problem is left to your own ingenuity. Perhaps you will make a habit of keeping a log of your course changes. That little gimmick will always help you find your way around.

In fact, this whole game is a great exercise in navigation methods. Ultimately, the game is best played by those who take the trouble to chart their courses and course changes, using the minimal amount of information sometimes available on the display.

A SHORT COURSE IN FINDING AND REPAIRING NAV BEACONS

As mentioned earlier, you are carrying out your mission in a day when the earth's space program has fallen into a state of disarray. One of the objectives of the mission is to repair all four navigation beacons, thereby making it easier to navigate through the universe.

There are four navigation stations in space that are running on their last legs. The only information available from them is their range. At the beginning of the mission, you haven't the slightest idea where they are or just how far away they are.

So part of the game strategy is to blast off from earth and set up a course that causes the range figures for the NAV BEACON objects to decrease steadily. As long as those figures are decreasing, you know you are at least moving in the right general direction.

Why not start out after the navigation station having the smallest range figure? Play around with course changes until you notice the range figure for that station decreasing steadily.

You will notice that the range figure changes very slowly at first, but decreases more rapidly as you approach the nav station's beacon.

As you close in on a nav beacon, you will most likely reach a point where the range figure no longer shows a steady decrease. Rather, it remains steady for a while and then begins to increase. That is a sure sign you are overshooting it. It's time to stop and make a change of course.

The first change will have to be an educated guess. You are flying blind and by the seat of your pants. Play around with your direction controls until you see the range figure decreasing again. This takes some real patience and analytical thinking on your part.

When you get within 2 space units of an inoperative navigation beacon, stop (strike the S key) and fix the thing. How do you repair a broken navigation beacon? It's simple, really. Just strike the N key. That'll do it.

You know you've fixed the beacon when your status readout suddenly begins showing the X and Y coordinates of that beacon. From that time on, you can use those figures to fix your position in space *relative to that nav beacon*. If you want some more practice finding and repairing nav beacons, blast off from the repaired one and search out another inoperative one.

While you are learning to find and repair navigation beacons, you will occasionally pick up some radar information from the ADVERSARY and the HULK objects. Tracking them down can be pretty tricky and, worst of all, chasing after them can make you lose track of the beacon you're trying to find.

For the purposes of this exercise, then, you ought to ignore the other objects. They're harmless, anyway.

To this point in your training, you should be able to blast off from home, find and repair all four beacons and (here is the real catch) find your way back home. Keep track of how long it takes you to do this job, and you'll begin getting an idea of how long it takes to play the whole game.

Think about some strategy now. Wouldn't it be most helpful to make up a chart of the universe—a large sheet of coordinate paper showing HOME at the lower left-hand corner? Before leaving home, you could inscribe large arcs having radii equal to the range of the navigation beacons. If you keep track of your course changes, you can get a fairly good idea of where those beacons are located relative to home. After you repair the last one, you will have an idea about the course to fly in order to return home.

In fact, if you don't keep a log of some sort, it is going to take many hours of trial-and-error flying to get within the 100 space-unit range of the HOME radar. You can find your way home by systematically following the "edges of the universe," though.

A SEEK-AND-DESTROY TRAINING MISSION

The final lesson in your basic space ranger training program is to seek out and destroy the ADVERSARY or one of the HULK objects. Unlike the NAV BEACON objects, ADVERSARY and HULK objects are in continuous motion in space as long as they live.

These "live" objects aren't easy to find, either. You haven't the slightest notion about where they are until one of them moves within the 100 space-unit range of your radar. That means you have to cruise space, perhaps setting up a systematic search pattern of motion, until one of these objects moves within range.

If you think it was hard to track down a stationary navigation beacon, wait until you have to chase down a moving target. You have two elements in your favor, however. First, your ship can fly twice as fast as ADVERSARY or one of the HULK figures. The second point in your favor is that these objects always travel in straight lines. So in spite of sloppy controls, your spacecraft can outmaneuver the moving objects rather well.

For the sake of carrying out this training mission, run the program from the start, blast off from earth, and set a course diagonally (U and R controls) across space. Sooner or later, one of the objects will run into your 100 space-unit radar range. When that happens, the display will also start giving you range and relative coordinate information.

Remember that a −X value means the object is to your left, and that you must set a course with an L component in order to approach it. A positive X value means the object is to your right. By the same line of thinking, −Y values means the object is below, while positive values of Y means it is above.

When an object falls into your radar range, start making the course corrections necessary for catching up with it. It isn't an easy task, especially while the object remains close to the 100 space-unit limit.

Close in on the target. When the range figure is within 10 space units, strike the F key. Striking the F key sends out your deadly destructive force field. If you hit the object, the status display will show the message DESTROYED.

If you have carried out your lessons with the NAV BEACON objects properly, you shouldn't have too much trouble closing in on one of the moving objects. The real problem is finding the one you want to destroy. In keeping with the way things seem to go in real life, finding the last one is the most difficult task of all. You simply have to cruise around in space until you find it.

PLAYING THE GAME OF SPACE RANGER MISSION

The objective of the game is to leave earth, repair all four navigation beacons, destroy all moving ADVERSARY and HULK objects and then return to earth. In the light of your training sessions, you can appreciate the difficulty in carrying out the complete mission.

It can take a skilled player several hours to complete the mission, and sometimes it cannot be done in one session. If you must leave the game for any length of time, simply strike the S key to bring your spaceship to a halt. The ADVERSARY and HULK objects that are still alive will continue to roam about freely, but that won't spoil the game at all.

There is some merit in having three people playing the game. One can act as the pilot, operating the control keys and making critical decisions. Another player can work as a navigator, attempting to keep track of course changes and the positions of stationary objects. The third player can be a radar operator, keeping an eye open for unexpected intrusions of the moving objects. Having a radar operator is especially important when the pilot is preoccupied with the job of repairing a navigation station or tracking another moving object in space. Table 15-1 summarizes the key controls for this SPACE RANGER MISSION game.

DECLARATIONS, FUNCTIONS AND PROCEDURES FOR SPACE RANGER MISSION

The complete program listing for SPACE RANGER MIS-SION offered earlier in this chapter is written to conserve memory

Table 15-1. Summary of Key Controls for SPACE RANGER MISSION.

```
U—upward motion relative to HOME
D—downward motion relative to HOME
L—left-direction motion relative to HOME
R—right-direction motion relative to HOME
N—repair a NAV BEACON
F—fire a force field
X—abort the mission (same as striking the BREAK key)
```

space. Clarity of programming procedures and the formal methods for writing structured programs were sacrificed in order to get the source program into the memory space available. The bottom line of this tradeoff is that the declarations, functions and procedures are rather hard to follow, let alone understand.

For the benefit of readers who are interested in understanding the workings of the SPACE RANGER MISSION game, the listing in this section shows the formal, clearer programming format. Please understand that the program cannot be entered with this format. You must stick with the format shown earlier in this chapter. Attempting to enter the game in this fashion will turn out to be a waste of time for you. Once the 4.5K of program space is used up (by entering an excessively long source program), the system latches up without warning. All the work you've done to that point will be totally lost.

Listing

Here is the listing, excluding the mainline program, written in a clearer fashion:

```
(* SPACE RANGE MISSION *)
VAR OBJ,N,SEED,CHANGE,CFLAG,PHASE,ENGO,DELAY:INTEGER;
(* DECLARE ARRAYS *)
XCOORD:ARRAY(10) OF INTEGER;
YCOORD:ARRAY(10) OF INTEGER;
XVEC:ARRAY(10) OF INTEGER;
YVEC:ARRAY(10) OF INTEGER;
TYPE:ARRAY(10) OF INTEGER;
LIVE:ARRAY(10) OF INTEGER;
(* RANDOM NO. *)
FUNC RND(RLOW,RHIGH);
VAR M,P:INTEGER;
  BEGIN
  REPEAT
    M:=N*3125;
    IF M<0 THEN M:=ABS(M);
    N:=M;P:=M;
    P:=P MOD RHIGH
  UNTIL (P>=RLOW) AND (P<=RHIGH);
  RND:=P
END;
(* RELATIVE COORDS *)
FUNC RCOORD(ELESHIP,ELETARG);
BEGIN
  RCOORD:=ELETARG-ELESHIP
END;
(* RANGE *)
FUNC RANGE(XSHIP,YSHIP,XTARG,YTARG);
VAR XDIST,YDIST,SCALE,RAD,ROOT:INTEGER;
  BEGIN
  XDIST:=ABS(RCOORD(XSHIP,XTARG));
  YDIST:=ABS(RCOORD(YSHIP,YTARG));
```

```
    IF XDIST>=10*YDIST THEN
      RANGE:=XDIST;
    IF YDIST>=10*XDIST THEN
      RANGE:=YDIST;
    IF NOT((XDIST>=10*YDIST) OR (YDIST>=10*XDIST)) THEN
      BEGIN
      IF (XDIST<=100) AND (YDIST<=100) THEN
        SCALE:=1
      ELSE
        BEGIN
        SCALE:=10;
        XDIST:=XDIST DIV 10;
        YDIST:=YDIST DIV 10
        END;
        RAD:=SQR(XDIST)+SQR(YDIST);
        ROOT:=0;
        REPEAT
          ROOT:=ROOT+1
        UNTIL SQR(ROOT)>=RAD;
        IF (SQR(ROOT)-RAD)>(ABS(SQR(ROOT-1)-RAD)) THEN
          ROOT:=ROOT-1;
        RANGE:=ROOT*SCALE
      END
END;
(* OBJECT STATUS *)
PROC ENESTAT(XSHIP,YSHIP,XENE,YENE,LIVE,TYPE);
VAR ENEDIST:INTEGER;
  BEGIN
  ENEDIST:=RANGE(XSHIP,YSHIP,XENE,YENE);
CASE TYPE OF
  0:IF ENEDIST>100 THEN
      WRITE('OUT OF RANGE')
    ELSE
      WRITE('RANGE:',ENEDIST#,' X=',RCOORD(XSHIP,0)#,
      Y=',RCOORD(YSHIP,0)#);
  1:IF NOT LIVE THEN
      WRITE('DESTROYED')
    ELSE
      BEGIN
      IF ENEDIST>100 THEN
        WRITE('NOT IN RANGE')
      ELSE
        WRITE('RANGE:',ENEDIST#,' X=',RCOORD(XSHIP,
        XENE)#,'      Y=',RCOORD(YSHIP,YENE)#)
      END;
  2:IF NOT LIVE THEN
      WRITE('RANGE:',ENEDIST#,'  NAV INOPERATIVE')
    ELSE
      WRITE('RANGE:',ENEDIST#,'      X=',RCOORD(XSHIP,
      XENE)#,         '  Y=',RCOORD(YSHIP,YENE)#)
    END; (* OF CASE STATEMENT *)
  WRITE(13)
END; (* OF FUNCTION *)
(* MOVE SHIP *)
FUNC SHIPMOVE(ELESHIP,DIRSHIP);
VAR NEWDIR:INTEGER;
BEGIN
```

```
  IF(ELESHIP+DIRSHIP<0) OR (ELESHIP+DIRSHIP>1000) THEN
    SHIPMOVE:=ELESHIP
  ELSE
    SHIPMOVE:=ELESHIP+DIRSHIP
END;
BEGIN
END.
```

DECLARE ARRAYS Section

As usual, the mainline program variables must be declared at the beginning of the program. They do not have much meaning at that point, so begin your analysis of the program with the section commented DECLARE ARRAYS.

The game uses six 10-element arrays, each element representing a subscripted variable associated with objects in the game. Table 15-2 shows that each element in the arrays is associated with one particular object. Element 0 in each array, for example, represents variables associated with your spaceship. The 2-elements represent the adversary, the 3-elements represent HULK #1, and so on.

Table 15-3 then defines each array. For example, the array XCOORD holds the absolute X component of every object's position on the screen. Carrying the example a bit further, element 4 in the XCOORD array holds the X position of HULK #2. Element 5 of that same XCOORD array, on the other hand, holds the X coordinate of HULK #3.

So there are 11 relevant objects in the game program, ranging from your own spaceship (element 0) through NAV BEACON #4 (element 10). And there are six different variables associated with each object in the game, ranging from their X coordinates (XCOORD) through an indication of whether or not the objects are "alive" (LIVE). Arrays such as these must be declared early in the program, but in this case they don't have much bearing on the analysis until a bit later in the listing.

Table 15-2. Definition of Elements Within Each Array.

0—PLAYER'S OWN SPACESHIP
1—HOME
2—ADVERSARY
3—HULK #1
4—HULK #2
5—HULK #3
6—HULK #4
7—NAV BEACON #1
8—NAV BEACON #2
9—NAV BEACON #3
10—NAV BEACON #4

The next major declaration is the one for generating some random numbers. This begins at the comment, RANDOM NO., and it is virtually identical to the random functions used quite often in earlier sections of this book. There is no need for further discussion of the random function at this time.

RCOORD Function

The comment RELATIVE COORDS brings up the next important declaration section. RCOORD is a fairly simple Pascal function, doing nothing more than calculating the X and Y coordinates of some object relative to your own space ship. If, for example, an object happens to be 10 units above and 4 units to the left of your spaceship, this function is responsible for generating the numbers 10 and −4—the values ultimately assigned to the X and Y coordinates displayed on the screen for that particular object.

The RCOORD function requires two variables at the outset, ELESHIP and ELETARG. ELESHIP represents the absolute X or Y coordinates of the spaceship, and ELETARG represents the absolute X or Y coordinates of the other object within radar range. By "absolute" coordinates, I mean the actual X and Y distances from HOME, the origin of the entire universe coordinate system.

So all that RCOORD does is to subtract the X or Y component of your spaceship's location from the corresponding X or Y coordinates of the other object. The result is a number, one that is positive or negative, showing the relative bearing of the object from your spaceship.

As an example, suppose the spaceship is at absolute coordinates X=100 and Y=250. That means the ship is 100 units to the

Table 15-3. Definition of Arrays.

```
XCOORD—X coordinate of distance from HOME
YCOORD—Y coordinate of distance from HOME
XVEC—X component of motion (1, 0 or − 1)
YVEC—Y component of motion (1, 0 or − 1)
TYPE—Type of object (0, 1 or 2)
          Where 0 is HOME and players own spaceship
                1 is a movable, but destructible object
                2 is a stationary NAV BEACON
LIVE—operational status (0 or 1)
          Where 0 is DESTROYED or INOPERATIVE
                1 is alive or fully operational
```

right and 250 units above HOME. At the same time, an object within radar range might have absolute coordinates X=120 and Y=245. Cranking these two sets of X values into the function, RCOORD(100,120), yields a relative X coordinate of 120-100, or 20 space units. The object, in other words, is 20 units to the right of you.

Working the same function, using the Y values in this example, the function turns out a relative Y bearing of -5. That means the object is 5 space units below you. In a manner of speaking, function RCOORD translates absolute coordinates of your spaceship and some object into relative coordinates, which are relative to your position in space.

RANGE Statement

The declaration statements commented RANGE turn out to be a bit more involved than RCOORD. In this case, the problem is to solve a square root using integer arithmetic. The general idea is to use the relative X and Y coordinates generated by RCOORD to solve the Pythagorean theorem and come up with the range.

In any X-Y coordinate system, the distance between two points can be calculated by this equation:

$$\sqrt{X^2 + Y^2}$$

where X is the horizontal component of the distance and Y is the vertical component.

It is difficult to come up with a precise solution to the range equation when you're limited to integer values. We simply have to live with some inaccuracies. The answers will be whole numbers, even though most situations call for fractional parts. Being forewarned that this function will produce estimated range values, take a look at how it can be done.

The variables declared for RANGE include XDIST, YDIST, SCALE, RAD and ROOT. The meanings of these variables will become apparent as you go along here.

Calculating XDIST and YDIST

The first operational statements call for running the RCOORD function a couple of times. The first time that function is called, the idea is to determine the absolute value of the X distance to the object. For the sake of calculating the range of the object, the sign of the X components (whether it is negative or positive) isn't relevant. So XDIST, the absolute value of the X distance, is calculated by a relatively simple process. YDIST, the Y component of the distance to the object, is then calculated the same way, using the same RCOORD function.

Now here comes the first bit of range estimating. There is little point in going through a lot of careful calculations whenever one component of the distances is more than 10 times the other. Any right triangle having one side more than 10 times longer than the other will always produce a hypotenuse that is very nearly equal to the length of the longer side. Hence, you have the two conditional statements that test the relative values of XDIST and YDIST. In the first case, if XDIST turns out to be 10 or more times greater than YDIST, the program simply sets RANGE equal to XDIST. The function is done. By the same token, if YDIST is 10 or more times larger than XDIST, the function immediately sets RANGE to the value of YDIST.

Those are the simple solutions to the matter of calculating range. The tricky part comes in whenever XDIST isn't much larger than YDIST, or YDIST isn't much larger than XDIST. The remainder of the RANGE function is devoted to solving the triangle.

The first step in solving for RANGE at this point is to test the values for distances of 100 or more. Supersoft Tiny Pascal cannot handle numbers larger than a 16-bit binary format allows. That's about 32,000 in the positive and negative directions. By checking for XDIST and YDIST values greater than 100, the program is eliminating the possibility of having an oversized number crop up later in the function.

So if XDIST and YDIST are both less than or equal to 100, a variable called SCALE is set to a value of 1. Otherwise, SCALE is set to 10, and the two distances are divided by 10. Dividing larger numbers by 10 ensures none of the later operations will yield a sum greater than the system can handle.

RAD and ROOT Variables

Now you should be down to the statement RAD:=SQR(XDIST)+SQU(YDIST). This one squares the two values and sums them, effectively performing the $X^2 + Y^2$ part of the range finding job. Variable RAD thus stands for "radicand," the number under the root symbol in the basic range equation.

The function then sets a trial root, variable ROOT, to 0. Then a REPEAT statement causes ROOT to increment UNTIL its square is equal or greater than the RAD value. At that point, ROOT is pretty close to the square root of the RAD value, and that's what this whole thing is about.

The function could be ended shortly after this point, but an extra IF. . .THEN statement provides a bit more accuracy to the operation. That conditional statement compares the differences between the squared ROOT value and RAD under two different conditions. The first part gets the difference between $ROOT^2$ and RAD, while the second part backs up the value of ROOT by one number and does a similar comparison: $(ROOT-1)^2-RAD$.

In essence, the statement is asking, "Which value is closer to being the square root of RAD? ROOT or ROOT—1?" It looks for a possible "overshoot" during the ROOT-incrementing phase of the operation, making the ROOT:=ROOT—1 correction if that value turns out to be closer to the square root of RAD than ROOT is.

By this point in the function, ROOT is as close to being the square root of RAD as integer arithmetic will allow. The remaining operation is to set RANGE equal to the ROOT value. But wait! Weren't very large values of XDIST and YDIST divided by 10 earlier in the program? Yes, they were; and a variable SCALE carried a value of 1 or 10, depending on whether that division-by-10 took place or did not.

Recall that SCALE was set to a value of 1 if there was no division by 10, and it was set to 10 if the division was carried out. So the statement RANGE:=ROOT*SCALE straightens out— scales the final value—by multiplying ROOT by SCALE.

This is the first time a root function has been described in this book. You might want to mark the page so you can find it for your own programs at some later time.

The function RANGE is thus called whenever it is necessary to compute the range between your spaceship and some other object in space. The variables that must be carried into this function are XSHIP, YSHIP, XTARG and YTARG. Those represent the X coordinates of your ship and the target, and the Y coordinates of the same.

ENESTAT Procedure

Procedure ENESTAT begins under the comment OBJECT STATUS. The main purpose of this procedure is to determine whether or not an object is within radar range and figure out whether the object in question is dead, alive, inoperative and so on.

As a procedure, ENESTAT does not calculate any values that are carried back to the statement that calls it. That is always the purpose of a Pascal function. That is not to say that calculations aren't carried out within the procedure, however.

Variables that must be available when running ENESTAT include XSHIP, YSHIP, XENE and YENE. These are the absolute X and Y components of your ship and the "enemy's" position in space. LIVE is a value 1 or 0 that indicates whether or not the object in question is fully operational. A value of 1 indicates the object is indeed operational, while a value of 0 means it is destroyed or inoperative.

The TYPE variable is an integer between 0 and 2. The 0-type object is HOME, the 1-types are the five moving objects (ADVERSARY and the four HULK things), and the 2-types are the four NAV BEACON objects.

The only variable used solely within this procedure is ENEDIST, actually the range between your spaceship and the object in question. So upon calling procedure ENESTAT, it first calculates the range to the object being considered. This is a simple matter of calling the RANGE function just described.

Then the program uses a CASE statement to sort out operations according to the TYPE of object being studied. If the object is type 0 (HOME), the first consideration is the distance to HOME. If the distance to HOME is greater than 100 space units, this procedure writes the message OUT OF RANGE on the screen. If you have already played the game, you are quite familiar with that one.

On the other hand, if HOME distance is less than 100 space units, the program calls for writing RANGE:, followed by the calculated range figure, the X distance to HOME and the Y distance to HOME. The X and Y components of the distance to HOME are both calculated by calling the RCOORD function. RCOORD (XSHIP,∅) provides the X distance, and RCOORD(YSHIP,∅) yields the Y component of the distance to HOME.

Type-1 Object

If this procedure is being run with a type-1 object, case value 1 applies. Here, the first test is to see whether or not the object is "alive." If it is not alive, the program calls for writing DESTROYED on the screen. This message occurs after you've killed the ADVERSARY of any of the HULK objects.

But if a type-1 object is alive and well, the ELSE part of the statement does a couple of things. First, there is a test to see whether or not that particular object is within the 100 space-unit range of your radar. If not, the system prints NOT IN RANGE. Otherwise, it calculates the range, X component of the distance and direction and the Y component of distance and direction. Those values are simultaneously printed on the screen.

NAV BEACON Objects

Type-2 objects, the NAV BEACON objects, follow CASE 2. If the objects are still inoperative (not alive), the statement simply prints the range and the message, NAV INOPERATIVE. Otherwise, the program prints out the range *and* the relative bearings in an X-Y format.

Taking an overall view of this ENESTAT procedure, it is responsible for providing the data presented to you on the screen. In the process, it calls most of the functions described to this point in the analysis.

The final segment of this declaration phase of the program is labeled MOVE SHIP. In the simplest terms, this function is the one that makes the spaceship move around in space. To run the function, you must provide variables ELESHIP and DIRSHIP. ELESHIP is the absolute value of the ship's distance from HOME as expressed, in turn, as X and Y coordinates. DIRSHIP is a value of −1, 0 or 1, indicating the direction of motion relative to HOME. As you will see in this function, those DIRSHIP values are generally added to ELESHIP, thereby changing the X and Y coordinates by 1 unit, −1 unit or no units at all.

The only point of minor complication is that SHIPMOVE also determines whether or not your spaceship is at the edge of the universe. If your absolute coordinates for X or Y are trying to go less than 0 (you are at the very bottom or left-hand edge) or greater than 1000 (you are at the top or right-hand edge), the function disallows further motion in that direction.

SPACE RANGER MISSION MAINLINE PROGRAM

The mainline programming for the game is listed in the first version of the program. Refer back to the first part of this chapter.

The first part of the mainline program is labeled with the comment SEED. The WRITE statement under SEED clears the screen and prints the heading, ENTER TO START THE GAME...

This heading is really a delay tactic used for generating a seed number for the random number generator, function RND. While the player is sitting around reading the heading message, the SEED sequence counts values of variable SEED between 99 and

999. When the player finally strikes the ENTER key, the WHILE INKEY<>13 statements causes a break from the sequence, with SEED equal to some number between 99 and 999.

Object Initialization

The next step in the mainline program is to INITIALIZE GAME. Here, variable N is set to the SEED value, variables CFLAG and PHASE are set to 0 and 1 respectively, and the screen is cleared once again by a WRITE (28,31) statement.

Then there are a number of initializing steps involving variable OBJ. OBJ is going to be an integer between 0 and 10, representing each of the elements within the game arrays outlined in Table 15-2. The overall idea is to set the initial values of each object's position in space, direction of motion (if applicable), object TYPE and operational status.

Now that is a lot of variables to initialize. But the job is kept to manageable proportions by using the arrays declared at the beginning of the program.

So the first OBJ initializing operation involves objects 0 and 1, PLAYER'S OWN SPACESHIP and HOME. For both objects, this part of the initializing program sets their coordinates to 0,0 and establishes them as TYPE-0. They are both set as LIVE objects as well.

The second phase involves objects 2 to 10, everything except SPACESHIP and HOME. Here, the initial X and Y coordinates in space are set to random numbers between 100 and 900 space units from HOME. This means that the ADVERSARY, all four HULK objects and the four NAV BEACON stations are scattered at random in space.

The third phase of object initialization involves objects 2 through 6. These are the moving objects, and the program initializes them as LIVE and TYPE-1 objects. After that, they are given random motion vectors that exclude a pair of zeros. If these objects were permitted XVEC and YVEC values of zero on both counts, they would be motionless in space throughout the game. And we don't want that to happen. Hence, the need for a REPEAT sequence that continues picking random values until XVEC and YVEC are not both zero. One of the two motion vectors can be 0, but not both.

The last segment of the object-initializing operation involves the navigation beacons, objects 7 through 10. You can see that they are not LIVE initially. They are set to their INOPERATIVE condition as long as LIVE=0. They are also classified here as TYPE-2 objects. Finally, their motion vectors, XVEC and YVEC, are set to zero so that they do not move in space.

Printing Sequence

That concludes the initializing portion of the game. The next item on the agenda is commented START GAME.

The major task of the program is that of printing the current navigation status on the screen of the CRT. The printing sequence opens with a REPEAT statement that implies the program is going to cycle through the process continuously until something happens to stop it. If you read down to the end of the program, you will find that the UNTIL part of this statement calls for a variable CHANGE being set to character X. Recall that you abort the entire game by striking the X key. This is the REPEAT . . . UNTIL sequence that key interrupts.

After the intitial REPEAT line, you find a WRITE statement that formats the message, CURRENT NAVIGATION STATUS, near the center and top of the screen. After dropping down two lines, the program enters another REPEAT sequence. This is the sequence responsible for updating the navigation information on the screen. It begins with a WRITE(28, 13), which returns the cursor to the upper left-hand corner of the screen and then line feeds it down one line below the CURRENT NAVIGATION STATUS message.

Also, take careful note of the fact that a variable CHANGE is set to 0 at the beginning of this information updating sequence. The next line reads: FOR OBJ:=1 TO 10. This implies that everything within the subsequent BEGIN ... END series of operations will involve all 10 game objects in sequence.

CFLAG Variable

The next set of statements are built around that CFLAG variable. If the CFLAG is not set to 1, the system uses a WHILE ... DO statement to cycle through an INKEY operation up to 10 times. This cycling of the INKEY operation takes place until the operator strikes some key on the keyboard or the 10 INKEY cycles are done. If the operator does indeed hit a key during this cycling interval, variable CFLAG is set to 1. So variable CFLAG is equal to 1 or 0 at this time, depending on whether or not the operator strikes some key during the INKEY-cycling process.

CASE Statement

Setting aside CFLAG for the moment, the next set of operation are built around a CASE statement. What happens here depends on which object is being considered at the time. Recall that variable OBJ is being cycled between 1 and 10 as all this takes place. That means one of the 10 CASE messages are going to be printed on the screen.

If, for instance, the system happens to be working with OBJ=5, that means it is dealing with terms associated with HULK #3. When the program gets down to this CASE statement, it prints HULK #3—.

When the CASE statement has been executed, the program calls the function ENESTAT. That function, described in the previous section of this chapter, calculates ranges, relative coordinates, checks LIVE status, TYPE and prints the appropriate information on the screen. And it prints that information right after the message printed during the preceding CASE statement.

So if the system is running OBJ=5, ENESTAT is dealing with the relevant parameters for HULK #3. The CASE statement prints HULK #3. The following ENESTAT function fills out the rest of the same line.

Object-Moving Sequence

A section of the mainline program called MOVE THINGS comes next. As the comment implies, the purpose here is to change the coordinates of the moving objects according to the values of their motion vectors, XVEC and YVEC.

The first motion always deals with OBJECT 0, your own spaceship. The two lines update the x and y coordinates of the spaceship by means of function SHIPMOVE which, in turn, carries variables established by executing four other functions: XCOORD, XVEC, YCOORD and YVEC. In short, those two lines move the spaceship.

The next few lines are responsible for moving all the ADVERSARY and HULK objects that are supposed to move. To do this, variable ENGO is cycled between 2 and 6, object numbers for the movable objects. Their positions in space are adjusted in much the same way that those of the player's spaceship are by function SHIPMOVE. The main difference here, however, is that the vectors are automatically reversed in direction whenever the object comes into contact with the edge of the universe. See, for example, the statement:

```
IF  (XCOORD(ENGO)<0)  OR  (XCOORD(ENGO)>1000)
THEN XVEC(ENGO):=XVEC(ENGO)*(-1)
```

If the X coordinate of the object attempts to drop below or go above the edges of space, the motion vector is reversed. It is not set to 0, or stopped, as is the case for the player's spaceship. In any event, it turns out that the current value of VEC is added to the object's present position, thus causing it to move through space.

Variable PHASE appearing around this object-moving sequence is responsible for setting new object positions just one time for every two times the player's spaceship coordinates are updated. The effect of this every-other-time feature is that the ADVERSARY and HULK objects move no more than half as fast as the player's spaceship.

Then there is an UNTIL CFLAG=1 statement. The UNTIL refers back to the screen updating operations. Recall that CFLAG is set to 1 only if the player strikes a key during an INKEY cycling process. Otherwise, CFLAG is set to 0.

So whether or not the system executes the CASE CHANGE OF statement depends on whether or not the player has hit a key to set CFLAG equal to 1. If not, the system repeats the screen updating and moving operations. But if the player did hit a key, CFLAG is equal to 1. It is time to take some action based on the key the player hit.

The CASE CHANGE OF statement effectively decodes the key operation, taking action appropriate to the situation. These operations can alter the motion vectors of the player's spaceship, fix a navigation station if the RANGE function shows that the nav station is in range, or fire the weapon and "kill" a moving object.

After taking that action, the program returns to the beginning of the screen updating operation. In short, the mainline program updates the navigation information on the screen. It gives the player an opportunity to signal a change of status is in order, to move his spaceship position twice as fast as any other moving object and to take any action specified by striking a control key.

Chapter 16

Translating
BASIC Into Tiny Pascal

Now that you know more about Pascal than ever before, you might have a notion about converting some of your favorite BASIC programs into Tiny Pascal. I have for you some good news and some bad news.

The good news is that there are a lot of BASIC commands and statements that can be carried over directly into Tiny Pascal. The bad news is that Tiny Pascal cannot deal with string statements and floating-point arithmetic very well, so it is difficult to translate BASIC programs having those statements and functions in them.

Another bit of bad news is that so many BASIC programs are written in a haphazard, albeit workable, fashion. The Tiny Pascal compiler doesn't like haphazard programs, so you might end up rewriting portions of the original BASIC program. In spite of the bad news, it is possible to salvage a good share of many BASIC programs, thereby allowing you to rewrite portions of your favorite programs into Pascal with little effort.

DIRECT CONVERSIONS FROM BASIC TO TINY PASCAL

There are a good many keyboard commands and program statements in BASIC that have direct, or nearly direct, counterparts in Tiny Pascal.

Keyboard Commands
BASIC: CLOAD *"file name"*
Tiny Pascal: LS *file name* or LP *file name*

These commands load programs from cassette tape into the machine. Both the TRS-80 BASIC and Tiny Pascal versions call for a file name, but BASIC has the added requirement of enclosing the file name within quotes.

Tiny Pascal offers the option of loading either source-code versions (LS file name) or previously compiled P-code versions (LP file name). Of course, a program written onto cassette tape as a source-code must be loaded as such, and the same goes for the P-code loading operation.

BASIC: CSAVE *"file name"*
Tiny Pascal: WS *file name* or WP *file name*

These commands write programs from the computer's program memory onto cassette tape. Tiny Pascal programs can be written onto tape in either the source-code or P-code formats. WS file name saves the source-code version, while WP file name saves the P-code version.

BASIC: DELETE *mm-nn*
Tiny Pascal: D *nn*

The idea here is to delete a certain number of program lines. In TRS-80 BASIC, you can delete the lines numbered mm through nn. If, for example, you want to delete BASIC program lines 100 through 200, the command would be DELETE 100-200.

Since Tiny Pascal does not have numbered program lines, the command D nn deletes nn lines downward from the current pointer position. To delete the next five lines of Pascal programming, you would do D 5.

In either language, omitting the mm or nn numbers deletes only the current line.

BASIC: NEW
Tiny Pascal: D*

These commands delete the entire program.

BASIC: LIST *mm-nn*
Tiny Pascal: P or P *nn* or P*

It is important to be able to view selected portions of a program on the CRT. That is the point of these commands. In

BASIC, doing a LIST mm-nn lists the program from line number mm to nn, LIST -mm lists the program up to line number mm, LIST mm-, lists the program from line mm to the end, and LIST displays the entire program, from beginning to end.

Not having numbered lines, Tiny Pascal's version of the BASIC LIST mm-nn is somewhat restricted in its application. It is possible to achieve the same results, however, with some practice.

In Tiny Pascal, entering P lists the current line, P nn lists the next nn lines, and P* does a complete listing of the program. These listing commands in Tiny Pascal can be used only with a source program and in the system's edit mode.

BASIC: RUN *mm*
Tiny Pascal: R

In BASIC, doing a RUN mm command begins execution of the program from line number mm. If you omit the mm number, the execution begins from the lowest-numbered line.

By the very nature of Pascal programming, it is virtually impossible to run a program from anywhere but at the very beginning. Thus, the execution of a compiled Tiny Pascal program can begin with nothing but a single command, R.

BASIC: EDIT *mm*
Tiny Pascal: E

These commands put the system into its edit mode, making it possible to alter the program without having to dump the whole thing and start over from scratch.

TRS-80 BASIC allows you to edit one line at a time by entering EDIT mm, where mm is the line number for the statement that needs some work.

Entering E in Tiny Pascal begins the editing operation at the first line of the program. Again, the fact that Pascal does not use line numbers makes the editing operation seem awkward at first. Tiny Pascal, however, makes up for the lack of line numbers by allowing you to skip around within the program rather easily.

The following summary of Tiny Pascal editing commands allows you to get to a specific program line without an undue amount of trouble:

- U—move up one line in the program.
- U*nn*—move up *nn* lines in the program.

- U*—move up to the first line in the program.
- N—move down line in the program.
- N*nn*—move down *nn* lines in the program.
- N*—move down to the last line in the program.

Edit-Mode Operations

BASIC: strike the ENTER key
Tiny Pascal: Q

These keyboard operations terminate the edit mode and return operations to the command mode or monitor.

BASIC: X
Tiny Pascal: X

Display the remainder of the current program line, move the cursor to the end of that line, and allow insertion of additional characters.

BASIC: I
Tiny Pascal: I

This command allows the insertion of new material. In BASIC, this insert operation lets you insert new characters into the current line only. Inserting a whole new line in BASIC is a matter of entering an appropriate line number and statement from the command mode.

In Tiny Pascal, I is used for inserting a whole new line of program text. In the current versions of Tiny Pascal, it is not possible to insert characters within a line without deleting and re-entering everything else to the end of that line.

Input/Output Statements

BASIC: PRINT *expression*
Tiny Pascal: WRITE (*expression*)

These program statements print characters on the CRT.

In BASIC PRINT *math expression* causes the numerical results of a math expression to be printed. PRINT X+2, for instance, prints out 5 on the CRT if X happens to be equal to 3 at the time. WRITE (math expression#) does the same thing in Tiny Pascal.

PRINT *"string"* in BASIC lets you print out any string message or character enclosed in quotes. WRITE ('string') accomplishes the same thing in Tiny Pascal.

It is possible to write multiple-expression printing statements in both languages. There are some differences in the ways the two languages respond to punctuation between the expressions.

In BASIC, for instance, expressions separated by commas cause those expressions to be separated horizontally on the screen by one standard print zone. Tiny Pascal has no single-expression statement for a print zone format. In fact, expressions within a single Pascal WRITE statement must be separated by nothing but commas.

Another difference between the two languages (when it comes to multiple-expression printing statements) is that Tiny Pascal must be told to do a line feed/carriage return. The same sort of BASIC statement must include a semicolon between expressions to avoid an automatic line feed/carriage return.

To print multiple expressions without a line feed/carriage return, do:

PRINT *(expression; expression* in BASIC

and

WRITE *(expression, expression* in Tiny Pascal

In these instances, the two expressions will be printed side-by-side on the CRT.

Printing expressions on separate lines can be done this way:

PRINT *(expression*):PRINT *(expression*) in BASIC

and

WRITE *(expression,* 13, *expression*) in Tiny Pascal

The number 13 in the Tiny Pascal version is interpreted as the ASCII control code for doing a line feed/carriage return on the CRT screen.

BASIC: INPUT *variable*
Tiny Pascal: READ *(variable)*

These statements bring execution of the program to a halt until the operator enters some value for the variable from the keyboard. In Tiny Pascal, the variable is generally limited to numerical values, although it is possible to enter single-character strings.

To assign some value to variable G, the appropriate BASIC statement is INPUT G. In Tiny Pascal, it is READ(G#).

Like the PRINT and WRITE statements, it is possible to assign values to more than one variable within a single INPUT or READ statement. Both languages call for separating the variable names by commas.

PROGRAM STATEMENTS

BASIC: DIM *array(dim)*
Tiny Pascal: VAR *array*: ARRAY(*dim*) OF INTEGER;

Setting the dimensions of an array in BASIC is one of the few declaration statements in that language. In both instances, *array* is the variable name assigned to the array, and *dim* is an integer specifying the size of the array.

Although TRS-80 Level-II BASIC permits multi-dimensioned arrays, Tiny Pascal allows only 1-dimensional arrays. So if you see DIM *array(dim-1, dim-2, dim-3)* in a BASIC program, you know you are going to have to get pretty clever to do the same sort of 3-dimensional array operations in Tiny Pascal.

BASIC: LET *variable=expression* or *variable=expression*
Tiny Pascal: *variable:=expression*

These are the fundamental assignment statements that attach the value of expression to a designated variable. If you see something such as LET A=X+23 in BASIC, you can do the same thing in Tiny Pascal with A:=X+23.

BASIC: END
Tiny Pascal: END.

These statements mark the end of a program. They return the system from the program to the command/monitor mode.

BASIC: ON *expression* GOTO *line 1, . . ., line n*
Tiny Pascal: CASE *expression* OF
                               line 1:
                                   .
                                   .
                                   .
                               line n:

The equivalence between these statements in BASIC and Tiny Pascal is a bit tenuous. It is offered here because it works under many circumstances and at the hands of a programmer who is thoroughly acquainted with the nature of the two. The general idea is to skip to a certain line of programming, based on the value of some expression.

BASIC: FOR *variable=expression* TO *expression* . . . NEXT
                 variable
Tiny Pascal: FOR *variable:=expression* TO *expression* DO

In their simplest forms, these two statements perform the same kinds of looping operations. As presented here, they both increment the value of variable, one integer value at a time, from the first expression through the second expression.

The BASIC version has the advantage of allowing the programmer to add a STEP value, thereby allowing the statement to increase or decrease the variable value by steps other than 1. These two examples do the same thing:

FOR Z=25 TO Ø STEP −1   . . . NEXT Z in BASIC

and

FOR Z:=25 DOWNTO Ø DO   in Tiny Pascal

Stepping at values other than 1 or −1 in Tiny Pascal calls for programming several statements. Suppose the BASIC statement reads:

FOR F=Ø TO 1ØØ STEP 1Ø . . . NEXT F.

The Tiny Pascal counterpart is:

```
          F:=Ø;
    WHILE F<=1ØØ DO
          BEGIN
             .
             .
             .
          F:=F+1Ø
          END;
```

BASIC: REM *message*

Tiny Pascal: (* *message* *)

Neither of these statements are executed during the running of a program. They simply allow the programmer to insert explanatory text into a program listing.

BASIC: IF *expression* THEN *statement* ELSE *statement*

Tiny Pascal: IF *expression* THEN *statement* ELSE *statement*

These common conditional statements are identical and work exactly the same way in both languages. The ELSE clause is optional in both instances.

BASIC: CLS

Tiny Pascal: WRITE(28, 31)

These statements clear the CRT screen and send the cursor to the upper left-hand corner.

SET/PLOT Statements

BASIC: SET(x, y)
Tiny Pascal: PLOT(x, y, 1)

The SET/PLOT statements print a rectangular spot of light on the CRT at horizontal coordinate point x and vertical component y. The value of x is limited to integers 0 through 127, while the value of y must be between 0 and 47.

BASIC: RESET(x, y)
Tiny Pascal: PLOT(x, y, 0)

These are the complements of the SET/PLOT statements just described. The idea is to "erase" a rectangle of light previously drawn on the screen by a SET or PLOT statement.

POKE/MEM and PEEK/MEM Statements

BASIC: POKE *location, value*
Tiny Pascal: MEM(*location*):=*value*

These statements write a 1-byte value into a 4-byte memory location. Tiny Pascal has the advantage of allowing location and value to be expressed either in decimal or hexadecimal form. BASIC allows decimal integers only.

Unless specified otherwise, the location and value integers in Tiny Pascal will be taken as decimal values. By adding a percent sign, %, at the beginning of the integers, they can be expressed in hexadecimal form.

BASIC: PEEK(*location*)
Tiny Pascal: *variable*:=MEM(*location*)

These are the complements of the POKE/MEM statements just described. Instead of writing data into a memory location, however, these PEEK/MEM statements read data from the specified memory location.

Port Number and Value Statements

BASIC: OUT *port number, value*
Tiny Pascal: OUTP *port number, value*

The idea here is to send a value to an external device having some specified port number. The statements are very nearly identical in both languages.

BASIC: INP (*port number*)
Tiny Pascal: INP (*port number*)

The statements are identical in form and application. In either case, they return a value present at the designated port number.

Cursor Moving Statements

BASIC: TAB n
Tiny Pascal: $192+n$

These statements move the cursor n places to the right. Used most often in conjunction with PRINT/WRITE statements, they generally take the form PRINT TAB(n) expression or WRITE($192+n$, expression). In both instances, expression will appear on the screen, beginning n character spaces to the right of the present cursor position.

In Tiny Pascal, the value of n is limited to the range of 0 through 63.

ARITHMETIC FUNCTIONS

Most arithmetic functions in TRS-80 Level-II BASIC are difficult to translate into Tiny Pascal. The main problem is that so many of the BASIC math functions call for floating-point arithmetic, and Tiny Pascal has no such provisions. One notable exception is the ABS(expression) function, which is identical in form and application in both languages.

Some of the BASIC math functions can be "faked" by means of Tiny Pascal subroutines (functions), but the form of the subroutines depends on the application at hand. The scheme for finding the square root of a number in the SPACE RANGER MISSION game (Chapter 15), for example, is quite suitable for that particular game. But it might not have the precision required for other kinds of applications.

CHANGING PROGRAMS FROM BASIC INTO TINY PASCAL

While it is possible to make a number of direct translations of BASIC statements to equivalent statements in Tiny Pascal, it is often very difficult to take an entire BASIC program and translate it, point for point, into a proper Tiny Pascal format.

Take any short BASIC program as an example, and see if you can make a direct translation into Tiny Pascal. In some cases, you can do it with some success, but most attempts are bound to fail somewhere down the line.

One thing that signals a difficult, if not impossible, task is the appearance of numerous arithmetic function such as SIN, TAN and EXP. These transcendental functions are possible in Tiny Pascal only with the greatest amount of effort and mathematical know-how. The problem is that such functions very rarely fit into an integer-based system.

Another kind of BASIC statement to avoid is any involving the manipulation of string variables. While UCSD Pascal can handle strings, Tiny Pascal cannot.

Finally, there is the matter of program structure. BASIC does not demand the same high degree of careful structuring that is the hallmark of Pascal. Some BASIC programmers do, indeed, apply formal structuring processes during the development of a program; if that is the case, there is a good chance you can make a fairly easy transition from BASIC to Tiny Pascal.

But the nature of BASIC allows some pretty sloppy programming to yield satisfactory results. Many BASIC programs, even those sold commercially, are really patchwork quilts assembled from bits and pieces of programs. Such programs can work quite nicely, but closer inspection shows they were assembled in a trial-and-error fashion, with that old GOTO statement getting the programmer out of just about any conceivable logical dead end.

Unstructured BASIC programs are just about impossible to translate into Tiny Pascal. If you can do it, you can probably fit square pegs into round holes.

Unfortunately, getting a BASIC program into a Tiny Pascal format calls for tearing the BASIC version to pieces, figuring out how it works, generating a flow chart and writing the Pascal version from scratch. Incidentally, if you think I am being a bit harsh about sloppy, but workable, BASIC programming, try a little experiment for yourself. First, try translating some BASIC into Tiny Pascal. It won't take long to find out how difficult the job can be.

Then try going the other way. Try translating a Tiny Pascal program into BASIC. Things run a lot more smoothly all down the line.

The Pascal program must be highly structured and well organized before it can even be compiled. So starting out with a well organized program makes it much simpler to translate into a different program format or language.

Who knows? Maybe you will never do a whole lot of programming in Pascal. But after working your way through this book, you are bound to become a much better BASIC programmer than most.

Appendix

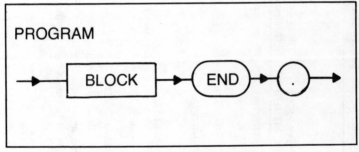

Fig. A-1. Syntax diagram for a Tiny Pascal PROGRAM.

Table A-1. TRS-80 ASCII Cursor Control Codes.

Code (Decimal)	FUNCTION	TINY PASCAL STATEMENT	Code (Decimal)	FUNCTION	TINY PASCAL STATEMENT
8	Backspace and erase current line	WRITE(8)	29	Cursor to beginning of the current line	WRITE(29)
13	Linefeed/carriage return	WRITE(13)	30	Erase to end of the current line	WRITE(30)
24	Backspace	WRITE(24)	31	Clear to end of frame	WRITE(31)
25	Advance cursor one space	WRITE(25)	192-255	Tab n spaces to the right, where n is an integer between 0 and 63	WRITE(number) where number is 192+n
26	Downward linefeed	WRITE(26)			
27	Upward linefeed	WRITE(27)			
28	Home the cursor	WRITE(28)			

NOTE: Only those cursor codes considered appropriate or useful for TRS-80 Supersoft Tiny Pascal are shown here. Consult your TRS-80 manual for other codes that might be of experimental interest.

Table A-2. ASCII Character Codes.

CODE Decimal	Hex	CHARACTER	CODE Decimal	Hex	CHARACTER
32	0020	space	64	0040	@
33	0021	!	65	0041	A
34	0022	"	66	0042	B
35	0023	#	67	0043	C
36	0024	$	68	0044	D
37	0025	%	69	0045	E
38	0026	&	70	0046	F
39	0027	' (apostrophe)	71	0047	G
40	0028	(	72	0048	H
41	0029	)	73	0049	I
42	002A	*	74	004A	J
43	002B	+	75	004B	K
44	002C	, (comma)	76	004C	L
45	002D	-	77	004D	M
46	002E	. (period)	78	004E	N
47	002F	/	79	004F	O
48	0030	0	80	0050	P
49	0031	1	81	0051	Q
50	0032	2	82	0052	R
51	0033	3	83	0053	S
52	0034	4	84	0054	T
53	0035	5	85	0056	U
54	0036	6	86	0057	V
55	0037	7	87	0058	W
56	0038	8	88	0059	X
57	0039	9	89	005A	Y
58	003A	:	90	005B	Z
59	003B	;	91	005C	↑
60	003C	<	92	005D	↓
61	003D	=	93	005C	◄
62	003E	>	94	005D	►
63	003F	?	95	005E	—

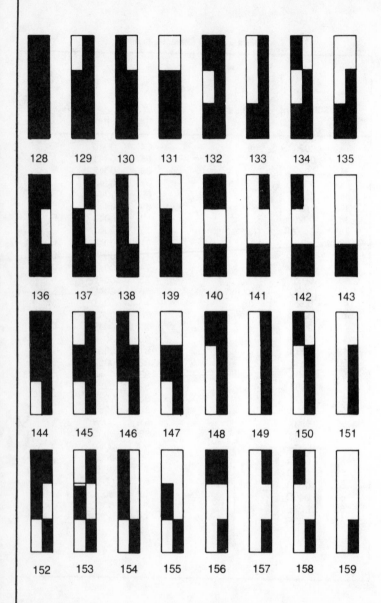

Fig. A-2. TRS-80 graphics code format.

Table A-2. ASCII Character Codes.

CODE Decimal	Hex	CHARACTER	CODE Decimal	Hex	CHARACTER
32	0020	space	64	0040	@
33	0021	!	65	0041	A
34	0022	"	66	0042	B
35	0023	#	67	0043	C
36	0024	$	68	0044	D
37	0025	%	69	0045	E
38	0026	&	70	0046	F
39	0027	' (apostrophe)	71	0047	G
40	0028	(	72	0048	H
41	0029	)	73	0049	I
42	002A	*	74	004A	J
43	002B	+	75	004B	K
44	002C	, (comma)	76	004C	L
45	002D	-	77	004D	M
46	002E	. (period)	78	004E	N
47	002F	/	79	004F	O
48	0030	0	80	0050	P
49	0031	1	81	0051	Q
50	0032	2	82	0052	R
51	0033	3	83	0053	S
52	0034	4	84	0054	T
53	0035	5	85	0056	U
54	0036	6	86	0057	V
55	0037	7	87	0058	W
56	0038	8	88	0059	X
57	0039	9	89	005A	Y
58	003A	:	90	005B	Z
59	003B	;	91	005C	↕
60	003C	<	92	005D	↕
61	003D	=	93	005C	◄
62	003E	>	94	005D	►
63	003F	?	95	005E	—

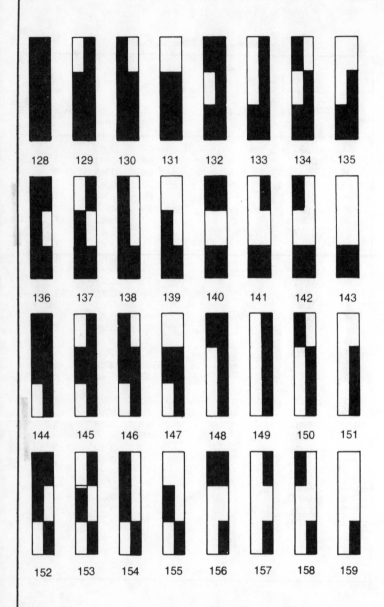

128 129 130 131 132 133 134 135

136 137 138 139 140 141 142 143

144 145 146 147 148 149 150 151

152 153 154 155 156 157 158 159

Fig. A-2. TRS-80 graphics code format.

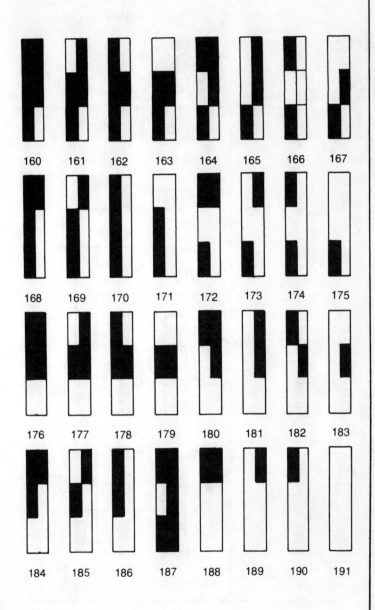

160 161 162 163 164 165 166 167

168 169 170 171 172 173 174 175

176 177 178 179 180 181 182 183

184 185 186 187 188 189 190 191

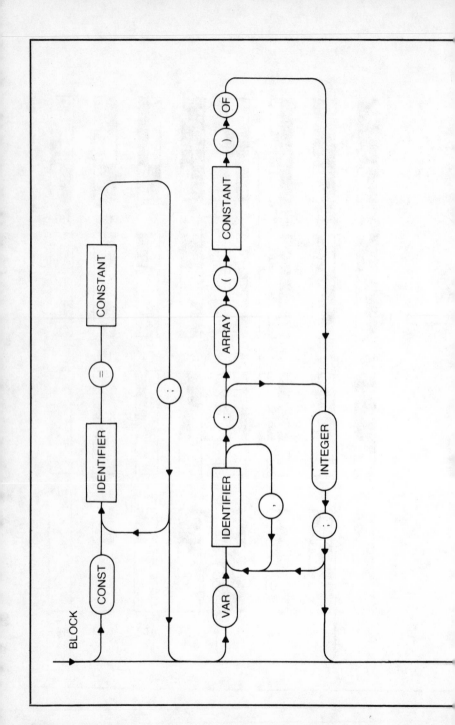

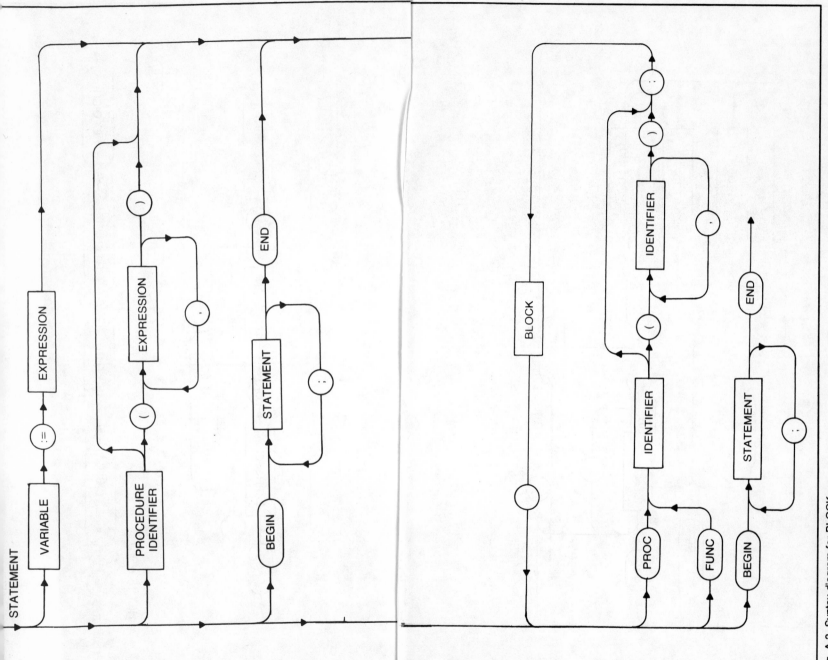

Fig. A-3. Syntax diagram for BLOCK.

341

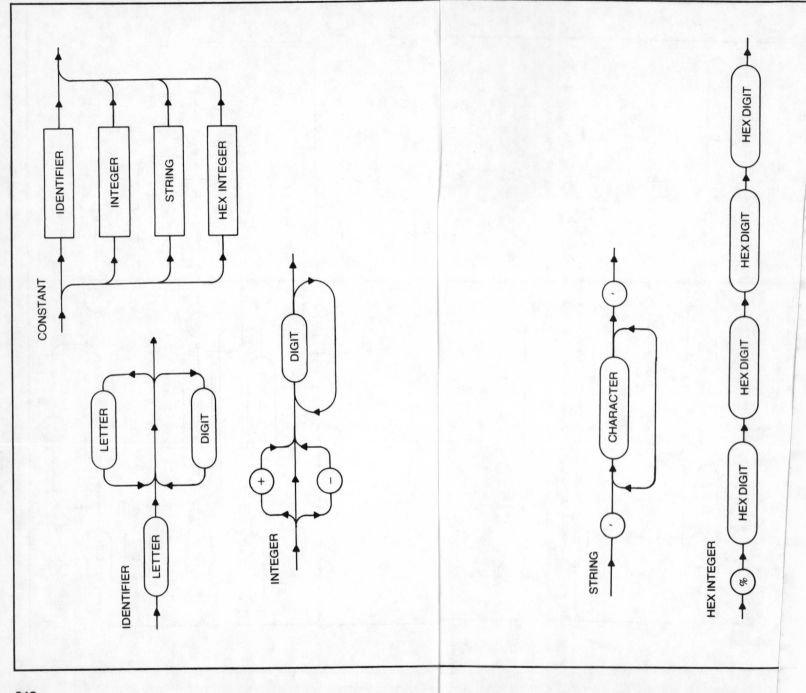

CONSTANT

IDENTIFIER

INTEGER

STRING

HEX INTEGER

IDENTIFIER

LETTER

LETTER

DIGIT

INTEGER

DIGIT

+

-

STRING

CHARACTER

HEX INTEGER

%

HEX DIGIT

HEX DIGIT

HEX DIGIT

HEX DIGIT

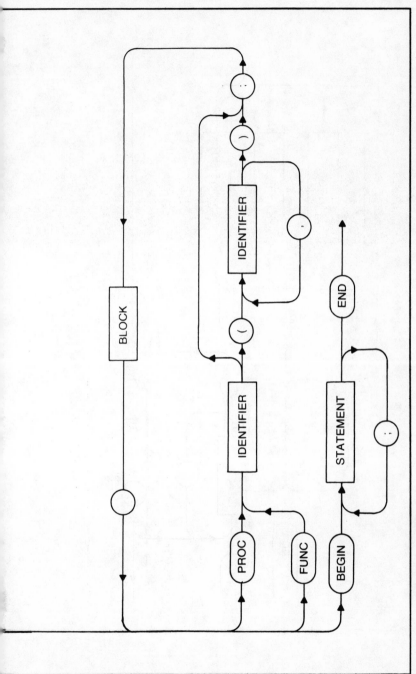

Fig. A-3. Syntax diagram for BLOCK.

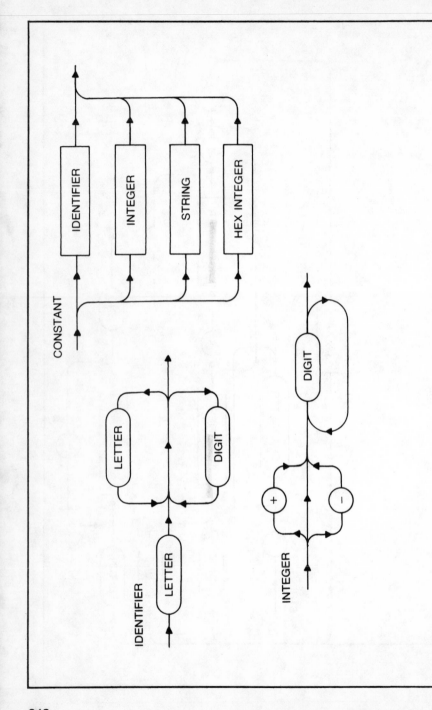

CONSTANT

IDENTIFIER

INTEGER

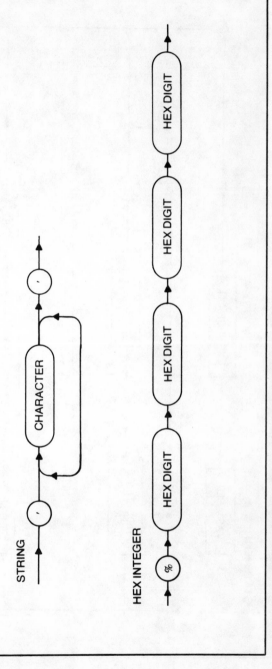

Fig. A-4. Syntax diagram for IDENTIFIER, CONSTANT, INTEGER STRING and HEX INTEGER.

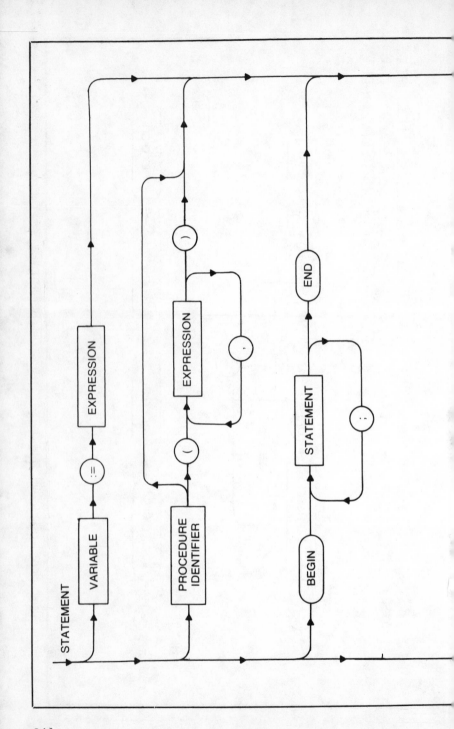

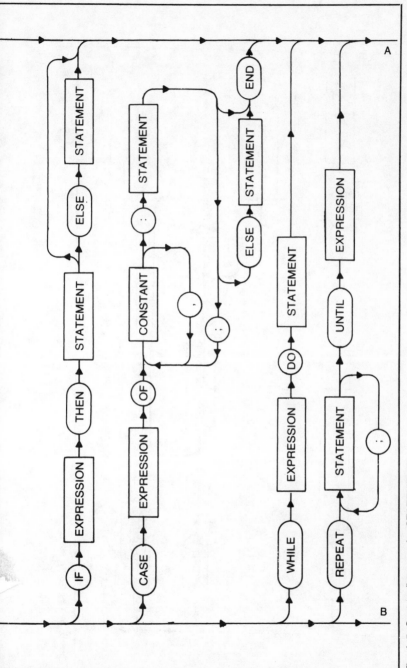

Fig. A-5. Syntax diagrams for STATEMENT.

345

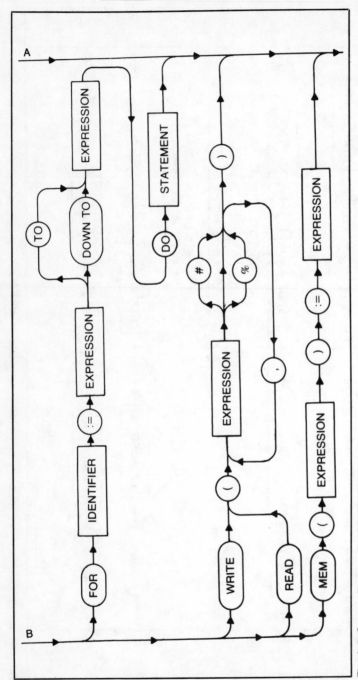

Fig. A-5. Syntax diagrams for STATEMENT.

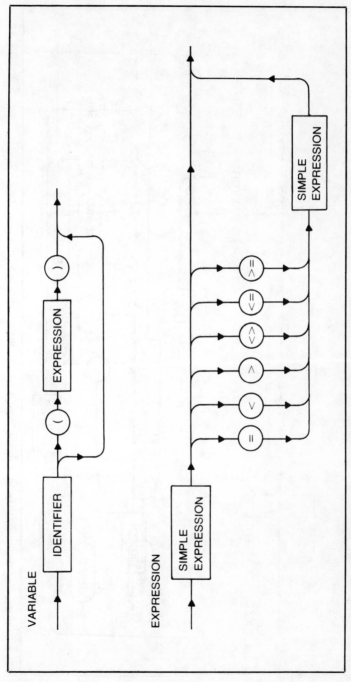

Fig. A-6. Syntax diagrams for VARIABLE, EXPRESSION, SIMPLE EXPRESSION and TERM.

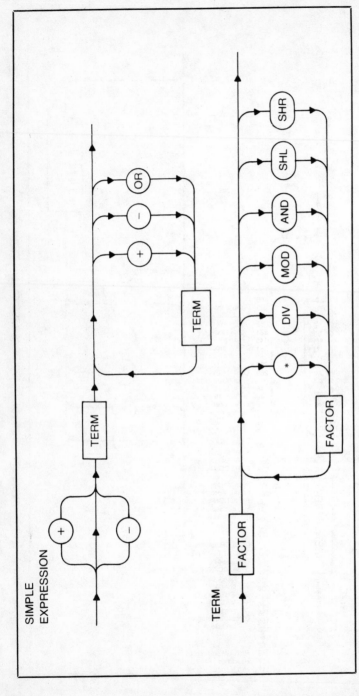

Fig. A-6. Syntax diagrams for VARIABLE, EXPRESSION, SIMPLE EXPRESSION and TERM.

Index

Index